THE LIBRARY
ST. MARY'S COLLEGE OF MARYLAND
ST. MARY'S CITY, MARYLAND 20686

POWER

IS

OURS

BY

HON. M. Gatsha Buthelezi

BOOKS IN
FOCUS Inc.

© 1979 Books In Focus Inc.

All rights reserved. No portion of this book may be reproduced or transmitted in any form, mechanical or electronic, without written permission from Books In Focus Inc., except by a reviewer who may quote brief passages in connection with a review.

Library of Congress Catalog Card Number 78-74593

ISBN 0-916728-08-0

COVER AND BOOK DESIGN: PAULETTE NENNER
TYPESETTING: HERTZ DATA CORP.

Books In Focus, Inc.
Suite 31B
160 East 38th Street
New York, N.Y. 10016

Telephone: (212) 490-0334

CONTENTS

INTRODUCTION

I appreciate this opportunity to introduce this compilation of speeches by Gatsha Buthelezi. I first heard of this unusual man about five years ago. At that time, Buthelezi was not generally known in this country, however, recently, he has become an effective spokesman for his people in the Republic of South Africa. To say that Buthelezi has been controversial is an understatement. It is clear that his critical lashings at government leaders and apartheid have enraged the Nationalist Party which sees him as a "nuisance." It would be more correct to refer to him as a "thorn in the government's side."

Gatsha Buthelezi should be read for several reasons. In the first place, he is a significant Black spokesman in the Republic of South Africa. He is a part of that country and inhales what he calls its "polluted air." His speeches represent a realism and reflect a grasp of the radical restlessness of a growing number of South African Blacks radical position. He is one of the few vocal indigenous Black leaders in the Republic of South Africa whose voice is clearly heard.

Why is Gatsha able to speak in that social context? It seems contradictory that a Black can be as outspoken as Gatsha and be able to survive in that society. How does one account for this? I believe the answer can be found in what some call the "popular authenticity of his leadership." It cannot be denied that he has a very significant following. Inkatha, an organization of which he is a leader, has a reported membership of over 150,000. Inkatha is not only important because of the quantity, but also because its members come from several nationalities and races. This is anathema in the Republic of South Africa and Buthelezi reportedly has been chided for his violation of apartheid policy. Add to this, the fact that Buthelezi is also the Chairman of the South African Black Alliance, an inter-racial political organization. Finally, you must remember that he is the operating head of the Zulu nation whose population is over 5 million. There is no question that he is a significant leader which is suggestive that he is a force that cannot be taken lightly.

The independence of Buthelezi has created problems for him with a large number from the liberal community. Gathsa has taken the unpopular stand of not calling for "disinvestment of foreign business." How is it that this man, who is completely dedicated towards the elimination of apartheid, can be "conservative" on this issue? Gatsha is quite aware of the dilemma. He said: "In thinking about investment in South Africa, I find myself increasingly involved in a conflict of a very fundamental nature. On the one hand, I cannot bring myself to tell the poor and the suffering of this country that I am working for the cessation of foreign investment in South Africa. Investment means increased prosperity and it means jobs for the unemployed, clothes for the naked and food for the hungry. That is why I regard white liberal groups who are well disposed toward the suffering Black as showing a lack of political sensitivity when they condemn us for inviting foreign investment."

This position of Buthelezi does not come without pain. He goes further in describing the dilemma when he said, "Investment increasingly appears to me as having a supportive role within status quo politics." Gatsha is a man of the future and sees clearly that apartheid has failed and the task of the Black man is to start building for tomorrow. Buthelezi does not say whay we want him to say. His position alienates the South African government and the foreign white liberal sees him as compromising with the establishment. Hopefully, persons will carefully read Gathsha's speeches and allow their hearts to feel the spirit of an earnest and powerful leader.

Before one judges Buthelezi, remember that he has called for a convention to consider how foreign investment can be used to establish social justice. It should be pointed out that the call for investment is not an endorsement of traditional capitalism. Gatsha has said, "The days of unfettered capitalism, whose self-interest is served by supporting repressive governments, are numbered, particularly in the Southern Africa that is unfolding before our eyes."

The speeches of Buthelezi provide a tremendous source of material for those interested in getting additional insight on the South African problem. Gatsha is obviously a well-informed person. He seems to be comfortable speaking to a group of businessmen in Johannesburg, conversing with Henry Kissinger, addressing a church convention and speaking at a rally in Soweto. Each time the reader will gain new insight as he is led by this gifted mind and articulate person. Buthelezi shows an understanding of business economics, history, and especially politics. As one reads his speeches, he is amazed at Gatsha's proficiency in so many disciplines. A careful reading of these speeches can give one an acquaintance with several important areas in trying to understand apartheid and its effects.

One final thing I wish to say about Buthelezi, and that deals with what appears to be his strategy, he is a very capable organizer with unbelievable political sensitivity. Gatsha has launched a very controversial organization, Inkatha. It was primarily a call for black unity. Inkatha is the building of black nationhood so that there would be in place a capable and enlightened leadership to deal with the future of a new South Africa.

Inkatha is not merely futuristic for it is involved in limited moves for political and social change. This can be seen in its somewhat sophisticated politcal analyses and discussions about issues in the Republic of South Africa. The government would be taking serious risks not to give due regard to Inkatha.

There are many strong black leaders in South Africa and several of them have different points of view, some of them are mentioned in this book, but none can doubt the effectiveness of Gatsha's Inkatha leadership.

Finally, I want to be emphatically clear that I respect Gatsha Buthelezi. Since the world has announced its interest in the Republic of South Africa, it is extremely important that Gathsha Buthelezi is heard and understood. It may be that you will not agree with him, but give him your attention and then state your opinions. I am convinced that Gathsha Buthelezi is a courageous man and has a heart which pulsates with love for his people. He has earned the right to be heard.

Reverrend Leon H. Sullivan
Director, General Motors Corporation
Minister, Zion Baptist Church, Philadelphia
Author of the Sullivan Code of ethics
for American companies operating in
South Africa

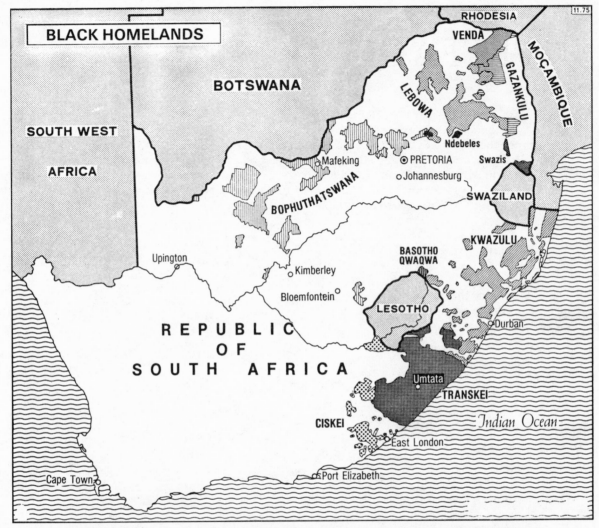

This map shows the area designated as homelands by the South African Government. The fragmented nature of the areas is clear. KwaZulu for example, is divided into 29 separated pieces.

PREFACE

The Zulus are part of the Nguni branch of the Bantu people. The Ngunis are said to have originated in Saharan West Central Africa.

This land was originally fertile, but as the Sahara desert encroached further southwards, the Ngunis began migrating toward the south. They followed a course through present day Zaire, Zambia, Mozambique and Rhodesia, eventually crossing the great Limpopo River through present day Transvaal, to settle among other areas, in what is now Natal, and the Eastern Cape. There were hundreds of Nguni clans settled in what is now Natal, in South Africa, among which was the tiny Zulu clan. In the Zulu language the word ZULU means "heaven" or "universe." The Zulus inhabited a small territory until the advent of Shaka Zulu, the great African military genius. Through the invention of the short stabbing assegai, a ruthless attitude toward the enemy, a system of absolute discipline and training and an advanced view of social order, Shaka achieved military conquests unparallelled in Africa, culminating in the establishment of the Zulu empire as the absolute power in the area. Starting with 500 people and 100 square miles, Shaka assimilated 500,000 persons and controlled all of Natal, and more. In the process of destroying his military foes he accomplished the feat of forging over 240 unruly Nguni nomes (or clans), into one unified Zulu nation. Though the birth of the Zulu nation was by fire, and was accomplished within twelve short years, its results have been long-lasting. The national order survived the assassination of King Shaka and the nation continued to grow in power. Shaka's revolutionary concepts of war and society were so powerful, that offshoots of Shaka's military impis (regiments) began major emigrations to the north. Mzilikazi (translated: path of glory) one of Shaka's generals, founded the Ndebele nation of Rhodesia. Other offshoots went as far north into Africa as Kenya and founded the Watusu nation, the Shangane nation and kingdoms in Central Africa.

In effect Shaka reversed the direction of Nguni emigration. During the 1800s the Zulus and Afrikaners clashed, but except at Blood River never met head-on in really significant ways. The Boers were generally content to occupy the lands of the Transvaal, left partly vacant due to the emigrations caused by Mzilikazis' march north.

The British Empire, however, went after the rich Zulu lands of Natal, and thought they could dictate to the Zulus at will. They learned differently at Isandhlwana, when a force of 1600 British soldiers was totally annihilated by regiments of King Cetshwayo's army. This was one of the greatest blows inflicted on the British army in its entire history until then. It was not until the battle of Ulundi, in January 1879, that the British were able to break the power of the Zulu armies, through the use of artillery which killed them at a distance. Still

ix

it was not an unconditional surrender, and King Cetshwayo was later received as a ruling monarch at the British throne. To this day most of the highly fertile lands taken from the Zulus in Natal are in the hands of British plantation interests, many controlled from London.

The Zulus continue to be known for their bravery and fearlessness, and the highly orderly character of Zulu society survives to the present day, as does the dynasty advanced by Shaka. There has been an unbroken line of Zulu kings until now, with the throne at present filled by King Zwelethini Goodwill, ninth in the line of Shaka. The Zulu king is a constitutional monarch and the symbol of the Zulu nation. The political leadership of the Zulus resides in the Chief Minister, who is Hon. M. Gatsha Buthelezi, the author of these speeches.

Chief Minister Gatsha Buthelezi

Gatsha Buthelezi, the chief executive officer of the Kwa Zulu homeland is also president of the National Cultural Liberation Movement (Inkatha) and chairman of the South African Black Alliance. His leadership of these organizations makes him one of South Africa's most influential political leaders.

But Buthelezi is also one of South Africa's most controversial figures. Some people do not understand how he, an outspoken critic of apartheid, can give credibility to what he opposes by serving in the homeland administration which apartheid has established for his people. However, those who asked Buthelezi to accept nomination and who voted for him see no contradiction in the role he plays.

After the Sharpeville Shootings of 1960, the government banned the African National Congress and the Pan-Africanist Congress. A political leadership vacuum developed which the government hoped to fill with the leadership of co-operative chiefs. The Africans of Natal (the Zulus) requested Buthelezi to stand for election in order to prevent the election of pro-government chiefs. They knew that he was a leader who could rally his people after the Sharpeville Shootings, re-dedicate them to the ideal of nationhood, and lead them onwards from where the ANC and the PAC had been stopped.

Buthelezi and some of his supporters were convinced that the government would seek to destroy all opposition. Therefore in order to survive, the African nationalists in Natal had to gain control of the segregated institutions and transform them into instruments against apartheid.

On November 10, 1973, Buthelezi attended a meeting of chief executive officers of the main homelands administration in Umtata, capital of the Transkei. At this gathering he made a powerful plea for an alternative to the independent homelands which the government promoted. The heads of the segregated homelands adopted the ideal of the Federal Union of the Autonomous States of Southern Africa as their alternative to apartheid.

Four years later, Police Minister J.J. Kruger called Buthelezi to Pretoria to warn him that if he did not desist from admitting non-Zulus into the membership of Inkatha, he, Kruger, would take action against the African organization. Buthelezi said he saw no reason why he should keep members of other African language-groups out of Inkatha when Kruger's Afrikaner National Party had English, Greek, Jewish and other members.

Within South Africa Buthelezi's following cuts across rural and urban differences, educational differences, and ethnic differences. In July 1978 a study by the Arnold Berrgstrasser Institut of Freiburg, West Germany showed that fully 44% of the urban blacks in South Africa supported Buthelezi.

Buthelezi's main concern, as his followers say, is to build an effective political power base, so that if and when his people decide to bring South Africa to her moment of decision, they will not simply end up as cannon fodder.

This calls for a policy which includes a great degree of patience. It exposes Buthelezi to attacks from the Left, the militants and the government on one side, and to suspicion from liberals, in South Africa and the West.

The present collection of his speeches is a declaration designed to enable the world to obtain a fairer idea of the goals Buthelezi has set himself and the strategy he believes the crisis in his country calls for.

*Dedicated to the men and women
who are striving for justice and peace in South Africa.*

Chapter 1

THE SOUTH AFRICAN SITUATION

TO A GROUP OF VISITING AMERICANS

Johannesburg, October 1976

I thank my friend Mr. Stephen Zarlenga by whose effort I have been enabled to share my thoughts with you on this subject.

I think it was the chief protagonist of the Nazi regime, Dr. Goebbels, and the Fuehrer himself, Adolf Hitler, who stated that a lie told often enough soon becomes accepted as the truth. To me, in no other matter is the truthfulness of this illustrated more than in what has been accepted as the "homelands" policy of the present government. The government needs no propagandist because its best propagandists are in mass media opposed to the government's policy.

In the first place, we Africans have been changing names as no pet ever does, from Kaffirs, to Natives, and now to Bantu. The word Bantu means "people," and can also designate a group of African languages. This whole exercise of calling us by all these names, which make us non-persons, is a symptom of a white attempt to define us out of the South African Nation. It is a conscience-salving technique of my white countrymen to call us these names so as to cover themselves with a moral blanket by pretending that we are other things than just South Africans like themselves. They have been at this game ever since they entered our country three hundred years ago. It therefore always intrigues me that the white opposition press and politicians, and particularly those who regard themselves as ultra-liberal, will always speak of people like myself as "Bantustan Leaders" or "Homeland Leaders." This they do ostensibly to ridicule the government's policy, but they unwittingly give it authenticity and credibility in so doing. It would take almost half the time of this address for me to explain to you why it is so much poppycock and a sign of being ensnared by Mr. Vorster's sleight-of-hand politics to regard a person like myself as if I were a

1

creation of Vorster and his government or of whites, in any sense. Apart from the time factor, it is also somewhat embarrassing for one to be explaining who one is, as if one had to explain one's pedigree like that of a prize horse, or exotic cow, or pedigreed poodle, or Siamese cat. The trouble is, if the National Party propagandists have succeeded in mesmerizing their opposition's mass media, I realize how much more confusing this must be for you, as foreign visitors.

That is why at the outset I want to make it very clear that blacks in this country have one homeland which they all share together: South Africa.

The myth that we blacks have no rights in so-called white areas can no longer be sustained. South Africa will never be divided into a number of black mini-states dominated by a sprawling white monster-state. This is a figment of the white man's mind, which is more a symptom of his political megalomania than of political reality.

The power of the black masses is now awakened, and inequality will be put to an end. This will happen however astronomical the defense budgets may be.

Whites from various parts of the world settled in South Africa and seized land by imperial edict supported by military superiority. It is by that same military superiority that they have so far been able to maintain the status quo, as we shall see in a moment.

After squabbling among themselves for a century, they eventually came together in the Act of Union in 1910 to consolidate their white interests. Although they were a hotch-potch of cultural affiliations, it suited their scheme of white domination to regard themselves as one white nation.

In preparation for 1910 various commissions studied the South African situation. By 1913 the Native Land Act was passed setting aside so-called scheduled areas in which we blacks were allowed to live. This 1913 act was a formalization of a practice that was already in existence. In the various colonies and republics that came together in 1910, blacks had already been forced to live in restricted areas and were kept there at gun point.

Blacks never accepted this position and tried to break out of the system by wars and rebellions.

After the 1913 Native Land Act, blacks in some areas still had residual rights to purchase land outside their so-called reserves and scheduled areas.

This residual right was opposed by the 1936 Bantu Trust and Land Act.

This Act was an arbitrary division of land between blacks and whites, by whites in white self-interest. It excluded blacks from having any land rights in all the economically developed areas, and all known mineral deposits were included in white areas.

We blacks were not consulted at the various times colonies were proclaimed and republics established. We blacks were not consulted when the 1913 and 1936 Acts were passed. We were not consulted when the Bantu Authorities Act of 1951 was passed and when the Promotion of Bantu Self-Government Act of 1959 was also passed.

We were not consulted and we do not feel morally bound by these acts of white self-interest. These white acts certainly did not create a feeling of common loyalty in South Africa as a whole.

2

If ever the seeds of revolution were sown, the whites of South Africa sowed those seeds.

These acts of exploitation were given a veneer of moral respectability by playing with words. "Baaskap" turned into "Homelands."

This veneer has not fooled blacks. We can say authoritatively that the playing with words has not made any real difference to our position. To be in white areas, blacks need bits of paper from white bureaucrats. To work in the industrial centres, blacks need bits of paper, and even to move from one area to another, blacks need bits of paper from white officials.

Every year the police enforcement of these regulations, which curb black movements, results in thousands of prosecutions, as can be seen from the following table:

Prosecutions Under The Pass Laws

The Report of the Commissioner of the S.A. Police for the year ending 30 June 1973 contained information about certain cases sent for trial under the intricate laws and regulations that are commonly known as the Pass Laws. There was a notable decrease in the number for that year.

Nature of Law Infringement:	1972-3 Number of Cases:
Curfew regulations	131,464
Registration and submission of documents	203,492
Bantu (Urban Areas) Consolidation Act	148,703
Bantu Administration Act not elsewhere specified	15,472
Masters and Servants Act	16,477
	515,608

These totals represented 31.8 per cent and 24.2 per cent, respectively, of the total number of cases sent for trial for law infringements during the year concerned. In spite of the decrease, the figure for 1972-3 is equivalent to 1,413 trials for Pass Law offences every day of the year. Articles in THE STAR on 3, 4, and 5 July described what was termed a system of "conveyor belt justice" in the Bantu Affairs Commissioners' courts in Fordsburgh, Johannesburg, where each court might have to deal with between 80 and 130 cases a day.

Whites seized land by power and they cling to their privileged position by power.

This whole process of exploiting blacks was strongly sustained by colonial economic interests. Investors have for more than a century and a half had great rewards in participating with whites in South Africa and in their exploitation of the blacks.

This is one side of the South African coin. The other side is of human endeavor in taming untamed land, of economic progress. The fact that there has been exploitation must not blind us to the fact that there has been progress through exploitation.

South Africa is the economic giant of Africa. For the sake not only of the poor in South Africa, but for the sake of the development of the whole of southern Africa, that development must continue.

I have, for moral and Christian reasons as well as pragmatic reasons, chosen the path of peaceful change. I must confess, however, that after a meeting I had with the Prime Minister on the 8th of this month, I am now even more skeptical that those of us who believe in a peaceful change can ever succeed in the face of such white greed, and white intransigence as came throuqh so distinctly in the attitude of the Prime Minister to all our suggestions about a peaceful change.

We blacks cannot afford to precipitate a holocaust in our own country. Change that destroys the base of future development would be self-defeating. On the other hand, being pragmatic in this sense also means I must be pragmatic in another sense. My people have been abused beyond the point of human endurance. They can no longer tolerate their insufferable position. My leadership will cease to mean anything to them if they cannot receive tangible benefits from it. Besides, I love my people and share their suffering.

When nothing is left but to fight a just war, people all over the world down through the centuries of history have done just that. We black South Africans are people among the rest of humanity.

I am not talking about these things lightheartedly. I know what this means to an unarmed people like ourselves. Let me take a look with you at the kind of defense force and armoury white South Africa has for the current year. In the April issue of a London Magazine entitled AFRICAN DEVELOPMENT (April 1976) South Africa has an army of 38,000 (31,000 conscripts), and 138,000 in the active reserve (citizen force); reservists serve 19 days annually for five years. NAVY: 4,000 (1,400 conscripts), reserves 10,400. AIR FORCE: 8,500 (3,000 conscripts), 3,000 reservists, and 75,000 territorial commandos. MAIN WEAPONRY: 140 tanks, 20 Comet medium tanks; about 1,400 armoured cars, including 250 Saracens, 54 Tigercat SAM's and a variety of light and medium artillery. There are 108 combat aircraft including six Canberra light bombers, 10 Buccaneer light bombers with AS-30 SAM's, 32 Mirage fighters plus 16 used as fighter-reconnaisance aircraft, seven Shackletons, 20 Pia-glio Albatrosses, four transport squadrons and 20 Alouettes, 20 Puma and seven Wasp helicopters, 32 warships including two destroyers, six frigates, six corvettes, and three (Daphne class) submarines. In the same magazine, Major-General Neil Webster, Director-General of Resources in the South African Defense Force, was quoted as saying that his countrymen, like the Israelis, "must get used to the idea of living with a warlike situation for some years to come."

This is the extent to which the country is on a war-footing. You will agree with me that we are already in an extremely volatile atmosphere. We have seen in

SOUTH AFRICAN SITUATION

the last four months the extent to which the forces of nationalism are on the move — white nationalism because it feels threatened and besieged — and black nationalism because it has to find expression. Those of us who adopted a non-violent stance despite so much provocation by our gun-wielding countrymen, attempted to keep these forces off collision course. It is quite clear now that to keep them off this course today is almost an impossible task.

South Africa has reached the stage in which white intransigence is playing brinkmanship with total disaster.

Even so, I still hope that it is not too late for a peaceful solution to dominate over a violent solution. I must cling to this hope as long as this is possible.

The role of the foreign investor is crucial in South Africa. Injections of foreign capital are vital to the survival of the South African economy. I am not unaware of the dilemma posed by the fact that it is the very strength of this economy which props up the white military might that is used to maintain the status quo.

If, however, such investments are made to prop up an increasingly vulnerable white-only cash economy, they will be lost in the chaos which is bound to arise. Military might by itself can never be a decisive factor where there is such interdependence, and where blacks outnumber whites by so many millions of souls.

It is for pragmatic reasons, as well as moral reasons, that I have clung to the hopes of non-violent solutions. The owners of capital in South Africa, however, do not sustain me in that hope. So far, they have played the white government's game.

This partnership between capital and repressive legislation must now be terminated!

I think that it is not yet fully realized that in South Africa people will conquer capital if capital opposes the will of the people. Investment at this time in South Africa must take sides in the central political struggle — apartheid versus full participation in the government of the country by the majority of the country. Capital has sided with forces maintaining the status quo. It is, therefore, a political factor which must take its chances in the open political arena. The neutrality it claims is a fiction.

Everything in South Africa is now sliding willy-nilly into a melting pot. Apartheid, white political dominance, white technological advantages over their black counterparts, a virulent black consciousness, the Westminster-type political model, white and black trade unionism, the black work force, tribal land tenure systems, and white rights to freehold property, are all ingredients in this melting pot. None of them will emerge untouched.

It is, therefore, foolhardy in the extreme to discuss investment in South Africa as though the past will continue into the future. It is also foolhardy to say that the existing economic order will not undergo radical changes.

I have lately been subjected to arguments that only a fool cannot see that change is going to take place in South Africa. Those who have argued in this line have done so in an attempt to move my political stance backwards by years.

My stance was that apartheid would fail. My stance now is that it has failed. My stance was that homeland development would suffer from lack of white sincerity. My stance now is that it has suffered irreparably from white insincerity.

We cannot say that we should return in time to the point when homeland development could become something real for blacks. The homeland vehicle has crashed. It is smashed beyond further use.

Everyone is agreed that change will come in South Africa. Unfortunately, this change means many different things to many different people. Those who say I am becoming too hasty are invariably those who think about change in terms of making the bitter apartheid pill more palatable by sugar coating it.

The change I want for millions of blacks in the country is the scrapping of apartheid and the so-called homeland policy. I am impatient with those who build a South African conflict situation which in actuality will be a conflagration.

Whatever we mean by change, we start from a given point in reality. We will have black rural residential and peasant farming areas in the foreseeable future. We will not have them because whites in this country want it that way. We will have them because in the foreseeable future the cash economy will not be able to transform peasant society into a farming and industrial society for a considerable time.

Any illusion, however, that the economically poor will remain politically disenfranchised is misplaced. Any idea that the elite will not have to involve themselves in a radical redistribution of wealth is wishful thinking.

The dynamic driving force of politics in this country is the black man's will to fight for equality of opportunity — not in their urban ghettoes, nor in their impoverished reserves — but in the suburbs, streets and market places of the cities.

Blacks have realized that without political power there is no equality of opportunity.

In thinking about investment in South Africa, I find myself increasingly involved in a conflict of a very fundamental nature.

On one hand, I cannot bring myself to tell the poor and the suffering of this country that I am working for the cessation of foreign investment in South Africa. Investment means increased prosperity and it means jobs for the unemployed, clothes for the naked and food for the hungry. That is why I regard white liberal groups who are well disposed toward the suffering black, as showing a lack of political sensitivity when they condemn us for inviting foreign investment. For example, the Students' Wages Commission circulated advertisements in the so-called homeland areas a couple of years ago implying that those of us involved in the sufferings of our people were literally saying to investors: "Come on and rape us, we are lying on our backs." To me it is proof that however much they may empathize with us, they can never comprehend the enormity of black misery. It does not matter how much they empathize; they have never experienced life as one of the suffering blacks. By saying so, I am not questioning their bona fides. I am merely saying that it is such an overplay that prompts some blacks to reject all whites and to be suspicious of all white sympathy. I thank God, because it is only by His grace that despite the innuendos suggesting I am involved in the economic prostitution of my own people, I have not yet reached the state of rejecting all whites merely because of the misplaced and passing enthusiasm for our cause by some of them.

On the other hand, I cannot bring myself to support an economic order within a political system which creates poverty and hunger.

Investment increasingly appears to me as having a supportive role within status quo politics.

Look through one of the South African windows. See Mr. Kruger announcing publicly that whites have the right to shoot blacks in the defense of their property, and in the same breath he tells those whites that the police cannot be everywhere and that they should take collective self-help steps to ensure the safety of their factories. The safety of factories and the safety of investment does not lie in the barrel of a gun. It lies in meaningful political change, which is long overdue in this country.

The circumstances in which Mr. Kruger spoke arose because of political reasons. He was faced with political problems, and he should have given political answers.

The industrialists whose properties are threatened have no hope of securing their interests through gunfighting. They must come to realize that their vested interests will best be preserved by meaningful change.

We are aware that big business has negotiated concessions from government departments in areas of training, manpower-utilization and housing. However, real political developments are forging so far ahead that these concessions, and the negotiations which led to them, will soon become indictments.

Homeland development and the future of the homelands as such are bound up with these considerations. Investment, whether in the cash economy or in the peasant economy, is an investment in one integrated socio-economic and political system. I, therefore, cannot separate investment issues in the homelands from investment issues in the cash economy. My dilemma remains there.

I must pause to emphasize that the dilemma I talk about is not self-inflicted. It is not a product of an ideological or even simply a political stance I may have adopted. The dilemma is established by reality in South Africa — a reality that neither you nor I can escape. We certainly cannot talk it out of existence.

I belong to my people. I have their ears and their hearts. I know them and I am aware of what draws them to become involved in the struggle for liberation from oppression. Their oppression is real — and my dilemma originates in their oppression.

I return to my previous remark that it is not yet fully recognized that people will oppose capital if capital opposes the will of the people. Whenever this has happened, the road to the rejection of capitalism has been tortuous and difficult. South Africa, I believe, has already commenced that journey, and tragically so. But I do believe that this is a fact of life in this country which demands recognition.

Frequently, those who are the most ardent in their defence of the capitalist free enterprise system are the greatest enemies of that system. If ever there is a demise of capitalism here, white capitalists will fully share in the blame.

The South Africa we have known is crumbling. It is not too late to do something to ensure a continuing democracy within which a responsible free enterprise system can evolve. It is, however, too late to perpetuate the status quo.

Faced with inevitable changes in the future and with the present situation in a state of flux, it is not possible to reduce the question of investment to a simple formula. There are, however, some things that must be stated about the acceptability of foreign investment in South Africa.

The first is that blacks no longer can give blanket approval to foreign investment on the simple grounds that investment creates jobs for blacks. That could be a very important reason for a particular investment being regarded as acceptable if a number of other criteria are met simultaneously. For blacks to support any kind of investment simply because it offers jobs could, in some circumstances, amount to blacks participating in their own exploitation.

The second thing that must be stated about investment is that the question cannot be pronounced upon in discussions such as we are having here. We must stop saying to blacks: "You must welcome investment; it is good for you." The call has gone out in many black circles for disinvestment. The question of whether or not to invest has become a contentious political issue.

There have been gross acts of exploitation under the guise of investment for the sake of developing the economy. How investors can act responsibly in the totality of the South African situation has yet to be explored. And this responsibility cannot be explored by the dialectical use of words and concepts in theoretical debates.

If one had to develop a framework within which the explanation of investor responsibility could take place, the following two areas would have to be included.

Responsibility in Partnership between Labour and Management

There can be no responsible investment which does not lead to a partnership between the owners of capital and labour.

That partnership cannot now exist because the Industrial Conciliation Act excludes blacks by the definition used for employee.

A consequence of this is that there is no possibility of disputes between labour and management being settled by arbitration.

The Works Committee system is no substitute for a free trade union movement.

Responsibility in Partnership between Community and Investor

There will be a strong tendency for investment to be exploitative if investment is not mutually beneficial to both the community in which it takes place and the investor himself.

Investors must by now realize that the black majority in this country will, in the foreseeable future, have the power to grab any investment they like and do with it what they will. If and when this happens, everybody will lose. To avoid that, investors must start thinking about the situation now.

Earlier this year, I called for a convention at which the whole question of investment would have been discussed in detail. The unrest in the country, and particularly the way the government has handled that unrest, has made the holding of any convention impossible.

At the earliest opportunity, such a convention must be held and dialogue between blacks and investors must commence. Irresponsible investment now will be met with irresponsible action later. Again I must remind you that I am not making these kinds of statements from an ideological viewpoint. I am, I hope, sharing a glimpse of reality with you.

In calling for a convention on investment, I am of course, recognizing that there is a need to share views on investment and a need to define a developmental role for investment. My own contribution to the discussion at such a meeting would be along the following lines:

I would argue that some form of a free enterprise system in which the private sector is permitted to play a creative role would be the best option for South Africa. I would, on the other hand, argue against unrestrained capitalism in which the dependency of the South African economy would be perpetuated.

Such restraints as would be imposed on free enterprise should be determined by:

—the needs of self-sufficiency in the economy, and

—the developmental role the South African economy should play in the wider southern African context.

I would argue that development should:

—be based on the home market,

—encompass a wide range of industries,

—not be reliant on foreign finance, except where such finance is subjected to local control, and

bring about independent technological progress.

Home Market

There will be no economic progress in South Africa unless there is political stability. That stability depends upon the people's involvement in the economy and their gains from it.

The majority of black South Africans do not feel that they have benefited from South Africa's economic development. There must be further and rapid expansion of the home market, if people are to feel that their new political dispensation has any meaning for them.

Industrial Diversification

A growing economy, drawing from an ever increasing percentage of the peasant community, can only come about by maximizing diversification. The development of the home market must go hand-in-hand with diversification if the growing peasant population's dependency on rapidly depleting resources is to be minimized. Free enterprise can make a significant contribution to the development of the home market and the diversification of industry.

Foreign Finance

It is not the origin of money which creates problems for a developing economy. Foreign capital brings with it managerial skill and technological expertise which every developing economy requires. The control over foreign funds is, however, problematic.

If one looks at the Zambian experience, one realizes the extent to which foreign funds controlled by expatriates were not employed to the best advantage of the indigenous population, until there was forced Africanization.

It is essential that foreign finance be controlled to ensure the involvement of the local population in its employment.

Independent Technological Progress

Independent technological progress is an essential requirement of real grass roots economic development. Blacks in South Africa up to now have been excluded from full participation in technological development. Only now, when there are too few whites for certain skilled jobs, are blacks being trained in the various trades. Even today, whites are protected by legislation from black competition. Investors have, so far, participated in this exploitation of economic opportunity to the enhancement of white privilege and to the detriment of black workers.

Private enterprise can play a significant role in the progress of independent technological development. This development can best take place on the factory floor. Training and human development does cost money but it also makes money. Making money out of people, without exploiting them, is possible.

If commodity production is important in the development of the home market and the diversification of industry, and if free enterprise is involved in those developments, it should also be involved in the development of independent technology.

Thus, to conclude, I would restate the more important points I have made.

South Africa and its economy up to now have been exploitative. The black section of the population has been used and abused to the point where they have been pushed to the edge of human endurance.

In the explosive South African situation, it is still possible that peaceful solutions may prevail, and it is still possible to continue South Africa's economic growth to become a significant developmental factor in the whole of southern Africa. For that to materialize, however, black cooperation in South Africa is needed. That cooperation now can be gotten only by intentions of radical change in which blacks will fully participate in the government of the country.

Investors who have been a party to oppression in the past must be a party to change in the future.

A partnership must now be developed with blacks. A U.S./South African partnership which excludes blacks only can bring about a final conflagration which will destroy the base from which progress can continue. This is a decisive factor which Americans in particular must note.

Investor responsibility must go beyond palliatives and must involve the investor in confrontation with authority.

Unless this takes place, and unless change results, and unless after change partnership between labour and capital is established, and unless there is rapid economic growth which decreases South Africa's dependency on capitalism as we now know it, capitalism will pass from the South African scene forever.

From what I have said it is clear that this means nothing less than the complete elimination of apartheid and racism from South Africa. Unless a move in that direction is made now, it will be senseless to blame blacks if the view held by some of our brothers that it is better to destroy everything and for all of us to start from scratch, triumphs. That view is not without merit, but the suffering entailed for so many people must, if possible, be avoided.

Chapter 2

THE FUTURE OF INVESTMENTS

OPENING OF THE AKULU CHEMICAL COMPANY

ISITHEBE, May 1977

Nothing gives me more joy than to come to an occasion such as this, where I participate in a ceremony that I know means a nibble of bread for one or two mouths, amongst millions of blacks who comprise the poorest section of our South African nation.

When I visited Holland in September 1975, I was under great pressure from the mass media as they wanted me to answer the question whether or not I had been consulted, as was reported, by representatives of this industry. Most of the interested people wanted me to speak against your making this investment in this country. I, of course, confirmed that I was in favour of this investment. And yet what do we see in the latest issue of the right-wing magazine which goes under the title DEVELOPMENT — SOUTHERN AFRICAN EDITION 1976 no. 4. The following is a quote from this magazine:

> Despite his reported views that overseas investment in KwaZulu was politically undesirable, Chief Minister Buthelezi, commenting on the new investment plans, declared that it was the policy of the homeland government to encourage local participation in enterprises such as those of BATA and BIC.

On the other hand, let me read to you a statement from a background paper, SOUTH AFRICA: A POLITICAL PROFILE, written by a journalist by the name of John de St. Jorre for the Carnegie Endowment for International Peace in New York, dated 16 March 1977.

> The most interesting controversial figure among the homeland rulers is Chief Gatsha Buthelezi, the leader of the Zulus. Buthelezi has consistently opposed the government from his base in the KwaZulu Bantustan, another fragmented and impoverished homeland. He opposes

independence for these areas; insists that the Bantustan leaders do not, and can never represent the urban blacks; and, in a marked shift of his position a year ago, called for majority rule. There is no doubt that Buthelezi is a thorn in the Nationalist government's side. Treurnicht and the Verkramptes detest him and Vorster would give a lot to have him replaced by a more pliant Zulu leader. The government, however, cannot muzzle him for his legitimacy and platform are the creation, and indeed the centerpiece of the Separate Development concept. Yet, to a certain extent, Buthelezi plays the government's game. He is strongly opposed to violence as a means of change, he encourages local and foreign investment in the homelands, and his constituency is principally Zulu. . . a fact which dovetails with the government's notions of ethnicity and tribal nationalism.

And a little later the writer continues:

For the blacks there has been a qualitative change since June 16, 1976, a date that will surely acquire historic proportions. "We are no longer afraid and we feel time is on our side," might sum it up. Many Africans are now convinced that it is a question of all or nothing, black rule or death in the attempt. Their attitude of mind is curiously similar to the Afrikaner partitionists in that both groups have reached radical yet mutually unacceptable conclusions. Others, however, feel the center, where compromise between black and white and black and black is still possible, remains worth one more try. Chief Buthelezi is the leading proponent and has matched his beliefs by forming the Black Unity Front, a loose alliance of his own Inkatha Movement with the leaders of the Urban Councils and other moderate blacks in the townships. He is also putting out tentative feelers to the all-white Progressive Reform Party, sundering a hitherto sacrosanct apartheid barrier. He and the PRP, backed by English industrialists, hope to garner support from the nascent black middle class which has grown considerably in the period since 1970, when real black wages rose faster, proportionately, than those of whites.

This compels me to examine, in depth, the whole question of investment each time I feel the opportunity presents itself for me to do so. This is one of those occasions. With the forces arrayed against me on both sides, I feel that I need to repeat over and over again my views on this burning issue and this I now propose to do.

When a feasibility study is done of an industrial undertaking such as this one, a great deal of thought and hard work has to go into the study. I think it is an assumption we have a right to make that the feasibility study must have included socio-political considerations. The people who formulated this undertaking were made aware of the fact that investments in KwaZulu, or for that matter in any part of South Africa, are under critical review by a great many people.

There is need to restate my general position on the matter: we have no option but to accept investments in South Africa because we are a starving people, but investments which have been made have been exploitative in nature. I have warned repeatedly that unless labour and management form a partnership, and unless the investor enters into partnership with blacks, our whole political and economic order is threatened.

I know that the social, political and economic air we breathe is polluted to the point of being foul.

I know also that we blacks have no option but to breathe this foul air. We do not breathe the clean Swiss air, German air, American air or Dutch air. We breathe polluted South African air because if we do not breathe it, we die.

We accept investment because we need jobs so that we and our children may live to struggle for justice.

No black has any other purpose in South Africa. We exist only to struggle for the total overthrow of apartheid and all the injustices it means in the daily lives of the black people of South Africa.

It is we who must stay alive in South Africa. I obviously understand the intentions and the motives of those who call for the cessation of investment in South Africa. I also understand the feelings of a man who watches his children grow thin from hunger. He is the man who has the right to say that investment must cease. Nobody else, not even I.

It is not yet realized that black South Africans have a political sophistication which was forced upon them by their black experience.

There are vociferous groups in South Africa and beyond its borders who clamour for action, any action at any cost. Black South Africans, however, have a sophistication that does not lead them to indulge in futile action at tremendous costs to themselves.

Cool heads must not be confused with political subservience. The cry goes out to make black South Africans conscientious. These cries attempt to create a political fervour which is not needed. We blacks are made conscientious by our daily sufferings. We need a workable plan—a strategy which will win—we do not need to be told we suffer. This we know. We also know that the time is ripening for effective political action. We also know that the hard work of organizing the people has arrived. The discipline of being organized is something we lack. We are attending to that lack because we have seen that mass disorganization cannot be thrown against the organized forces at the command of the state.

All this, everything I have said today, is pertinent to this occasion. If what I have said and am still going to say gives anyone heartburn and heartaches, let me say that my duty to my people comes before any considerations of their individual feelings.

We are opening a factory, and I am asking whether this factory will become a brick my people hurl at the state, or will it become a brick in a new social structure—a new economic justice.

I am here opening this factory because I defend our right to accept your investment. Whether we are right in doing so or whether we are wrong in doing so will depend upon the way this venture is managed, the way you, as management, make this place free of political pollution—as circumstances permit.

I would like to present a view today for serious consideration by those who denigrate us for accepting investments like yours. A Zulu economist presented a most interesting paper on the issue of foreign investments in South Africa on the 18th of May 1976. There is the radical view that if investments dried up, the moment of truth would come soon, because a revolution that should precede liberation would ensue. That is, of course, apart from the moral view that disinvestment means not having anything to do with the evil. I now present the view expressed by this economist without any comment:

Now then what tactics are suggested by Marxist theory with regard to the issue of foreign capitalist investments in South Africa? Do the tactics flowing out of this theory coincide with the tactics of fighting for the withdrawal of foreign capitalist industry from South Africa?

In Marxist perspective, all agitation aimed at restricting the spread of and growth of capitalist industry and capitalist intercourse, in a capitalist society, are wrong, and in fact are declared by Marx, Engels and Lenin to be reactionary. "Marxists do not defend a single reactionary measure such as banning trusts, restricting trade, et cetera," Lenin wrote to Gorky in 1911, chiding those people who were against the spread of capitalist industry in the colonies. Marx, Engels, and Lenin encountered and fought such views all their lives. True to their method, they first explained the class basis of these views, pointing out that they originate among the petty-bourgeoisie strata of capitalist society namely:

—the small business people and small independent farmers, who develop a hostility towards big capitalist farmers, because developing capitalism generally brings ruin to small business people and small farmers; and
—the mass of intellectuals (including students) of a capitalist society, who, though originating from the lower classes of society, get detached and lack firm connections with the major classes of capitalist society. Since these intellectuals lack the material, effective power to alter the structure of society, and are, therefore, left only with voicing moral indignation, and all sorts of sentimentalism, and are inclined to look at history in terms of inflexible yardsticks of good and evil.

The most important point made and emphasized by classical Marxists about capitalism, is that the development of capitalist industry, along with the destruction, distress and misery it brings along, also creates the material and non-material powers which will enable the oppressed of society to struggle successfully for their emancipation. "It is," wrote Engels, "the revolutionizing of all traditional relations by industry as it develops that also revolutionizes people's minds."

Lenin stressed again and again that the development of capitalism also brings about the "elimination of the slave mentality among the toilers", raises their educational level and self-confidence to the point where they begin to demand for their own inclusion in the decision-making process in society; what is more they develop the capacities for organizing themselves intelligently for waging the struggle against oppressors. Now this is precisely what is happening in South Africa. The novel feature of South African society in our time, is the emergence of the African industrial working class, and its entrance into political life. This is what menaces white domination in that country more than it has ever been menaced before, which will in a short time now, overthrow it. But the modern African working class is a product of modern capitalist industry in South Africa. The more capitalist industry develops, the more numerous, sophisticated, educated, self-confident and courageous, becomes this working class, and abler will it be to fight for democracy and freedom in our case, to strike the death blow to white domination.

As I stated when I started quoting this black journalist, I present his view without any comment from me.

I would like to take this opportunity to appeal to all industrialists in South Africa, with an emphasis in my appeal to the foreign investors to enter into discussion with blacks in South Africa on what can be done to bring about economic justice.

I appeal to everyone concerned to consider the possiblity of contributing towards the costs of establishing a study unit comprised of blacks and black nominees to go into the whole question of whether or not a joint effort between investors and ourselves can lead to responsible involvement in bringing about economic justice in South Africa.

We need such a unit. You need such a unit. South Africa needs such a unit. How do you as industrialists run your affairs so as to justify your investment in economic terms without perpetuating our poverty and the political subservience which is so clearly related to it? How do you share your investment with us? These are questions that need to be examined. The answers to them are not found merely in better working conditions for blacks, however important a factor that may be. The political context I brought into this discussion demands that we exercise a kind of constructive creativity which goes beyond just working conditions. We have to define our several and joint roles in the creation of a new economic order.

The days of unfettered capitalism, whose self-interest is served by supporting repressive governments, are numbered, particularly in the Southern Africa that is unfolding before our eyes.

For all of us it is a question of bold creativity or chaos. You do not want chaos. We do not want chaos. But there will be chaos unless we are given a say in our future. Industrialists have a right to protect their interests, but if that right is exercised in a spirit of benevolent paternalism, nothing you can do will suffice, in ultimate terms, to protect your interests. For that purpose you need us. We also need you in creating a new economic order, if that is going to happen without bloodshed as many of us hope is still possible, even at this eleventh hour.

The total investment involved here amounts to $3,150,000 including the investment on behalf of the BIC in building and infrastructure. It is a capital-intensive industry, being a fully automated chemical process. Thirty-five blacks will be employed, increasing to 45 in the second year of this project. West Germany's Akzo Chemie is a subsidiary of the international Dutch Company, Akzo Chemie belonging to the Akzo group of companies which employs some 96,000 people and has interests in 160 companies located in more than 45 countries. Chemical Holdings Limited, an associate of the Anglo-American Corporation, is a leading South African company in the field of special chemicals and services.

Having sung my piece, it is now my privilege to declare this AKULU CHEMICALS FACTORY officially open.

May God bless all whose who will work here, and also bless their families. I thank Akulu Chemicals Limited for siting this factory in KwaZulu. To me, personally, it is a balm to the hurt that I feel as a victim of the crossfires on this issue of investment and its relation to the black struggle for liberation.

Chapter 3

TELLING IT LIKE IT IS TO HENRY KISSINGER

AT THE U.S. EMBASSY

PRETORIA, September 1976

You are visiting South Africa at a time when the black rejection of apartheid has been so evident that any expectation of the system lasting can only be regarded as mischievous. Mr. Vorster has undoubtedly expressed faith in the future of apartheid society despite the fact that hundreds of people have died and hundreds have been arrested. White intransigence continues unabated and is the match which will light the future.

The day on which violence broke out in Soweto, and the form it took, could not have been predicted. It was not planned nor was it directed. Many of us warned of such a possibility, and we warn now that Mr. Vorster is leading South Africa into a bloody confrontation not yet witnessed in Africa.

If ever there was a need for detente as an alternative to runaway violence, it is in South Africa. Yet there is no detente between Mr. Vorster and black leaders—this despite Mr. Vorster's attempts to operate with a detente climate in external relations.

A considerable degree of international diplomatic activity is devoted to the Zimbabwe situation. From press reports the new initiatives appear to have sprung from American interests in Southern Africa. Whatever the eventual outcome of the diplomatic activity now taking place, there will be tremendous implications for South Africa's black population.

The position of blacks in South Africa is such that they have not been participants in the various initiatives taken by Mr. Vorster in the past, nor have we been involved by Mr. Vorster now. We are therefore not party to any decisions which may have been taken and as yet there is no indication that such participation is envisaged by Mr. Vorster.

Mr. Vorster cannot afford to recognize the explosiveness of the situation in the Republic of South Africa by asking us blacks to join him in defusing the situation. Such requests would be an admission that his policies had failed. They have failed—and I can assure you that the final Transkeian-type division of

South Africa into semi-autonomous mini-states which are manipulable by Pretoria will never take place. Even in the "homeland" leadership role, there has been no dialogue between us and Mr. Vorster.

Black South Africans are involved in a struggle for liberation from white oppression. In their political action, their motivation is not to do away with petty apartheid in order to produce some future state of affairs which is more acceptable to more people. The driving force among black South Africans is their anticipation of radical change in the foreseeable future. The West must note that the spirit of optimism which Mr. Vorster produced when he talked about doing away with discrimination was in vain. Not only has there been little done in this direction, but even if much had been done, the Soweto riots would still have taken place. Blacks in South Africa seek rights and equality, not a more comfortable form of bondage.

Those of us who retain a hope of the democratic process bringing about change, find that the mandate from the people, on which they act, is rapidly narrowing their options as leaders. Black views in South Africa are hardening and impatience is increasingly being expressed with discussions and representations as a means of bringing about change. Black people in South Africa want majority rule to be established as a basic principle in a unified South Africa. Mr. Vorster made it clear a few days ago that he rejects this option. Before that, he rejected our offer of a multi-national federal formula for South Africa.

Any steps which result in stengthening Mr. Vorster's hand within the republic will not carry the approval of blacks. Any steps which entrench white vested interests in opposition to the black majority will be resented. And it is only blacks who can decide whether black interests are being ignored by you in your peace mission. I plead, therefore, for you to further involve us, so as not to make us deeply suspicious of what is now taking place between yourself and Mr. Vorster.

The dominant black view is that the United States has been irresponsible in not having a clearly defined southern Africa policy. While we are aware that such a policy is developing, we are unaware of what that policy is becoming.

It is important for you to understand that unless you convince the banned African National Congress, and the Pan African Congress, and ourselves, and black South Africans of your good intentions in Southern Africa, you will have no success in reaching an understanding with the vast majority of black South Africans.

Word has come to us from our organizations in exile that the United States has not afforded them the recognition their legitimacy in South Africa demands. In adopting that attitude toward them, the question is, whose interest is the United States serving through this attitude?

You must be made aware of the fact that both the Congresses are highly regarded in South Africa. The internal difficulties these organizations have experienced recently will not detract from their ultimate appeal within South Africa. What they desire for the masses of our people, is what we who are struggling within South Africa are striving for, for ourselves and millions of black people, who form the majority of the people of South Africa.

20

... TO HENRY KISSINGER

Recent events have shown the importance of resistance within the country. We feel strongly that inasmuch as our leadership in exile has been ignored to a great extent by the West, so has black leadership within South Africa, not been heard by the international community as led by the United States.

Looking at the broader context of the black view of your role in southern Africa, we ask you to appreciate the fact that the struggle for liberation in this part of the continent must be seen to be taking place within the African context. We blacks in South Africa do not agree with Mr. Vorster that South Africa is the West's front-line of defence against communism. The West must recognize that right now we are struggling for our political emancipation and for all the freedoms and rights entrenched in the American constitution. Our liberation struggle will one day play an important role in how the people of South Africa finally line up in international strategies.

Thus, both from the point of view of the political reality within the republic and from the point of view of the broader context, we ask you to keep in mind that you need to persuade black South Africans of your good intentions by becoming a recognized factor in the struggle for liberation taking place within an African context.

We blacks are aware of the fact that Mr. Vorster so far has retained the power to force his apartheid ideology on us.

We are also aware of the fact that Mr. Vorster's attitude to Zimbabwe and Namibia has been important. He has helped to maintain Mr. Smith's illegitimate UDI government. We, therefore, are not blind to your need to talk to Mr. Vorster during your endeavors to stabilize the political situation in southern Africa.

This notwithstanding, we request you not to play a role in the Republic of South Africa until such time as a National Convention, which is truly representative, can be held to articulate the whole country's view of our country's foreign policy. All those in jail and all those in exile and all who have been silenced by banning orders have the right to join with those of us yet at large to articulate the will of the people.

I would suggest that a positive role that can be played by you is to increase the prospects of such a Convention and to assist in developing black-controlled mass media which will further the cause of constructive politics. But even then, it must be WITH blacks and not FOR them.

There is still time for you to help black leaders to exercise non-violent options and there is still time for a black-white partnership in the reconstruction of South African society.

There is, however, so little time left in which to employ non-violent means to effect a multiracial solution and there is so little to encourage one to continue in non-violent methods that for all practical purposes time has run out for South Africa.

American influences in Southern Africa, which do not dramatically strengthen the hand of those of us who have so far adopted the non-violent option, could assist to bring down the curtains on that option.

Any settlement of the Zimbabwe and Namibian political ills which strengthens the apartheid hand of Mr. Vorster will most certainly herald a new wave of despair that will make violent options the only options for political realists.

Jabulani Amphitheater, March 1976

Chapter 4
STORM WARNINGS

A SOWETO MESSAGE TO SOUTH AFRICA

SOWETO, 14 March 1976

My dear sons and daughters of Africa, I greet you in the name of Mother Africa, and in the name of freedom.

I have had yearly pilgrimages to Soweto for quite some time, and this is one of these; but I dare say that this is perhaps the most important if we look at it in the context of the present political climate in southern Africa.

It is almost a year since we last met here. I thank the God of our forefathers, and all the saints of Africa for the privilege of meeting with you once again on this spot. I thank the members of Inkatha, our National Cultural Liberation Movement, for making arrangements for all of us to keep this tryst (for this is what it is), which we as blacks have with destiny.

Last year, on the 22nd of January, I issued a friendly warning to the Prime Minister, Mr. Vorster, that if we as blacks did not reach fulfillment through his policies (as appeared to me to be the case), that we would have no option but unrest and possible civil disobedience. I did so with responsibility, as I sensed the euphoria that pervaded the whole of white South Africa, because of the Prime Minister's so-called detente policy with other African states. Whilst I encouraged its pursuance, I pointed out its inevitable bankruptcy if it was not correlated with detente moves within South Africa itself.

I recall that I was chided by the white press for what they judged as rashness on my part. Some even interpreted my warning to the Prime Minister as a threat. The truth of the matter is that my words were not meant to be either one or the other of these two things. Some white South Africans even saw my warnings as further evidence of what happens when a Kaffir has forgotten his place. This is a place assigned to us not by the Almighty, but by our white countrymen who for generations have used the only power they have to maintain the status quo—the barrel of the gun.

I have had two interviews in the past three years at ministerial level. At both, I was told in no uncertain terms of the irresponsibility of my utterances on the inevitability of violence in this country if we blacks were continually denied human rights. On each occasion, I made it quite clear that when I spoke as I did, it was because I was hoping that violence could be warded off as a result of my warnings. I said I was not advocating violence, as my accusers alleged at the time. Despite the present euphoria about the imminence of balkanized independence in some of our South African reserves, there is not even a ripple in the pen regarding the sharing of power and decision-making by all South Africans.

I would be curious to know if the Prime Minister, and all the people who condemned me, particularly certain sections of both the English and Afrikaans press, still think my warnings were a symptom of irresponsibility on my part.

My brothers and sisters, today we meet in what is no doubt one of the most dramatic moments of South African history. After a 300 year white presence in our land, we find not much for our comfort. We have been through 150 years of white domination, and have been subjected to 66 years of oppression. All this has become the South African way of life.

This has been perpetrated against us in the name of Western democracy, and Christian civilization, by white manipulation of the Houses of Parliament and members of the Assembly. Despite all this time during which the status quo has reigned, we find today more than ever, that the very foundations of the apartheid society have been stolen. After more than 10 years of scorn and ridicule of Prime Minister MacMillan's "Winds of Change" warning, who can deny today that these winds of change are blowing not north or west of us, but right on our own borders?

The Prime Minister's detente policy has not succeeded. Not only has it not succeeded, but white South Africa has burnt her fingers in Angola. There was a scream of applause throughout South Africa, and outside, when South African troops were withdrawn from Zimbabwe. But we have seen in a matter of months that score erased by South Africa herself, through her Angolan connection. The pace of events and the struggle for liberation in southern Africa is gaining momentum, to the extent that the country's all-white Parliament cannot dictate Namibia very much longer. Mr. Vorster's influence in Zimbabwe has proven to be less influential than his black counterparts'. What do we see all around us? Our white countrymen are developing a war psychosis and are in the very real danger of retreating into a last stand white citadel. Indeed, both at street level and at ministerial level white South Africans are heard in private conversations, boasting of their state of preparedness and of the sophistication of their armaments. This is true even though there have been some voices even at ministerial level pointing out that these things are not good enough without the moral support of the majority of the population. But these same voices are made inconsequential by actions in Angola and the reluctance of white South Africa to share power with us.

Every hour of the day the time is drawing nearer when we will see white South Africa's enemies encamped on South Africa's borders. It is becoming more apparent every day that what was seen as Mr. Vorster's very gallant attempt to keep black buffer states, which do not cooperate with surrounding South Africa, is proving to be a dismal failure.

I know that the Prime Minister will no doubt think that I am speaking as I do because I am "a Kaffir who has forgotten his place." This thought makes many white South Africans mad. There is nothing they loathe as much as a Kaffir who has not been successfully kept in his place. To tolerate this would be to promote a process of destruction at the very foundations of the South African way of life. We have seen many white elections in our lifetime which have been fought on the basis of who can best keep the Kaffir in his place. If the Prime Minister, or anyone, should consider my utterances here today as irresponsible, my answer to such a charge would be: Had this not been their attitude, what precluded the Prime Minister from consulting me about his so-called detente policy in the light of my contacts in black Africa?

I think it is about time the Prime Minister, and white South Africa as a whole, realize that they cannot expect support from black South Africans in their white struggle to maintain a position of white dominance in southern Africa. Mr. Vorster did not bother to consult a single black leader on his detente initiatives. If he thinks he can disdain black opinion in this way, and then hope that blacks will offer themselves to be cannon fodder, this is a grave mistake.

As I have reminded you, I told Mr. Vorster and the world in January last year, that unless detente began at home, it would not succeed across our borders. He has excluded blacks from the national decision-making machinery of the country just like his predecessors. He has thus excluded blacks from the process by which foreign policy is determined. By excluding us in this way he has excluded us from the responsibility of making his national policies work and making his foreign policy effective.

South Africa has a place in southern Africa. In fact, as I have pointed out in the past, it has a very important role to play in the continent of Africa. My brothers and sisters, history now demands that we take our rightful place in Africa. History also demands, however, that what is South Africa's rightful place should be determined by the majority of the people of this country.

In spite of these words, I repeat that I still believe it is not too late to call for a white change of heart. I believe this not because I think that whites are going to have a sudden spasm of benevolence towards blacks. I believe that now the whites can see the "writing on the wall" and surely they must now realize that the country must move towards majority rule.

It is this single principle that is central to any question about southern Africa's politics. This is the burning question in Namibia. This is the burning question in Zimbabwe, as much as it has been the burning question in Mozambique and Angola. And as you all know, before other countries became independent, it was the burning question in every other African state.

I realize what I am doing here today by saying these things. These are very blunt words, but at this time they must be said. If they were not said, I would not be responsible. If no one amongst almost 18 million of us said them, history would judge all of us very harshly. Those who have ears to hear what I say will understand that I am offering a black hand of friendship to the whites of South Africa. Yes, it is a black hand, but it is still a hand of friendship.

You all know that serious maladies may call for painful surgery if that is necessary to save life. South Africa's malady is the refusal to share power with blacks. Now it is our turn to tell them that whites in this country can do only one thing to help themselves, and they can do only one thing to help us help them. They must be prepared to share power. This must be said, and it falls to my lot to say it today.

I have great expectations about my address today because I am going to speak on your behalf. I am going to express your concerns, and I am going to talk with the Black Voice of South Africa. The apartheid society, nurtured with a plethora of discriminatory laws which we blacks have despised for more than a quarter of a century, has already been overtaken by history. In this eleventh hour, in this last hour, some things need to be said in this country. They need to be said by blacks and they need to be said very clearly and in unequivocal terms.

No man must be able to say that he did not know, that he did not realize, that he did not understand. It is my experience that whites do not look into the future. The future they are creating is too horrible to contemplate. It is ironic that the Prime Minister must have had this in mind when he spelled the alternative to detente, almost in those words, as "too ghastly to contemplate." We blacks can look into the future. In the black future there is hope, there is liberation and there is the realization of human dignity.

We blacks are concerned first and foremost with liberation. We want to be free from oppression. We want to be free from the stigma of being unworthy of full citizenship or of being worthy only of fourth class citizenship and unworthy of having a real vote in the country of our birth. We want to be free and equal to all other men. We want to be free to participate in majority decisions about the future of our country and our common destiny with other South Africans.

We disdain the political role into which the white minority has relegated us. The white minority has foisted on us political circumstances which make a mockery of our dignity and our responsibility.

Because we have no schools other than those grudgingly granted to us, we have no education other than by inferior facilities. We can make no real decision even on what language should be used to teach our children. We have no place to live other than the monotonous drab houses given to our use here in a place like Soweto. We have no jobs other than those given to us by frightened whites, whose insecurity makes them fear competition on a man-to-man basis.

We have no black administration other than that provided by a frightened government which will not allow us blacks to compete with their positions as members of Parliament on merit in the constituencies of South Africa.

We have no choice but to live where the whites say we must live, do work which the whites say we can do. We cannot choose where to live. Our children are not free to pursue their own lives and choose their own careers.

I sympathize with you, my brothers and sisters, because just like you, I am not free. Like you, I do what I can. Together we suffer oppression. Together we must throw off the yoke of oppression.

Separate Development

The whole world must be told that we despise what some people euphemistically call "a separate development" of "separate freedoms," which we know to be nothing more than white BAASKAP (apartheid). South Africa is one country; it has one destiny and it in fact has one economy. Those who are attempting to divide the land of our birth are attempting to stem the tide of history just as King Canute played with sand in a puerile attempt to ward off the waves of the sea. They are mistaken men and are fighting against the force of history that began marching across Africa's borders by 1976. They act like puny men. They have not the strength to hold history back. History will triumph over apartheid. It will triumph because, in the final analysis, history is made by majorities and not by minorities. Minorities cannot prevail forever. Nowhere in the world have minorities prevailed against the majority indefinitely. The minority in our country has already lost its grip on reality. It cannot succeed very much longer.

Let Us Look at What They Have Already Lost

Successive governments in South Africa since 1910 in broad terms have pursued rather single-mindedly a policy designed to increase and protect the position of the privileged minority power elite. White politics has always been about squabbles among the elitists who vie with each other to be top dog in championing the rich and suppressing the poor.

White policy in South Africa for decades has been leading to the present position in which:

—Political treachery stalks the land. Treachery by the government and secret police. Bribery, manipulation and detention without trial. The banning of people, the banning of organizations are political treachery as far as the majority of South Africans are concerned.

—Constitutionally, the politics of constructive reconciliation is not possible in our country if the government persists in its headlong plunge into what amounts to political stupidity.

—The machinery of oppression which is the most subversive element in our country does not make it possible for the black majority of the country to play a positive role in the corridors of power, where real and meaningful wielding of power takes place.

Since 1910, successive governments have planted seeds of destruction in our country. We blacks do not believe that the social and moral elitism produced out of the fabric of our society can be defended morally or theologically. Nor can this tattered society be defended militarily in a situation of real conflict. The majority of blacks will not find it in their hearts to die on the country's borders to defend a system which is to them morally repugnant, a system which dehumanizes them and which mocks God Almighty for creating us blacks also in his image.

When we blacks look at Africa, and southern Africa in particular, we desire to take our place with our black brothers in their new world.

We, the majority of blacks, are primarily concerned with our liberation. We are concerned with our liberation not because we want to exploit the white elite in the way in which they have exploited us for generations. We are primarily concerned with our liberation because we want to play a constructive role for everybody. We have seen enough oppression in this land we love.

Peace

We will not perpetuate oppression. We want to live in peace, and we will want to pursue policies which will bring peace in our land, as well as peace between the states of southern Africa.

Revolution

I know that to many of my white countrymen these words will be interpreted as if I were advocating revolution. This in itself is inevitable, but in the words of the late Senator Robert Kennedy:

> A revolution is coming—a revolution which will be peaceful if we are wise enough, compassionate if we care enough, successful if we are fortunate enough, but revolution which is coming whether we will it or not. We can affect its character; we cannot alter its inevitability.

It is entirely up to white South Africa whether the revolution that is unfolding will be peaceful or bloody.

Black responsibility and black contributions to peace can only come after liberation in South Africa. This liberation is not possible within the context of apartheid society.

I challenge anyone to prove to me that the majority of blacks want the so-called independence which is offered to our reserves now called "homelands." The people who have elected me have given me no mandate to opt for the so-called homeland. They have toiled for generations to create the wealth of South Africa and do not want to abandon their birthright. They intend to participate in the wealth of the land.

No single black leader will dare to go to his people to decide the independence issue on the basis of a referendum. Some people are prone to mis-assess the black political scene. Because there is conflict among black groups, they believe that there is not an underlying black solidarity when it comes to the question of liberation.

My brothers and sisters, you know as well as I do that there is no room for division among ourselves when it comes to the question of liberation.

The divisions that appear to be among us are only debates about the methods which should be employed in order to liberate ourselves.

The vast majority of blacks are united in their opposition to apartheid and its consequences.

Beyond any divisions which appear to be present in black society, there is a unity based on a deep-rooted black nationalism. It is a reality which political theoreticians cannot verbalize out of existence.

The bricks of black nationalism are many and varied. There are ethnic groups, there are tribes, there are trade unions, drama societies, black church groups, student organizations, cultural groups and many others.

28

STORM WARNINGS

Government Policies

We are not afraid to say what we think of government policies. Some of us have never been afraid to say so, and so no one can accuse us of trying to cash in on the present fluidity in the southern African political situation.

Therefore we tell the Prime Minister today that the policies of his government are unacceptable to us; we tell him that he will never persuade the majority of us to accept his policies because we all know that:

—The government's economic policy is designed to perpetuate the privileged position of whites.

—The government's social policy makes humiliating assumptions about the black man's dignity.

—The government's political policy is the moat of besieged white self-interest.

—The government's foreign policy pursues ends which support apartheid and discrimination.

We blacks must continue to tell the world where we stand in regard to such policies.

We want to go beyond just negative criticisms of the apartheid society we so despise. What is needed urgently is that we put ourselves in a position to provide alternative policies for our country. If we do not do this, history will catch us flat-footed.

National Conventions

I believe that it is absolutely essential that we hold a series of representative national conventions representing all shades of black opinion.

I have called for a black national convention on economic matters.* It is important that this convention take place in August if all goes as planned.

I also think that it is warranted to call for a national convention on the so-called homeland independence issue.

I also call for a national convention on South Africa's foreign policy.

Let us treat each of these areas of black concern independently and in depth.

Let us do for ourselves what Mr. Vorster's white parliament does not do for us. This white parliament does not and cannot serve the best interests of blacks. It is now time for the blacks of the country to recognize that in the divide-and-rule policy of the government, no provision is made for blacks to enter into the decision-making process on crucial national issues which affect the majority of the people.

*This conference did not take place after the Soweto riots of June 1976 occurred.

We cannot wait for Mr. Vorster's government to do something about black decision-making at the national level. He has said bluntly that he will never do so as long as he and his party are at the helm of South African affairs. He said this to us on the 22nd of January 1975 as I told you last year. We must therefore act unilaterally in defining South Africa's policies. It is the policies we blacks define that will be heard and heeded by our brothers in Africa as well as in many other quarters of the world.

I am hoping that we will invite international speakers to these conventions. We will hear their wisdom. We will then close our doors and go into a black caucus where we will deliberate among ourselves.

It has been reiterated over and over again by government spokesmen that there is peace and stability in South Africa. This fact makes me assume that they ought to welcome a series of national black conventions and they ought not to hinder us in our plans to get together in order to talk about our country, and our future, which is tied to their own. At this time I should assume that there should even be eagerness on the part of the government to want to know what is the black consensus on crucial issues. I expect that speakers we may invite from outside to address us will have no problems in getting into the country. I say this with such certainty, as I feel certain that the government cannot misjudge the mood of our people at this time.

My brothers and sisters, I am the last person to beat the drums of racial tension. I am only being constructive and responsible despite the racial tension that imposed government policies create in this beautiful land of so much plenty.

It is high time the privileged in this country heard the voice of the underprivileged. They have failed to do this so far. Theirs is, I am afraid, a willful failure. It is this willful persistence in social and political stupidity which is productive of despair and anger which in turn create racial tension. These have seeds of our own self-destruction.

This is the country of our birth and in our country there is only one majority. I see very serious problems arising in the very near future if the government's policies result in the black majority's rejecting the contributions of the white minority. It is good that black nationalism, born in 1912 in Bloemfontein with the founding of the African National Congress, has filled the emergence of black consciousness. It is only through these factors that the dignity of the black man, so trodden under for so long, can be salvaged. This dignity must recieve the respect it deserves. It is my hope that the operative majority in this country will be a multi-racial majority. I have not yet despaired, despite so much that is certainly nought for our comfort. I do not believe for one moment that God created men to be divided among themselves. There was no apartheid in the Garden of Eden, and there is no apartheid in heaven. Why should there by apartheid in between?

The Son of God who came to save the world, is described by the Prophet Isaiah as a man who was despised. "Who knows?" as the late Senator Robert Kennedy asked when he visited South Africa. "What if God Himself is black?"

STORM WARNINGS

The Church

Let the church in South Africa support the majority in their movement towards constructive unity. The Church has in the past only paid lip service to this ideal. Some churches have not even done that much. It is perhaps necessary for black Christians to recognize that they have to take the lead at a national level. There may be protests from some white churchmen when they hear what I have said today about the Church. My answer to these protests is that the Church is rapidly losing credibility among blacks in South Africa. If churches are convinced that they have acted properly, then they have only convinced themselves. The Church has not been effective in its support for the black liberation struggle. I do admit that there have been outstanding individual churchmen who have witnessed. I say again that it is time for black Christians to take the lead in this matter.

The Church must take active steps towards reconciliation in this country before it is too late. There will be no true reconciliation until the blacks are liberated. In this matter the churches must act with conviction and what is more they must act in public.

> Let the people be free.
> Let the land be free.
> And let the Church be free.

In apartheid society people are divided against each other and the Church is torn by conflicts. In the name of God let us put our priorities in their proper order. In the interest of the Church, churchmen must support the black struggle for liberation.

Federal Formula—A Compromise Proposal

I have in the past called upon the whites to come to their senses. I even offered them a federal formula which mapped out their road towards responsible government. The whites are politically underdeveloped and they need assistance. The federal formula I offered them was the assistance they need if they are to develop politically. This was a compromise proposal. I must say now, and I must say with considerable emphasis, that such reconciliatory offers as were contained in my federal formula will be increasingly difficult to make in the southern Africa which is now emerging.

We blacks tell the whites that Mozambique and Angola are watershed events in Africa's history. Zimbabwe and Namibia will in the very near future broaden that watershed. South Africa will never be the same again. I implore the whites to turn away from the kind of future the government's present policies are creating. That kind of future is "too ghastly to contemplate."

31

Political Prisoners

As I have done so several time in the past, I again implore the the white government to release black political leaders now in jail.

As I Lie Awake

My brothers and sisters, when I lie awake, wide-eyed and staring because I am thinking about you and your suffering, many things come into my thoughts. In the small hours of the morning I lie awake; I know that thousands upon thousands of you get up in the dark to get on crowded buses and crowded trains to go to do a menial job for what in most cases, is a pittance. I know most of you work without security and social benefits. I know that you are denied real trade unions, and I know you are exploited.

As I lie awake at night, I know many of you also lie awake because you are cold, because you are hungry, because your child is sick, because you are worried. I know you are worried about your children. I know you are worried about tomorrow's food and tomorrow's rent. I know you feel anger because there seems to be no hope of improving your circumstances.

My message to you is that history has overtaken apartheid. There is hope for the future. Justice will prevail, and you will be given the opportunity to participate in the building of a better South Africa.

My message to you, however, is also that there is no magic formula to change the parade ground of the present racist regime into a Garden of Eden overnight. It was the sweat of the black man which built the economic wealth of South Africa that is denied to the sons and daughters of South Africa. It will be by the sweat of black man's brow that a new future will be built.

I appeal to your sense of realism, and I appeal to you in the name of your children, and in the name of future generations, to act constructively. We do not build a better South Africa by doing something in the future. We build a better South Africa by what we do now.

INKATHA

Before we can begin doing everything we need to organize ourselves into a disciplined body. We need to come together to support each other, plan with each other and act with each other.

My brothers, my sisters, we cannot wait until the Parliament in Capetown falls before we achieve that dignity which comes from self help and from making the best of the miserable mess we find ourselves in. Blacks in whatever corner of the country they find themselves are shrugging off the dependent mentality and philosophy, an act which has been expressed in the formation of Inkatha yeNkululeko yeSizwe.

STORM WARNINGS

In Inkatha people are getting together. It is a movement of ordinary men and women in ordinary walks of life, such as you see here today. As this movement gains momentum we will produce a ground swell which will bring about change in South Africa. Of this, I am absolutely convinced. Nothing can break my people's determination to shake off the chains that shackle them.

We see the need for reconciliation in a balkanized society, but there can be no reconciliation between a master and a servant, between a lord and a serf.

Reconciliation is a concept which applies only to equals. Equality in dignity is achievable now. Colonial and even feudal elements in the ruling elite will in future expect in vain that we remain beggars for the things which are our birth right.

I would like to stress over and over again that Inkatha is enabling ordinary men and women to articulate their positions, to formulate resolutions to their dilemmas and to seek answers to their questions. We are aware of the fact that as the insistence of Inkatha increases and as we move from questioning to statement and demand, there is danger of our being misunderstood. We are quite clear about this possibility. That is apart from the process already taking place of deliberately trying to misrepresent us in order to confuse people and to create more confusion amongst ourselves to serve the interests of our oppressors.

We accept that danger because there is greater danger yet in perpetuating a dependent and subservient mentality. The South African government wants us to be independent, as they say, and yet they have boycotted us as communities; they have thrown us on our own resources, but they will never succeed in making us perpetuate our own subservience. I hope my colleagues in other provinces will use their limited political dispensation to make Inkatha proliferate throughout South Africa. Inkatha has grown phenomenally during the past year and will continue to grow steadily.

I realize that some people might think that when I talk of freedom and liberation that I am thinking of the Zulus as distinct from my other African brothers in South Africa. In fact, our enemies are deliberately trying to propagate this falsehood. This is far from being the case. There is no Zulu freedom that is distinct from the black man's freedom in South Africa.

Black oppression has no ethnic boundaries. We have a common destiny as black people. We have indeed a common destiny even with our white countrymen who have rejected this idea for several generations. These are the implications of a just and non-racial society. The black man's struggle has to begin somewhere and quite clearly it has to begin right where each one of us is. The main thing to bear in mind is to have clear perspectives as to what the goals in our struggle are. We are victims of white exclusivity. We have been taught by our black experience to hate exclusivity, as exclusivity has been used as a base from which we have been victimized by probably the most wicked system ever devised by human beings to discriminate against other human beings.

In KwaZulu we have founded Inkatha, a National Cultural Liberation Movement, because we have learnt from experience that it is no use to wait and hope that others will come and help us in our predicament. We have concluded that in helping ourselves where it is possible to do so, we are taking an important step on the road to liberation. We hope that our brothers throughout the length and breadth of this land will get out of the apartheid straitjacket, as we are trying to do, and set up Inkatha as we have done. We are quite prepared to assist if there are problems about this because we believe that if this happens, black brotherhood will in due course become a reality in some kind of an all-embracing South African Inkatha. Two of the stated aims of the Inkatha Constitution are:

—To establish contact and liaison with other cultural groups in southern Africa with a view to the establishment of a common society.

—To cooperate locally and internationally with progressive African and other nationalist movements and political parties which work for the complete eradication of all forms of colonialism, racialism, neo-colonialism, imperialism and discrimination and to strive for the attainment of African unity.

We need not wait for the collapse of the white man's parliament for this development to grow.

Inkatha plainly declares itself to be an instrument of liberation. If others have difficulty in the activities of Inkatha let them form their own Inkathas. We are prepared to cooperate, as the business of black liberation is our business as much as it is their own. The important thing I wish to stress here is that to me it seems absolutely vital in our struggle for liberation for every organization which emerges among blacks to make possible unity with other black organizations. Division and the chewing of the cud of mutual recrimination have been the bane that has thwarted our freedom struggle for far too long. It has gone for so long and our oppression has gone on for so long because we allowed it.

There is nothing to stop us from having a number of Inkathas which, because their structure is similar and their constitution is similar, can join together in a national movement towards liberation. This is urgent as the time for talking is getting less every day and every hour. The era of action has dawned in southern Africa, and nothing, and not even military might, can succeed in snuffing it out. This is the challenge we face, my brothers and sisters.

In character and spirit Inkatha is not peculiarly Zulu or even peculiarly Natal. It is a constitution of the type which has emerged in black Africa to meet the deficiencies of the Westminster type constitution: a democratic system with the stamp of mother Africa, which has consensus as its core.

History now does not permit sectional leaders to create their own stamping grounds. All responsible leadership is faced with national questions which must be handled at the national level. These are matters which are above personal edification. These are matters of life and death for any people, which any people must face not as fragments but as one whole people.

My brothers, we must face this future. We must organize now as effectively as we can. I saw this need two years ago and I began organizing. I have always known that we need structures which span rural and urban areas and which span provinces. This kind of structure now exists in the form of Inkatha.

34

STORM WARNINGS

Africa needs you, my brothers, Africa needs you, my sisters. Yes, Africa needs you and me. This may turn out to be Africa's finest hour. The time has come for you to organize and act. This is the challenge you face, and this is the challenge I face. I WISH THEM WELL IN THE PATH THEY HAVE NOW CHOSEN IN THEIR WISDOM.

It seems to me to be a most unfortunate coincidence that as this hour beckons to us, to come and face this greatest challenge, we have also to lose at this very hour some of our brothers and sisters through a balkanization which can only give white domination a breathinq space and further prolong our people's suffering. I say these words not in a spirit of castigation. I respect my brothers in the Transkei and Bophuthatswana far too much to attempt to do this. This is a lament because my heart bleeds; for who knows what lies in store for them, or for us, in this ideological separation imposed on us by the white minority power elite through their unilateral parliamentary decisions? When a daughter in our society goes to get married, for some it may be a day of jubilation, for some it still remains a day of sorrow on account of the black future in a new life people face in each and every new situation. These are not words of condemnation but words of deep sorrow. I have always said and repeat here today that I wish them well in the path they have now chosen in their wisdom. It will only be tragic if the path they are treading is never trodden by the majority of blacks after them. I say so on the basis of the nationalist government's own stand, if I am to go by the discussions we have had with Mr. Vorster. His stand seems to spell a life of perpetual destitution and step-children status for black people within their so-called independence, as defined within the confines of 13 percent of South Africa's surface area. Whatever happens, I hope it will never be too late for us as brothers to save one another from the political wilderness where there can only be want, insecurity, and desperation.

God Bless Africa.
God Bless All Her Children.
Strength in the Struggle.
Hope for the Future.
Power is Ours.
Amandla! Ngawethu!
Matla! Ke Arona!

Chapter 5

DIALOGUE OR CONFRONTATION?

TO AN AFRIKANER CLUB

Umbongintwini, 30 April, 1976

I know how much in the modern world we are all nearly like automatons in the hands of mass-media. For this reason, I appreciate only too well the extent to which each one of you has his or her image of me, as it filters through the mass media. I therefore welcome this opportunity which has been given to me to present myself to you, so that you can confirm for yourselves whether your image of me is or is not a correct one.

I think it is most fortunate that I had this invitation not so long after I made my "notorious" Soweto speech. Various reactions to that speech, which I will be referring to more specifically a little later, proved how essential it was for me and other blacks to come to occasions like this in order to start the now overdue dialogue between white and black in South Africa. It is important to note here that we blacks have been denied the opportunity for such dialogue by our white countrymen all these years. In our society, which is so bedevilled by racial discrimination, this absence of meaningful contact has worsened relations between South Africa's various peoples. We just do not know each other as South Africans. We have known each other only as masters and servants. When a curtain is drawn between people, only disaster can result, as it is so very natural to fear and hate what one does not know. Fear and Hate! Those twin pillars of disaster between which prospects of a peaceful future for all South Africa's people will be crushed if we are not vigilant and diligent enough to do something concrete about this situation now. We do so now, or never.

I must apologize for using a language which is neither my own nor your own, in conducting this dialogue. I know it would mean so much more to you if I addressed you in your own language. I want you to know that this is one of the regrets of my entire life that I was not able to learn Afrikaans at school. This was not my fault. During my childhood, black education fell under the Natal Provincial department of education, and at the time, it was not possible for us to learn Afrikaans. This was mainly because this is a predominantly English-speaking province, and industry and commerce were also in the hands of English-speaking South Africans, almost exclusively. So English was at that time the only language of bread. It must be remembered that this was long before the Afrikaners reached political ascendancy in South Africa. There were also no teachers in black schools who could teach Afrikaans to Africans. I am afraid, even at present, that we struggle with very few teachers who are really proficient in Afrikaans.

I have explained the cause of this handicap at such great length because I realize that it is one of the greatest causes of the lack of such dialogue as should have started long ago between us. What is more, many Afrikaaners take it as a slight that we are unable to speak their language when they are in power in South Africa and when they comprise more than 60 per cent of South Africa's white population. Many Afrikaners quite erroneously take this to be a result of deliberate negligence on our part. Some interpret it as the very measure of our being more prejudiced against them than their English-speaking compatriots. When our utterances come through the English press, it is a most intolerable thing from the point of view of Afrikaaners. It appears to some of them as arrogant that we should address them through "die Engelse pers." I realize that we are operating under terrific handicaps, as this immediately makes many Afrikaners draw blinds across their hearts and minds, and fail to pay any heed at all to what some of us say.

I first realized that I was thus handicapped amongst my Afrikaans-speaking countrymen when I met a prominent Afrikaner journalist and now a friend. This was Otto Krause. He asked me the question:

"Gatsha, what do you think of the Afrikaners?"

My response to him was: "Otto, I have no blanket opinion on the Afrikaners; they are individuals, with good and bad like all other people. I have many close friends amongst Afrikaners."

Mr. Krause's reply was: "Come on! Gatsha, you are now being just a good politician!"

It never occurred to my friend that I was answering his question sincerely, that in fact I meant what I said. This was during a break at an international symposium in Johannesburg which we attended with Paramount-Chief K.D. Matanzima, the Chief Minister of the Transkei, and Chief L.M. Mangope of Bophuthatswana. I was therefore quite horrified when I was later referred to as a "black Englishman," and Chief Mangope as a "black Afrikaner"! This was only three years ago. It should indicate to you the lack of dialogue and understanding between us.

That is why I accepted without any hesitation the invitation by Kajuitraad to come here and address you. The Chairman of Kajuitraad suggested that it might be of interest for you to know from me the Zulu view of whites, and specifically of the Afrikaner, and this view in relation to development and progress towards self-determination. These were just guidelines which the Chairman of the Kajuitraad thought might be of great interest to you.

There was a time when blacks bent backwards in attempts to present themselves in the light in which whites would like to see them. We have now

DIALOGUE OR CONFRONTATION

fortunately reached a stage when we do not believe that it serves any purpose to pose or posture in order to gain acceptability in white circles. We have reached the point when we should really know each other as we really are, warts and all. Whilst it is important in our society to reach a common understanding, I think it is important for us to acknowledge that for white Africans, such as you are, it is of primary importance for you to come to terms with nearly 200 million black Africans who populate this continent, of which you are longing so much to be seen as a part. White South Africa is engaged in rather feeble attempts to come to terms with black Africa. I call these attempts feeble, because they remain meaningless and hollow so long as black and white South Africans have not come to terms first. Africa having come into her own, has forced white South Africa to bend backwards in seeking common ground with the majority of the inhabitants of the continent of Africa, rather than with Europe of which you pride yourselves as being a part, culturally and ideologically. I do not want to appear to be debunking the reality of those sentiments, but Angola and Mozambique, I hope, have stripped whites of their comfortable blinkers. I therefore hope that you are no longer under any illusion and that you appreciate that in Africa you have to come to terms with millions of other inhabitants of Africa and not via any foreign country or through foreigners. This must be on an eyeball to eyeball basis.

This is the reason why I regard my invitation here tonight as very important. One of the objectives of Kajuitraad is "creating better insight, appreciation, and understanding on current and important matters of our day. . . . To make a positive contribution towards the promotion of better human relations, respect and understanding between the Afrikaans-speaking population and other population groups in our republic."

I regard this assignment as one of the most important and historic ones of my entire career. I have always known that if one is to get through to the powers-that-be, it should mostly be through direct dialogue with the Afrikaners who wield power over me and my people. It has so far been unfortunate, as you will see later, that through the machinations of your mass-media, I have been either ignored or if any attention was paid to me at all, it was only when I have been condemned for the things I have said, and for the things that I stand for. This, in itself, is not a bad thing, that there should be blacks like me who are condemned for their convictions.

On the other hand there is a strong school of thought amongst my people, which does not believe that any dialogue of the sort we are having tonight serves any purpose whatsoever. They believe that only through confrontation can South Africa's problems be solved. This view has been greatly strengthened by what has happened in Mozambique, Angola, and what is now happening in Namibia and Zimbabwe. The psychological effect on black minds of liberation in Mozambique and Angola through bullets rather than ballots has been tremendous. It is these events, more than any other factor, that make many blacks feel that the era of dialogue is now past, and that the era of confrontation has come as the only MODUS OPERANDI through which black men can attain liberty in southern Africa. When blacks look at the history of the Afrikaner, they see Afrikaner leaders of yesteryear as men who helped Afrikaners to reach fulfillment through confrontation and revolution. Leaders of the Afrikaners such as General Hertzog, General De Wet, Dr. Malan, spoke blood and thunder. Afrikaner heroes include men who led Afrikaners not only via sweat, but also through blood and tears. The Africans who feel that the age of dialogue is gone remember that Afrikaner saints such as Japie Fourie, Roby Leibrandt and others who were seen by the powers of their day as rebels and revolutionaries, stand tall on the pages of the Afrikaner's history books because they were prepared even to lose their lives to move the Afrikaner toward his fulfillment. The Africans who hold the view that the time for dialogue is past feel that Afrikaners do not have to look too far back to see where all these sacrifices led them. They think it is even a betrayal of the black man's cause to pretend that blacks can attain what the Afrikaner has attained for himself, except via the same route, strewn with blood and lost lives, which the Afrikaner traversed. I believe that even at this late hour, the time for dialogue is not gone. If all South Africans seized their courage and got together, we would have meaningful dialogue, as distinct from the exercises in monologue which I see at present.

On a day like this, I might have been expected not to go beyond certain boundaries in saying what I have to say. I feel certain that with the kind of beginning I have made, you can see that I do not regard tonight's event as just a social event during which one would be expected to give a "be nice to the Boers" speech. The object in doing this would be not to upset anyone in the audience by raising his blood pressure, particularly after the sumptuous meal of which we have just partaken. I could easily confine myself to portraying a certain profile of myself which I thought you would find acceptable.

I am not coming here in any spirit of penitence for daring to attack some of the white sacred cows at Jabulani Amphitheatre last month. So let me say, I am very sorry if there are any people here tonight who may be expecting me to confine myself to a humorous vein, especially to illustrate that I still "know my place." This would mean that in the things I say here tonight, I would take my audience on a primrose garden path tour. It would mean confining what I say only to those areas in our co-existence least likely to cause controversy. This would mean peppering my speech with platitudes in the classic tradition of diplomacy.

There are many temptations that could have influenced what I have to say tonight. For instance, it would have been quite a simple matter for me to entertain you with an account of how the Afrikaans press took me to task for what I said in Soweto. There are plenty of funny cartoons that I could have shown you tonight, and that would have enabled me to pretend that the laugh is on me. This would have enabled you, when we go our separate ways after tonight's dialogue, to say, "Ai, on Gatsha! He's darem got a good sense of humour, hey?"

To be quite frank, if I were convinced that we had plenty of time in South Africa, I might have been tempted to do this, in the hope of softening you for more blunt words next time. But how do I know if there will be a next time? These are times of crisis, ladies and gentlemen.

There are alien soldiers on South Africa's borders, and there is very little time to decide what to do about their presence on those borders. The crisis asks, "What can people who are as alienated as white and black South Africans are, actually do people who are as alienated as white and black South Africans are, actually do about even belonged to one nation. Dr. Verwoerd did not mince words about not regarding blacks as part of what he called the South African Nation. This is not the fault of just the Afrikaner, but of all whites, including the English, over generations. The tensions which strain the very fabric of our society are worsening day by day. If they are to be defused, this must be done as quickly as possible. They can be defused through dialogue if we decide today to use to the optimum the limited time that we still have at our disposal.

African states, or the OAU if you like, through the Lusaka Manifesto of 1969, acknowledged the fact that we have a common destiny. It recognized that white South Africans are also indigenes of South Africa. This important document placed beyond dispute your right to be here.

We are living in times of trouble. There is great insecurity about the future. Throughout South Africa, family groups both black and white are searching their minds for the wisdom that can enable this country to avoid what is otherwise an imminent holocaust. Events around us are compelling us to make momentous decisions about our future. People are worried. Has this country a future? Do they have a future within the southern Africa that is now unfolding? It is tragic that in life prophets have no honour in their own countries. When I say this, I am thinking of how the late Professor P.V. Pistorius, amongst other Afrikaner prophets, earned himself abuse with his prophecies more than 20 years ago. I think here of his little book entitled NO FURTHER TREK. He stated in that book:

> There are groups and they do mistrust and fear and hate one another. But there is no further trek. Hate, unless arrested, must take its course. We are like heroes in some classical drama. We see our own doom inevitably approaching, but we are powerless to avert it. And it is a doom of our own making. Those whom the gods wish to destroy, they make insane. What gods have made the various groups in South Africa blind and insane? God could not have done so, since He has revealed Himself to the World as a God of love. But the gods of our own making have power. He who creates a tribal god will perish by the tribal gods of others. He who worships his own group and regards even injustice as good if it is thought to be in the interests of his qroup will perish by the injustices perpetrated by other groups. The stone in the pond can be removed, but no power can halt the undulations caused by its fall. They become ever wider.

Now this was said long before there were any Cubans on South Africa's borders. Professor Pistorius' theme was that human problems are not solved by running away from them. He illustrated his point by quoting the example of the exodus of the Huguenots from France, and the Voortrekkers from the Cape. How much better for them,"Huguenots or the Voortrekkers, if instead of going away from something, they had first solved their human problems and then had thought of going to, instead of going away from something."

The massacre of Piet Retief and his followers was an attempt at solving a problem, but it was no solution. The massacre of Zulus at Blood River in 1838 was also an attempt at solving a problem which was also no solution. The whole idea of keeping blacks out of decision-making ever since they were conquered, has been no solution. Decisions that have been taken for them have proved to be no solutions. The Anglo-Boer War was supposed to be solution, but it was not. Let us think deeply about these things in 1976, particularly after passing a defense budget which is astronomical. Can this solve our problems? I have great doubts, quite apart from what the Holy Writ tells us that "those who live by the sword shall perish by the sword."

The decision of the present government to pursue a "homelands policy" without the concurrence of blacks, is no solution. I will return to this later. I want to say that a number of good things have accrued to blacks as a result of the policies pursued by the present government, policies based on a philosophy which is repugnant to most blacks. I think, for example, of things like business opportunities in these areas and the opportunity, which Afrikaners had, to struggle for the attainment of one's self-realization. I would like, at this point, to pay tribute to many Afrikaners who work as functionaries in areas like KwaZulu, who are dedicated and have rendered inestimable service to blacks. The fact that these modest benefits have been achieved for the wrong reasons, cannot prevent us from honesty, and from paying tribute to these dedicated men who are not decision-makers but who are just doing a job that has to be done. These are men in our civil service and some planners in Pretoria and people who work in corporations that promote the economic development of these areas. These are men who bear the brunt of government policies because the wrath of my people at having these things rammed down their throats is felt by these men who come into contact with us. There are many people who expect us to be satisfied with crumbs, a thing which the Afrikaners themselves refused to do when they were dominated by the British. All these things prove that dialogue in South Africa has not even begun. Today there are voices that say we must work with the Afrikaner because he wields power and makes decisions. But in fact these would-be mentors forget that we have been doing this for quite a long time. But so far there is not dialogue within this straitjacket. I proposed a national convention a few years ago, and I was told by the government spokesman that there was no need for such a convention, as the present government knew what to do. I also proposed to the Prime Minister that we must have a multi-national council for South Africa such as exists in Namibia, and I was told by the Prime Minister that there was no need for such a council, that it was necessary in Namibia because South-West Africa was a special international issue.

Is it any wonder that the mood of uncertainty which is unsettling the great democracies of the world has begun to cast its shadow into South Africa? The fact that Providence provided added burdens here as a result of the cosmopolitan nature of our population makes these shadows much more ominous here than elsewhere. Despite the false sense of jubilation at imminent "homeland independence," we are just kidding ourselves if we think that our problems in South Africa will thereby prove to be soluble. Who can deny that fear is triumphing over us at this approaching hour of crisis? With so much fear in this country, who can really seriously believe that we have even begun to solve our problems? Fear is the most terrible of all our emotions. Professor Pistorius described it in these words:

DIALOGUE OR CONFRONTATION

Many of our fears are very deep-seated. Many of our fears have their origins in the distant past, and in this discussion we can at most point to facts and phenomena without attempting an exhaustive historical and psychological analysis. But fear is dynamic. It may be caused by objective factors. There may be good reason to fear. But it never ends there. Fear always goes further than the factors which caused it. It is creative and dynamic in the sense that it basically changes its victims. It destroys reason, even humanity itself. Under its influence, individuals become vicious, a rational and reasonable man becomes irrational and unreasonable. It engenders hatred and violence in one who fears and in the one who is feared, and society often finds it necessary, for its own safety, to put the victims of insane fear under restraint.

As a result of this fear what do we see? There are probably more than 300,000 whites who are now clutching nervously at their British or foreign passports as their only fire escape should the worst overtake us. Some whites are leaving the country fearing the worst. Some blacks, as can be seen in the pattern of cases in some of our courts, are leaving the country, fed up with frustration. Some whites are prepared to go to war. In fact, to say "some whites" is an understatement. We have, as I have indicated, a high defense budget this financial year.

There are some blacks who are not intimidated by this apparently formidable strength of the South African whites and who are therefore prepared to oppose them.

This makes it clear to anyone thinking of a prognosis for the next decade that whichever way the winds of change blow, the next decade will certainly see a most radical change in the history of our co-existence. The forces of nationalism are on the move—white nationalism because it feels threatened and besieged; black nationalism because it has to find expression! Our duty to future generations, therefore, is to force these forces off the collision course they are certainly on.

I have worked within the policies of your government despite my qualms of conscience because I tried to be a realist.

I realized that with the forces arrayed against us we blacks had to look up to the white man for our material needs, as something dictated by the economic realities of our situation. I realized that as the Afrikaner was, at this point in time, wielding power, we had to look up to him, whatever feelings we may have about him. This again was a matter which to me automatically flowed from the political dynamics of our situation. It is the Afrikaner that rules the sub-continent and therefore has been making decisions for us for almost thirty years now. I do not doubt that the Afrikaner may have been prepared for this role by the test of brimstone and fire he went through during the last 70 years. Despite all this, I wish to appear a bit immodest and say that the Afrikaner has to get out of his cocoon and understand me, or my people's aspirations, if the common survival of black and white is to be assured. This is not demanding the impossible, for did the British not finally have to climb down with so much grace to reach common understanding with the Afrikaner? This, as you have seen, is my main theme tonight and this is what I am talking about. I would like to continue to explore with you for the moment the relationship between the black man and the Afrikaner in general and the role of the Afrikaans mass-media, particularly the Afrikaans press.

We have, as I have indicated, some common ground to start from. I do believe that the Afrikaner shares with me my deep concern about the role of the press in shaping the minds of our people. It has always struck me that the Afrikaans press never bothers to cover events in KwaZulu, not even the proceedings of the KwaZulu Legislative Assembly, an Afrikaner creation. I only receive phone calls from the Afrikaans press if something that is construed as giving me negative publicity takes place; for example, when a red-herring about banned literature was introduced to cover up the rifling of my luggage by customs officials at Jan Smuts last November, I received phone calls even from some editors of Afrikaans newspapers. But before I go any further, I wish to quote from Marshall McLuhan's book: THE MEDIUM IS THE MESSAGE:

> The medium is reshaping and restructuring patterns of social interdependence and every aspect of our personal lives. It is forcing us to reconsider and re-evaluate practically every thought, every action, and every institution formerly taken for granted. Everything is changing — you, your family, your neighbourhood, your education, your job, your government, your relationship to "the others." And they're changing dramatically. Societies have always been shaped more by nature of the media by which men communicate than by the content of the communication.

Quite clearly the press in our modern society bears a responsibility which cannot be over-emphasized. The press finally determines the course of events because they are instrumental in shaping our thoughts. I have decided to single out the Afrikaans-language press tonight not because they are more guilty, but because they have to bear the added responsibility of representing to us a mirror of the mind of the ruling party. I believe that I can give you a valuable insight into the damage that can be done by an insensitive or irresponsible press. On the other hand it might help, vis-a-vis the attitude of the Afrikaans press towards me, for me to point out that I have been hauled over the coals twice at the highest level in this country, "for being used by the English press." Furthermore, there are some newspaper editors, I believe, who have also been reprimanded at the highest level in this country for giving "too much publicity to my activities and statements."

Having said so, let me hasten to add that some of the most lucid and penetrating political analyses in South Africa today, are done by fearless Afrikaans editors, who have embraced the finest principles of free speech so well enunciated in the First Amendment to the American Constitution:

DIALOGUE OR CONFRONTATION

Congress shall make no law respecting an establishment of religion, or prohibiting the free exercise thereof; or abridging the freedom of speech or the press; or the right of the people peaceably to assemble and to petition the Government for a redress of grievances."

I would like to emphasize that I have actually seen that ideal alive in certain sections of the Afrikaans press. I would like to add that I was once warned, also at the highest level, against some of the Afrikaans press. There is no doubt that our Afrikaans newspaper editors have a vital role to play in the scenario that is now unfolding before us. They are the people who live close to the pulse of our political organism. They are involved with the decision-making process, perhaps more so than most other newspapers in the world, as they have the trusting ears of their readers. This is a responsibility which ranks with the executive branches of government. That is why I thought that in my discourse tonight some useful purpose might be served if I gave you some insight into the relationship between myself and the Afrikaans press. I regard this relationship as tremendously important.

I would like now to deal specifically with my "notorious" Soweto speech of March 14th, and in particular the way that speech was handled by the Afrikaans press. I do this because even at this eleventh hour, I still believe in exploring all possibilities for a dialogue between us and whites, particularly those whites who are the Afrikaners who wield power over us. I believe that when you see how the Afrikaans press handled that speech, you will appreciate the extent to which such dialogue as I am talking about tonight is rendered completely impossible by the very instruments which should promote it or pave the way for it to take place. I regard this example as most illuminating in showing the complete breakdown in dialogue and communication between black and white and particularly between the black man and the Afrikaner.

I have here the crop of Afrikaans newspaper cuttings in the wake of my Soweto speech. Collectively taken, they add up to a very disheartening fact. I have been labelled and pigeonholed out of effectiveness by the Afrikaans press. Their final verdict amounts to the conclusion that I am not at all worth listeninq to. I am quite prepared, of course, to accept that in a democracy they are entitled to their own views. But when this becomes a chorus reacting in unison, then clearly there is something wrong somewhere. It is significant that I had predicted this very thing in my speech in Soweto.

The reaction of the Afrikaans press is best summed up in the following quote from an editorial in DIE TRANSVALER: "Chief Buthelezi does not deserve as much attention as he is now getting."

And Dr. Andries Treurnicht was quick to add that I owe my position to the government, while Voorslag, DIE VADERLAND'S political columnist, accuses me of ASTRANTHEID.

The subtle nuances of those expressions are not lost on me. I am not hurt so much as concerned about the psychology that produced them. What is a mystery to me is why the Afrikaans press reacted with such unanimous alarm over the fact that I wore a uniform in Soweto. The tragedy is that the Afrikaans press did not take the trouble to send a representative to Soweto. They described to their readers something they did not actually see for themselves or through representatives. I wish they had taken the trouble to send a photographer to take a photograph so as to give their readers a better description than "a safari suit with big pockets," if you will pardon the ASTRANTHEID.

Ladies and gentlemen, jokes aside. I am truly amazed that the Afrikaner, of all people, should react with such portentous consternation to my uniform. It is only a symbol you know, not unlike the symbols with which the Afrikaner himself brought his own nationalism to fulfillment. Was the Voortrekker uniform not a symbol of his nationalism? Is the powder horn (the KRUITHORING) not central to the Afrikaner nationalist philosophy? Does the Afrikaner expect me to check with him whether my choice of symbols are acceptable to him? Did he check his own symbols of his nationalism with the British who defeated him during the Anglo-Boer War?

I could, if I chose to, have worn my traditional Zulu regalia tonight, but listen to what DIE BEELD thinks of that:

> Impressions of power-ambition, probably already fanned by events on our borders, cannot but be strengthened by the Zulu leader's aim to convert the Zulu Cultural Movement, Inkatha yeSizwe, into a "National Liberation Movement," which all blacks can join. Or else it would be totally strange renunciation of the Zulu's tribal ethos from a man who, on Shaka days, participates in tribal dances with shield and assegai.

My question is, was the Nationalist Party, before 1948, not a national liberation movement? Is Volkspele not a tribal dance? Did the Afrikaner renounce his tribal ethos when he wore the Voortrekker uniform?

Let me assure you that there is nothing sinister about my uniform. It reflects values, aspirations, dreams, and hopes, not unlike those which moved your own people into the free interior of this continent, and later into the dominant force that you are on the subcontinent. So what is it that prompts Voorslag to imagine that I would make "the neck hairs of many rise?" Because I wear a uniform, and he says, "a beret like Savimbi likes to wear." Has Savimbi now been dropped after the triumph of the MPLA in Angola? Why not Lord Montgomery, who made the beret famous in the last war? Why not similar to the Boy Scouts, who wear a similar uniform? TEMPO says: "There is a new tone in his voice . . ." (How would they know, since they were not there?) And it goes on: ". . . his clothes were different, too different, and the message is different, dangerously different."

I would very much like to know how TEMPO'S readers interpret that!

People in the struggle need a uniform in order to identify. This is the uniform of our National Cultural Liberation Movement—Do I also have to explain the meaning of liberation to the Afrikaner when it is clear that he knows much more about it from his own past experience than we do? Did your

DIALOGUE OR CONFRONTATION

liberation not triumph over ours? Why does it have to be something sinister if we, in our political wisdom, decide to follow the same path?

I have decided to make quite a fuss about the uniform tonight for two reasons. The first is that the reaction of the Afrikaans press to my uniform represents to me the first spontaneous reaction to a new development. The second reason is that since it is spontaneous and unanimous, it highlights the fear psychosis which, as I have pointed out, is dominating the white man's reasoning in these troubled times. This is not a good omen for the future of South Africa or for that matter of southern Africa.

Considering the emotional tenor of that reaction it is hardly surprising that they also reacted by matching hysteria to my choice of terminology. Just listen to what DIE VADERLAND had to say:

> But measured against the truth, the following and other pronouncements by Chief Buthelezi can only be interpreted in one way by the ordinary reasonable person...

It goes on to quote my speech as follows:

> The era of action has dawned in South Africa and no one, not even military might, will succeed in snuffing it out. The time has arrived to organize and act.

I would like to remind you that these words of mine could just as soon have come from a speech by a Nationalist Party speaker at a rally prior to 1948, but see what DIE VADERLAND makes of it:

> To the reasonable listener — however Chief Buthelezi may have meant it — it must sound like a blatant invitation to revolution to overthrow the existing order with violence.

Where does he get that from? If he believes that there is only one kind of action the black man is capable of — violent overthrow of the existing order — must he burden his readers with the same bias and tell them that Gatsha Buthelezi said so? I said no such thing. The words are those of DIE VADERLAND, and I have to accept that its readers, not having had access to the original, will happily go to the polls believing that I am bent on a violent revolution. Is this responsible journalism? But he goes on:

> To make a speech which is open to such an interpretion is highly irresponsible for a homeland leader. It is the language of the haters of whites, Nyerere and Machel, the gate to anarchy.

We have a law in this country which makes it an offense to stir up feelings of hostility between races. Can DIE VADERLAND's readers be blamed if they hate me on the basis of that distortion? DIE VADERLAND continues:

Finally, there remains the question, "What role do white helpers like Beyers Naude, (with whom Buthelezi issues statements these days) and the Progs play?"

Isn't that strange? On the one hand DIE VADERLAND labels me a hater of whites, and on the other hand it muses darkly over the influence of my white friends —. Is it not the policy of this country that the white man should help the black man towards "emancipation"? Why then should I not get assistance from whites? Or is it because Dr. Beyers Naude happens to fall into the category of KAFFERSBOETIE. I find Professor Pistorius' comment on the word KAFFERSBOETIE worth sharing with you tonight. He says that it is indeed a strange comment in a Christian society that the mere word indicating love for one's fellowmen should be a term of abuse. But more pertinently, when the Afrikaner fought for his own liberation, would he have allowed anyone to tell him who he should get his advice from? Are we expected to spurn the friendship of everyone who does not subscribe to National Party policy? Is that the only way open to us to find acceptance from the Afrikaner?

Most of the readers of the Afrikaans press see me under these circumstances as someone who does not want to cooperate with the government. In this context let me recall that I am severely criticized month after month in THE AFRICAN COMMUNIST in London for being what they dismiss as "Vorster's stooge." And yet when the churches in Switzerland seconded a trained secretary, Miss Kathi Hartmann, to run my office in order to train my own staff, Mr. Vorster and his cabinet refused her permission to come to South Africa and work for me. A few months ago OXFAM, a development foundation, seconded a young man, Andrew Clark, a qualified expert on community development, and the Prime Minister and his cabinet refused him a visa. The fact that he is a Quaker did not help at all. Quite a number of resolutions of my assembly and cabinet, are often ignored or disregarded by Pretoria. Despite our cooperation, we get cold comfort and we are reminded of the definition black Americans in the South of America gave for the word "cooperation" as meaning where one party does all the "operating" and the other party only the "cooing." How can the world believe that there is self-determination under these policies? How can they believe us even when we talk of investments in these areas if we are forbidden to get even the least and most rudimentary expertise from abroad? How can people abroad believe that there is any intention to make these areas economically viable as the government claims? Must I take the same liberties as DIE VADERLAND and conclude that only those advisers who conform to the government's vision of our homelands will be allowed to assist us? How can people who suffered the worst arrogance of British colonialism do this to us? How can one talk of dialogue seriously within this straitjacket?

To come back to the point I am discussing, Piet Snuffelaar of DIE TRANSVALER took exception to my use of the word "Kaffir" in my Soweto speech. This is what I said in Soweto:

DIALOGUE OR CONFRONTATION

I know as I have indicated earlier today that the Prime Minister will no doubt, if I am to judge by his past attitudes, think, with many white South Africans, that I am speaking as I do because I am a Kaffir who has forgotten his place.

Piet Snuffelaar finds that "pestilential." Listen:

> It is pestilential to pluck so continuously at the string of the KAFFIR, like Chief Buthelezi — It has been years that Chief Buthelezi has been plucking at that string. Why doesn't he leave it? Every time he uses it, he lowers the level of the dearly needed debate on where our different nations stand with each other.

It may seem pestilential to Piet Snuffelaar, but I will continue plucking at that string for as long as the word remains in common usage in the living rooms of whites. When we moved our departments that operated in Pietermaritzburg to Ulundi, the new KwaZulu capital, I was informed by a white official in black and white, that certain white officials seconded to us by Pretoria were reluctant to move to Ulundi, as they "did not want to live in a Kaffir town" as they put it. So that it is sheer illusion to think that the use of the word KAFFIR is confined only to the members of the HNP. As far as I know the word KAFFIR means "an infidel or an unbeliever." The term offends my Christian ethic if the application is religious. In the colloquial South African context it offends my dignity. If it lowers the level of debate, do not lay that at my door. I did not bring the word into this country. I know that it was first used by the British imperialists in India as a term of derogation. The same people brought it into this country, and it later found its way into the Afrikaans glossary as well. Why should I be a hypocrite or play up to hypocrites when the dignity of my people is being trampled underfoot everyday when the white man calls them "Mr." in public and "Kaffir" in private? Who is bluffing whom? Piet Snuffelaar continues:

> He also has a way of reacting in a peculiar manner when there are replies from the Afrikaans side to his arguments. Then he tells us such replies are like a "BASS" talking to a "KAFFIR."

Well, here I am doing it again! But I will not reply to that one. I will leave it to Dr. Andries Treurnicht to respond. This is what he said when he addressed a youthful audience in Pretoria three days after my speech:

> In recognition of the Zulu's national awareness the National Party created room in which the Zulus and other population groups in the country can exercise their right to self-determination. It is this that Chief Buthelezi has to thank for his position.

And Aida Parker of THE FINANCIAL GAZETTE, which I classify under Afrikaans Press, had the following to say:

Other black leaders? Chief Buthelezi, nothing if not frank, has never been backward about publicly expressing his full and unflattering appraisal of men like Paramount-Chief Kaiser Matanzima and Chief Lucas Mangope. No matter what Mr. Buthelezi believes, I very much doubt whether these two among others carry any burning love for their would-be Zulu "liberator". No. For my money at least, Chief Buthelezi is playing a dangerous game at a most dangerous time. And he should beware of the proverbial backlash. In the days of Verwoerd, Malan and General Hertzog he would have got it — hard and fast. Mr. Vorster treads more warily, presumably to avoid any counter-reaction from an increasingly leftish English medium press. Such delicacy could in the end prove a mistake. Leaving all the replies to Dr. Hertzog and Jaap Marais could yet prove a political boomerang.

There you have it. It is quite clear what she meant when she said I would have gotten it hard and fast. Clearly what she was trying to suggest was that I may end up wearing a different kind of uniform.

I find it quite interesting that Dr. Wimpie de Klerk disregarded his own newspaper's warning not to pay attention to me. I respect him for at least attempting to get into the nitty-gritty of what my speech was about. In his PERSPEKTIEF he starts off with the following quote from my Soweto speech:

> I believe that now the whites can see the writing on the wall and surely they can now realize that the country must move toward majority rule.

Dr. de Klerk's comment is: "Short and sweet! Buthelezi says: a black majority government must be South Africa's destiny."

It is omitted in this analysis that I stated that I hoped that the operative majority will be multi-racial.

He goes on to say that there will be the "gaan bars" reaction which dictates that you pay no attention to black demands because it is "the barking of a war of nerves." And there will be the "skop-skiet-and-donder" reaction — the sooner we have a race war the better the chance of white survival. But he says another reaction is possible, and he divides it into "four accents."

The first is that "we" should not over or underestimate the demand for black majority government. "Let us rather overestimate it if we have to choose," he says.

The second point he makes is that it will do no good to blame each other. As he put it, every hand put into our bosom will emerge leprous.

He said many homeland leaders obstructed homelands development, and they failed to inspire their people into national consciousness and productivity. Yet, I ask you, was it not the Afrikaner's refusal to conform to the "national consciousness and productivity" the British envisaged for them that inspired the Great Trek? How can I do more than I am doing to inspire nationalism and productivity in my people if it is Pretoria ultimately that has a final say?

Dr. de Klerk and many others may not know the number of times my cabinet's decisions and those of the KwaZulu Legislative Assembly are vetoed or

DIALOGUE OR CONFRONTATION

rejected by the Minister of Bantu Administration and Development. The rejection of personnel that I get on my own initiative, as illustrated earlier in this address, is a good example of Pretoria's breathing down our necks quite unnecessarily. It is an example of how the development of the black man is seen by them as their sole prerogative and how the development of the black man by the black man on his own initiative is something frowned upon. It must be done on the basis of "dialogue" (that is, the word "dialogue" as understood by Pretoria), on Pretoria's terms of reference. It is not the question of whether the lion and the lamb must have a dialogue, not on whether the lion must or must not eat the lamb, but the question of the lion deciding to tell the lamb how it is going to go about the job of eating it.

I assume also that prominent South Africans such as Dr. de Klerk are well aware of a campaign of vilification by the Communist bureau in London against me each and every month of the year with each and every copy of THE AFRICAN COMMUNIST and through SECHABA. He should be aware of the campaign for investments in KwaZulu and in other black reserves I have been conducting for quite a few years now. He should be aware that in fact a few industrialists have opened up factories at our industrial growth point at Isithebe.

We have negotiated with a few South African entrepreneurs on the establishment of certain concerns in KwaZulu. I must say that although there are many good and dedicated Afrikaners with whom we have cooperated in trying to attract investors, Afrikaner investors who wish to come and invest in KwaZulu are not as many as one would expect. I would have thought, this being the policy on which Afrikaners have voted the government into office for almost 30 years, that their support of industrial development of KwaZulu should be more conspicuous than is the cause at present. I hope Dr. de Klerk is also aware that there is an international lobby that denigrates me as "Vorster's stooge". If this is not bearing the brunt of this vilification and denigration for the sake of the development of my people, I wish to submit that I do not yet know what is meant by "obstructing homelands development", and by phrases such as "failing to inspire their people with national consciousness and productivity".

Having said this, let me concede, and this is not grudgingly done, that Dr. de Klerk has always impressed me through his writings as a fair-minded man. He criticizes the Afrikaner just as much. There are too many delays, he says. Two little penetration, too much hesitation in the face of problems. And then he says:

> But recriminations are not going to help. There is still time to turn homelands development into a revolutionary concept. Because it is the only alternative to eventual black majority rule in South Africa.

Ladies and gentlemen, I do not think that you have to turn homelands development into a revolutionary idea, for it was a revolutionary idea from its very inception.

But there can be no alternative to majority government in the evolutionary context, even if we wait until all of us become coffee-coloured. Apartheid is a device of our time and place. It cannot survive. In a thousand years

51

hence, will we still have a lily-white whiteman's tan here, guarding its racial purity against the incursions of the infidel? Is that really possible, if we take into account the fact that South Africa has become an embarrassment even to her allies? In the famous phrase coined by DIE BURGER, South Africa is the polecat of the world. I had a chuckle to myself when I saw how DIE BURGER cartooned me after my Soweto speech with Mr. Colin Eglin in the company of the MPLA — as always represented in DIE BURGER as a skunk. I thought, well I have also graduated into the stinking fraternity to which South Africa belongs, or is this a separate fraternity of stinkers?

Dr. de Klerk expresses a third "accent." The homelands must be turned into a success story. And then he says something very seductive:

> The blacks will only identify with the homelands if the borders are acceptable.

And then in brackets:

> [Consolidation has been completed, the new phase is now further negotiation for the determination of borders according to a new scheme.]

When I saw this I really wondered whether this meant that Dr. de Klerk had access to information which we do not. Does he perhaps know something we do not know? Has the Prime Minister been bluffing each time he has said to us that he is not prepared to go beyond the 1936 Land Act? Is there another door open of which we are still to be informed? If one takes into account the reluctance of various governments to deliver the 1936 quota of land to blacks in the last 40 years, it is difficult to be so trusting as to believe that a new fever of benevolence is going to sweep across white South Africa all of a sudden to open a number of new doors despite the Prime Minister's determination not to budge one inch from the 1936 Land Act. I would like you to see the map of a projection of a fully consolidated KwaZulu.

I just do not and cannot accept this kind of sick joke. My people, if I read their mood accurately, as I hope I do, cannot accept that, not in a thousand years (if I may borrow a current phrase from a "statesman" north of us).

This is the Homeland in which, to use Dr. de Klerk's words, I am supposed to inspire my people with national consciousness and productivity! I am prepared to admit publicly, as in the past, that my people do need to be more motivated even within the limits of this LAPPIESKOMBERS. Dr. de Klerk rightly points out that the border industries hold more advantages for the white man. Not so long ago such words would have cost Dr. de Klerk his job, but he continues:

> If big cities rise as visible symbols of unity and the promotion of nationhood, [it will be preferable to] spending R73 million for the development of more than a hundred platteland towns.

And furthermore:

DIALOGUE OR CONFRONTATION

New overhead planning, and the determination of priorities, done by a knowledgeable advice committee outside the normal civil service channels, is a suggestion which is increasingly being made in influential circles.

I find this most fascinating. Who these influential people he refers to here are is a $64,000 question. I wish Dr. de Klerk had been more specific about this.

My feelings are not products of my ASTRANTHEID. They are based on how seriously I take Mr. Vorster when he talks to us. I take the Prime Minister seriously when he states so categorically over and over again that if we do not want independence on his terms (which is based on the 1936 Native Land quota), then we can remain as we are. This is the Prime Minister of South Africa himself speaking. We have no other hotline to him.

It is, of course, quite possible that Dr. de Klerk has information which is not for our consumption at present, but for a few trusted members of the Nationalist hierarchy. I do not know. I can merely speculate on this one. I can only take my stand on the facts before me and not on what editors of Afrikaans newspapers tell me. There is no better source of such information than Mr. Vorster himself. He is so far my only authority on these matters. There are many people who always say to me, "Do you not think that he says this for the consumption of his Verkrampte followers?" I have no reason to believe that South Africa's Prime Minister talks to us with his tongue in his cheek. Dr. de Klerk has more to say on this subject.

> The time has come to formulate constitutional suggestions through which the channels will be created for linking up of black and white common affairs, so that participation, co-responsibility and joint decisions can be arranged in these matters.

Do I read this correctly when I understand it to mean that we blacks are being invited here to participate in constitutional reform? Is this not what I have done so many times? Were my suggestions for a convention and for a multi-racial council for South Africa not attempts to make a contribution in constitutional reform? Does my speech on federation, which like the others was rejected by the Prime Minister, not fall into the same category? Does my Soweto speech not fall into the same category? This I believe is what I tried to do in Soweto when I said:

> I believe that it is absolutely essential that we hold a series of representative national conventions representing all shades of black opinion. Let us do for ourselves what Mr. Vorster's Parliament does not do for us.

If such conventions do in fact get off the ground, I wonder if Dr. de Klerk will also treat their findings as he has treated my contribution, by saying that I do not deserve attention. Will he say that their findings will not deserve attention like me?

I would like to point out something which is important here. In Soweto I called for black conventions. That is the only option open to black people, as the white man and particularly the Afrikaner has in the past shown that he has no interest in my idea of a national convention. In Soweto I stated to my people:

> I have in the past called upon the whites to come to their senses. I even offered them a federal formula which mapped out their road toward responsible govern- ment. The whites are politically underdeveloped and they need our assistance. The federal formula I offered them was the assistance they need if they are to develop politically. This was a compromise proposal. I must say now and I must say with considerable emphasis that such reconciliatory offers as were contained in my federal formula will be increasingly difficult to offer in the southern Africa which is now emerging.

There is a threat if you wish. It is a warning that no one can remain conciliatory when such gestures are not only met with rigid dogma but also ridiculed. It is a warning that our communication system has broken down at a time when we need it most. It is another way of saying that pontifications by whites, which have been the order of the day ever since they vanquished my people, are not acceptable to us as a basis for meaningful dialogue. They can never be that, and we as blacks reject dialogue if that is what whites understand by dialogue.

Are we once again, as is customary (if we knew our place), going to be expected to sit on the sidelines, while Dr. de Klerk's ."influential circles" go into an all-white huddle, in the name of white domination, to make decisions concerning the nationhood of black people? Is the Afrikaner once again arrogating to himself the prerogative of defining to us our national aspirations?

This is clearly what I understand this to mean. In other words, the white caucus will continue to be the order of the day. The black caucus I mentioned in Soweto is a logical outcome of our rejection from that exclusive white caucus or club.

It is simply incredible that the Afrikaner now decides to define nationalism on behalf of others, particularly if we recall that the Afrikaner had such problems in attempting to define his own nationalism, to such an extent that it was split down the middle less than four decades ago. I am curious to know if the de Klerks and the Treurnichts even today can sit down at the same table and arrive at a common definition of Afrikaner nationalism. Can they reach the same conclusions on what is meant by words such as "volkseenheid"(unity of the people) and "broedertwis" (conflict between brothers)? I have my gravest doubts. Nationalism and loyalties become extremely difficult to define in this land with such a motley assortment even within the Nationalist Party itself.

It is to ignore the great lessons of history for the Afrikaner to assume the role of devising for the black man what the black man's concept of nationalism should be. That is what in my opinion amounts to political underdevelopment. I am afraid I cannot put it more euphemistically just because tomorrow I have to lobby for favours from the same people. I have never believed in operating like that. If I did so, I would end up by beinq all things to all men. South Africa cannot afford too many of that ilk.

Let me admit that whilst I speak of white political immaturity, this is not a peculiarity of whites; Africa suffers under the burden of political underdevelopment but of a different sort. The world as a whole is in political shambles. Political mistakes are made and fingers can be pointed at almost any country even amongst the Western democracies. But in South Africa, we recklessly ignore the most important step to responsible, mature government and peaceful coexistence which is summed up in the word "dialogue". I stated at the beginning my admiration for Dr. de Klerk, for one so often comes across such refreshing sincerity in his writings. Although I have discussed what he had to say at such great length, he came to the same conclusion as I reached that a new deal is now called for. This is what I find so confusing and I then ask, "Does my uniform, my terminology and the colour of my skin make my person and message unacceptable?"

I would also like tonight to touch briefly on one of my statements in Soweto last month, which earned me the tag of "revolutionary." I said:

> The events in Mozambique and Angola and similar impending events in Zimbabwe and Namibia have brought a new sense of national awareness into the hearts and minds of South Africa's blacks.

I said this for no other motive except in the interest of truth as I believe this to be nothing but the truth. All the dark and weird interpretations of it do not make it invalid as an assessment of what the score is in the southern African of today.

Webster's dictionary defines nationalism as "advocacy of making one's own nation distinct and separate from others in social, cultural and political matters". I realize of course that nationalism can mean different things to different people. However the emotions which become operative do so in any colour. So I also said:

> In spite of these words, I repeat that I still believe that it is not too late to call for a white change of heart.

And I added that:

> We have a common destiny as black people. We have indeed a common destiny even with our white countrymen who have rejected this idea for several generations.

But this was not even reported, let along brought into context with my "revolutionary" words. Am I to continue offering the white man the hand of friendship? Am I to keep silent when my hand is spurned, knowing that if I objected I would then be branded a revolutionary. Is this not what is called "knowing and keeping my place?"

I am no revolutionary. But as I see a revolution coming, should I not say so? Am I to pretend it does not exist in order to curry favour with the white man? Am I to lie? Am I to say that there is no imminent revolution? Should I not state even the obvious that events north of us have stirred our own awareness? Should I lie and state that we are not frustrated and angered by our voicelessness? I was once again rapped over the knuckles at the highest level for daring to say blacks are voiceless in this country. Am I to lie and say that we as blacks are secure in the knowledge that the white man will make wise decisions on our behalf? Must I lie and say that the quality of our lives is adequate? That the education of our offspring is in good hands? Is that what it takes to be taken seriously? Africans, when talking amongst themselves, always concede the point that the Afrikaner is blunt. Why must I do what the Afrikaner himself has never done? Why should I be evasive about assaults on our dignity as blacks and on our being denied fundamental human rights? I merely repeated the Prime Minister's own warning when I said that if we did not do all these things to solve our problems, we were creating a future that is "too ghastly to contemplate."

Let us look together at my future as defined by Dr. Andries Treurnicht, Deputy Minister of Bantu Administration and Development and Education. The following are further points he made in the same speech, in which he chided me in Pretoria. I assume that the "new boy" did this on behalf of his government. Here they are:

> The biggest export product of the black nations is their labour. We should use this to put our homelands on a sounder basis. Labour must bring money in for the homelands, and it should be ploughed back.

> He also says that: the notion that South Africa is already integrated economically is false. The essential bond between the whites and the other nations is a contractual bond. So blacks must continue to contribute toward more and more development of this richest economy, and use all the fruits of their labour to develop these areas. In other words his own so-called "homeland" must continue to be neglected and undeveloped whilst the black man uses all his energies to develop the white man's "homeland." Even if one, for argument's sake, found this fragmentation acceptable, this formula would still be absolutely unacceptable. If this is not based on a formula of one group exploiting another, then there is no such thing as exploitation. We cannot accept it. I have already said that my people are aware of what is happening elsewhere in Africa. They know what is described as the government's "final plans" for them, and they find these unacceptable. As I stated in Soweto, "the majority of blacks will not find it in their hearts to die on the country's borders to defend a system which is morally repugnant, a system which dehumanises them and which mocks Almighty God for creating blacks also in His image."

DIALOGUE OR CONFRONTATION

In reply to this, Mr. Jaap Steyn of RAPPORT accused me of instigating the black disturbances in Johannesburg last month. Mr. Steyn goes on to say that clerics such as Dr. Beyers Naude, Archbishop Denis Hurley and Bishop T. Bavin should abandon their "paternalism" towards black leaders. Do you see this kind of twisted logic at play once again? When I fraternize with Harry Schwartz, DIE VADERLAND smugly dismisses us as "the heroes of Mahlabatini," Dr. Treurnicht tells his young admirers that Beyers Naude and I cooked the Soweto thing up together. And RAPPORT tells church leaders to abandon their paternalism towards us. To what extent is this logical and reasonable? Is only the Nationalst Party's paternalism acceptable? Does my rejection of these distortions make me a revolutionary? Should I advise my people to lap up Dr. Treurnicht's distorted pontifications? Must they accept his selfish vision which reduces the black man to a lifetime of servitude to white South Africa? Must I believe that when God created black people and placed them on this tip of Africa, he destined them only for this role?

Mr. Steyn continues:

> People who know Natal say they can clearly see the border between a white farm and a black KwaZulu farm. The white man's soil is properly tilled, the black man's looks like a desert. Whose fault is this? The white system? AIKONA!

In the interests of comparative analysis, I can give Mr. Steyn these distinctions:

KwaZulu is the most densely populated of all these so-called homeland areas.

KwaZulu is where in place of hot and cold water taps we must use bilharzia-infested streams.

KwaZulu is where Escom makes way for Eveready.

KwaZulu's children, unlike white children, have no free and compulsory education. Agriculture is a matter of education.

KwaZulu is where children pay fees, pay for their books, pay for privately paid teachers, pay for the construction of buildings, and where they do not board a bus to school but have to run to school, regardless of conditions of weather.

Perhaps Mr. Steyn does not appreciate that we moved to Ulundi because of the infrastructure that exists there. It was because of the railway line, possible Escom connection, water, etc.

In Soweto on the 14th day of March this year, I indicated that I knew that my words would be received in the manner they have been received:

I realize what I am doing today, by saying these things as I do. These are very blunt words, but at this point in time they have got to be said. If they were not said, I would not be responsible. If no one amongst 18 million of us said them, history would judge all of us very harshly. Those who have ears to hear what I say will understand that I am offering a black hand of friendship to the whites of South Africa. Yes, it is a black hand, but it is still a hand of friendship.

In view of all the strictures we have gone through, can there be any doubt that my hand of friendship has once again been turned down? Can we believe that the government of this country is seriously seeking a consensus when its newspapers reject me as a revolutionary and the wishes of my people as the "barking of a war of nerves"?

Am I not seeking that consensus when I offer you the hand of friendship and suggest that we talk things over? Am I not contributing to that consensus when I tell you what my people think and feel?

Black nationalism is not different from white nationalism provided the democratic principles apply. Professor Thomas I. Emerson's book TOWARD A GENERAL THEORY OF THE FIRST AMENDMENT has the following pertinent quotation:

> Any society must in order to function and survive, maintain within itself a certain unity. It requires sufficient agreement amongst its members not only to settle differences according to rules and without resort to force, but to make the formal rules work in practice. No mechanism for government can by its mere existence hold a society together. This is especially true of the modern industrial community with the interdependence of its parts and the complexities of its operation. Hence any society must seek to promote consensus among its members, and in this the government will necessarily play an important role.

Therefore failure to recognize that black nationalism is not different from white nationalism can only be seen as the beginning of our troubles, as it can only lead to confrontation, as has happened in other parts of Africa.

These are certainly times of great fluidity in southern African politics. Why should I not keep my own options open? This is not in the interests of any self-promotion or demagoguery, as has been alleged, but it is only in the interests of my people. We are categoric that the independence of KwaZulu, as presently conceived, is unacceptable to us. We also cannot see that it would be in the interests of our people as a whole to seek a complete amputation of KwaZulu, which would amount to a complete forfeiture of our birth rights. With such provocative writing on the wall, I do not believe that I would be doing my duty to my people and to South Africa, if I accepted such a LAPPIESKOMBERS, whilst everything around is in a state of flux. It is against that background that my call for majority rule should be seen. We blacks love this country. We blacks also take pride in our history. We blacks are proud of our contribution. We are also anxious to ensure a secure future for our children.

DIALOGUE OR CONFRONTATION

If we recognize South Africa as a unit, if we recognize that black nationalism will neither conform to the straitjacket designed for it by the Nationalist Party nor go away, if we recognize that equality is central to the definition of democracy, and if we recognize that peaceful coexistence between different groups is possible, then we do not have to follow in the bloody footsteps we have seen followed in certain parts of the continent. I realize, of course, that the history of black and white on this continent offers us scant assurance for the future. It breeds fear and mistrust. We have no reason at all to repeat the lunacies of history just in order to say that history repeats itself. There is absolutely no reason why we cannot plan a common future in a United South Africa. It seems silly to fragment our fatherland merely in order to accommodate our ethnic neuroses. We must abandon the master-servant relationship first, if we are to meet as equals around a conference table. I hope no one tonight thinks I am preaching revolution as has been alleged. I hope you will see my message as that of peaceful coexistence and of laying foundations for a secure future for all.

I made a speech in January 1975 in which I stated that the government's policies do not offer blacks real fulfillment. I was then dismissed by the Afrikaans press as an agitator. Let us sum up how this year's warnings have been construed:

—Dr. Treurnicht reminds me that I owe my status to the government.

—DIE VADERLAND accuses me of ASTRANTHEID and ridicules my uniform.

—Piet Snuffelaar says I am stirring cheap emotions.

—Dr. Wimpie de Klerk says there are other solutions than mine, but does not offer to share them.

—DIE BEELD accuses me of power ambition.

—DIE TRANSVALER says I don't deserve attention.

—TEMPO frets that I have become "dangerously different."

—Jaap Steyn accuses me of uttering "hollow phrases."

—Aida Parker proposes punitive measures against me by the Prime Minister.

—And all are agreed that I am a dangerous revolutionary.

As you can see this is, roughly speaking, the same treatment I got last year. I have now merely graduated from an "agitator" to a "revolutionary." I have in this way been branded, pigeon-holed and ignored.

It would of course be grossly wrong to blame the Afrikaans press alone for the discrepancies we have been looking at. My Soweto message was thirty-two pages long, so very little of my speech actually made the newspapers in any language. I have since taken the trouble to send copies of my Soweto speech to the Afrikaans editors concerned, in the hope that I would later have a say on the subject.

I thought that the scope the invitation to Kajuitraad gave me was wide enough to enable me to have such a say.

I have a message for the Afrikaans press and it is this:

You have the right to consider me irrelevant as that is entrenched in the principle of free speech. You are fortunate in that your views are respected by your readers.

We all bear witness that you are going through the process of discarding the shackles of secular interest. We have seen a new open-mindedness flourish on your editorial pages. But, internal dialogue has not yet begun, as your rejection of my Soweto speech testifies. If we are to avoid perpetuating the tragic tradition of black/white conflict on this continent, South Africans of all colours must reconsider their thinking on a number of fundamental issues within a very short time.

The mass media have a vital role to play in bringing about a change. This is the time for people to have the facts of life before them, and they need your help to make important decisions regarding their future. If this is a democracy, as you claim, the right of free speech extends to all citizens, even black non-citizens like myself.

You can, of course, continue to tell your readers to ignore Gatsha Buthelezi, but let me warn you that if you continue to do so, you do so at your peril. Because if your readers therefore come to the wrong conclusions, will you bear responsibility for it? In this regard, I would like to quote to you from the words of Chief Justice Charles Hughes of the U.S. Supreme Court in a landmark judgment on free speech, made in 1937.

> The greater the importance of safeguarding the community from incitement to the overthrow of our institutions by force and violence, the more imperative is the need to preserve inviolate the constitutional rights of free speech, free press and free assembly in order to maintain the opportunity for free political discussion, to the end that government may be responsive to the will of the people and that changes, if desired, may be obtained by peaceful means. Therein lies the security of the republic, the very foundation of constitutional government.

So that by stifling and belittling what blacks try to articulate as their contribution, the Afrikaans press infringed the letter and spirit of this great judgment. In other words, if blacks decide that only violence is left to them whatever the consequences for themselves and the country, your stifling of dialogue in this manner will have only led us to a bloody confrontation. These are not threats but logical outcomes of all the outcry against what I said in Soweto. You want to hear only what you think you and your readers would like to hear from blacks.

This is certainly not the first time there is such a breakdown in communication between us blacks and the Afrikaner. It was, after all, this government which banned the African National Congress and the Pan African Congress.

DIALOGUE OR CONFRONTATION

We live in times when history offers little for our comfort. The very foundations of democratic government are under attack. We have to be adventurers if we are to survive these onslaughts by venturing into the unknown. We have unique problems which call for unique solutions. There are bound to be fears, as it is natural to have fears heightened as one approaches the unknown. We need as a first step the admission of all shades of opinion into the marketplace of ideas, so that they can compete for popular acceptance.

Although each time I have attempted to make a contribution my ideas have been distorted, I am not bitter about this. I am only sorry and my heart can only bleed for my country. When my ideas are distorted in the manner you have seen, by the South African Broadcasting Corporation and through CURRENT AFFAIRS, white readers and listeners, have been deprived of the means of judging for themselves what I suggest, fairly and without fear. I have so far been denied in this way the right to present my thoughts in the marketplace of ideas.

I refuse to be denied a voice in determining my future. I am by birth and tradition, a leader of my people, separate development politics aside. By decisions of your government and legislature, in which black people do not participate, I am the Chief Executive of KwaZulu, and if an election were held tomorrow, I would be elected still as such.

I have been elected by the Assembly twice without any division. I am the President of Inkatha, the largest liberation movement of its type within South Africa. I am patron of various African organizations representing black interests. I have travelled extensively in Africa and abroad and have been received by some heads of state in Africa and by the members of the Secretariat of the OAU, in Addis Ababa in a manner befitting a son of Africa. I am a great-grandson of King Cetshwayo, a grandson of King Dinizulu and the son of Princess Magogo, the full sister of King Solomon ka Dinizulu, and am a member of the Zulu Royal House in my own right. I am a hereditary Chief of the Buthelezi Tribe, a great-grandson of Chief Mnyamana Buthelezi who was Prime Minister of the Zulus when we were a sovereign nation, and who was commander-in-chief of the entire Zulu army. My late father, Chief Mathole Buthelezi was the Prime Minister of KwaZulu during King Solomon's reign. I acted as Prime Minister to King Cyprian, who was my first cousin, for 16 years, before there was any separate development of politics in KwaZulu.

I am not mentioning these things to boast, but as a broad hint to Dr. Andries Treurnicht and those who may be misled into thinking that I owe what I am to the government, as he said a few days after my Soweto message.

Tonight has been a depressing event in itself as it has been proof, as I have said, that we have not yet begun to have dialogue as South Africans. These are times when we have to be blunt with each other. If we cannot establish any meaningful dialogue we will destroy each other through a bloody confrontation. That will be the only thing left. That is what the Prime Minister meant by the alternative that is too ghastly to contemplate."

I demand to be heard, as I represent millions of my people whose voice I am. My people demand to be heard. My people support these views as their attendance at my mass meetings bears out.

I am afraid I have not contributed much to the debate about the development and progress towards self-determination. However, I believe that in dealing with these matters in the manner in which I have, that I have rendered a service not just for Kajuitraad, but for South Africa. Development that is taking place in KwaZulu even on the modest scale I have sketched, is vital and must go on, even whilst the present political impasse exists. It can only contribute something towards a peaceful unravelling of the political situation in South Africa. As I hinted earlier, it would enhance the belief in the sincerity of the nationalist government, even if one does not agree with the philosophy behind its policy, if more Afrikaners than those I have mentioned earlier, appear to be eager to assist blacks in their own development.

With Pope Paul VI in Rome

Chapter 6

ROLE OF THE CHURCH

TO THE DIOCESAN CONFERENCE OF NATAL

October 1977

When one thinks about the kind of political and economic questions facing the people of South Africa, one can approach the subject from a people's point of view. Much of what I say may be offensive to some of my brothers here but I claim the right to feel free to speak in love, in the sense in which St. Paul spoke of speaking the truth in love in his letter to the Ephesians 4:15: "But speaking the truth in love, may grow up into him in all things, which is the head, even Christ."

I want to assure you that although I wear the two hats of President of Inkatha and of Chief Minister of KwaZulu, I have come here to share my thoughts on the subject of your discussion, as your brother in Christ.

Right at the outset I want to make the central point of my address. This is that the socio-political questions and economic questions which we face must be defined in terms of people's response to oppression rather the requirements of an existing institutionalized way of life. I make this point central because I do not believe that we in South Africa are fully facing the reality of the situation confronting us when we talk about economic development in terms of border industry growth, on-the-job training, increasing employment for blacks in the central economy, and so on. Nor are we facing the reality of the situation confronting us when we talk in terms of making homeland governments work, giving greater power to urban black communities, and the establishment of advisory boards at local, provincial and national levels.

Such talk as is necessary within these kinds of terms, is forced upon us while we face the avalanche of human needs thrown up by a fundamentally unjust society. Although on a day-to-day basis I am concerned with the hungry, and therefore with job opportunities available to my people, and I am concerned with eliminating the worst of my people's experience of being administered by an alien, white-clenched fist, this does not mean that I define the fundamental problems of South Africa in terms of these kinds of issues.

For those of us who suffer under the yoke of apartheid it is very real. It has to be dealt with. Its rough edges have to be smoothed wherever possible. For those of us who go hungry, a little improvement means a great deal to our children. There is a justified day-to-day involvement at this level. I am involved at this level because for me people are very important and people determine issues. I weather the storm of protest which from time to time breaks out against me for being involved in "homeland politics". Should my people die and suffer within the system of apartheid simply because we have a need for some kind of pseudo-purity? Must I be the butt of such strictures even from those who have not deserted the unjust premises of their white society? I do not expect people to pay a price that extends to their suffering and the hunger of their children in order that my soapbox oratory will be more acceptable in some quarters.

Beyond this involvement, I have seen myself as having another destiny beyond the issues related to the day-to-day alleviation of poverty and suffering within the limitations imposed on us. There are the deep, perplexing questions which we face in South Africa. These questions are not academic questions and they are not ideological questions. They are people's questions. They are questions of humanity's response to suffering in an oppressive society. The future of South Africa will be determined by suffering people and not by the external requirements of an existing industrial setup, banking institutions or organized labour. The real issues facing us do not arise out of the need to protect an existing order, an existing set of privileges, an existing advantage of man over man at the expense of man. The real questions facing us are not how to preserve a South African way of life as it has evolved up to the present. The real issues facing South Africa relate rather to a people's force at work demanding the demolition of the instruments of injustice and oppression.

One has only to look at the instability of the South African situation to realize that we in South Africa have built into our society forces which will tear it apart. The real issues we face are revolutionary issues and not reformist issues. The instability of our society at all levels precludes the possibility of our South African way of life enduring in perpetuity. Indeed, it precludes its continuation even through the foreseeable future. The outward stability to which government spokesmen have up to now referred is made possible only by the fact that the torture of prisoners takes place behind closed walls where no eyes see, and the intimidation of people in their daily lives is an almost secret thing, and by the fact that blacks have participated seemingly willingly in the most abhorrent of discriminatory practices in the economy designed to protect the privileges of our white minority.

People go to jail at gun point and they remain there because the doors are locked, and people go to work because they are at the point of starvation and they remain there because there is nothing else for them to do.

The fact that we have in South Africa what is in all probability an unparalleled range of discriminatory social practices and the most formidable range of oppressive laws, orchestrated by an administration which is jackboot in its nature, accounts for the on-going way of life in South Africa. A good example of what I mean is the crude sabre-rattling I was subjected to by the Minister of Justice two weeks ago.

The basis of our society in South Africa is not of God, and this very pertinent fact adds in a very particular way to the instability of that which is around us. Justice and truth are in a very real sense the allies of the poor and the oppressed. The privileged in this country can only fight for their privileges which are bought by a great deal of suffering on the part of the underprivileged. The defence of those privileges against the just claims of the underprivileged is not of God.

The real issues of South Africa are people issues and not institutional issues. The poor and oppressed in South Africa have awakened to be a force of change which is irresistible and which will continue mounting up pressure that must and will break through the barriers of change. The poor and oppressed are very well aware of this fact. They have a consciousness of themselves as people whose ultimate destiny is in their own hands. Black consciousness is, in part, this — an awareness of being men and women enough to control their own destinies.

There are in the poor and oppressed two diametrically opposed dimensions. One is a destructive anger where men search to put a stone in their hand or a gun in their hand, or where they search for the match, participate in the mob and are indiscriminate in their anger. The other is the dimension of togetherness. The human experience is giving rise to the phenomenon of an emerging brotherhood; in its dimension a new set of attitudes and values are in the making which put the spiritual and the human above the material.

If I had to enumerate the one issue which we were facing that was more important than all others it is the issue of whether or not the anger and violence will prevail over the humility and the spirit of brotherhood.

I believe sincerely that the Church is greatly privileged and enjoys a unique position which could be employed to bring about constructive change in South Africa. The Church is privileged and it has a unique power. There is no question of this. What is, however, questionable is whether the Church realizes the crucial role which it ought to be playing and the power it has to work for the good of man.

I have become deeply disappointed and perhaps even disillusioned about the Church's response to the South African situation. There is indeed very little to encourage me in the hope that I still have that God will lead us all to his own appointed destiny through the active participation of the church in the struggle for liberation.

I see in the broad context of South Africa a government growing in the harshness of its power. I see in the broad context of South Africa the increasing employment of brutality, the increasing negation of accepted Christian values. I see an ever-increasing unwillingness on the part of the white community to come to their senses and bring about change. I see the white community girding its loins for an armed conflict agains the poor and the oppressed. I see military preparedness reaching ever greater heights and I see civil defence becoming almost a way of life in the privileged community.

I see a greater and greater intolerance for opposition. Above all, I see a kind of blindness to the implications of white stupidity. I ask myself the question of where the church stands in these things. I ask what it has done in these circumstances, and I tell you when I debate these questions with myself, I am disabused of false hopes to the point of being disillusioned.

I want to make one observation: It is that the Church may have become so institutionalized that it has lost its prophetic vision. The Church at one level seeks to perpetuate itself as an institution. It runs itself as an efficient business machine. It is sensible and pragmatic in its own survival as an institution. The Church, if it is these things, must forfeit its right to be prophetic in its love for man.

The hand that builds the parish church and the mind that guides the parish council, the people who are inward-looking in these tasks, are inadequately equipped to dismantle the resilient structures of apartheid. The position could be described as a bunch of amateurs facing professional and highly trained oppressors. The Church as a voice is characterized by a feebleness which can be ignored with impunity. Its high-sounding resolutions have no bite because the people in the Church have no will to suffer and to testify to their commitment to Christ. BOSS (Bureau of State Security) says,"Boo!" and Christians shudder and shut up. They may pray more piously and become more concerned with the salvation of individual souls. I have nothing against piousness. Indeed, it is a great virtue of man reaching its highest expression in the Christian faith. The object of piety is the inner life of man and not his social responsibilities.

My own pursuit of piousness keeps me going in what is otherwise a dismally hopeless situation. However, even the pious man has a social responsibility and that responsibility is being neglected by the church.

I have said that the most important issue is whether anger and violence will prevail over humility and the spirit of brotherhood. I must strengthen this thought in your minds. Somehow I must convey to you its importance.

The blunt fact of the matter is the ever-increasing chance of violence prevailing because we are too afraid even to recognise its existence. The spirit of violence is accentuated with every bullet fired at children, with every arrest, with every act of torture, with every denial of man's responsibility to man, with every intention to maintain the abhorrent system of apartheid at all costs.

The maintenance of our society already rests heavily on the employment of violence. I have grave difficulties in believing that the South African situation will not continue to deteriorate in terms of the employment of violence, both in the maintenance of the status quo and in challenging the status quo. I believe the time has come to start considering our responsibility as one of primary concern with the limitation of violence. But if we cannot admit the existence of violence, we will never discharge this responsibility. Throughout all my political life I have stood for non-violent change, but this does not mean that I am blind to the existence of violence.

In the gravest of terms, I warn this conference that a time is rapidly approaching, and may already have come, in which violence will be opposed by violence. Recognising the inevitability of something is not a song of praise for it. When I am crushed beneath the wheels of a steamroller, the hardness of the wheel is real, and the flattening of my body is real. To say that my body need not be flattened in that context is stupid.

ROLE OF THE CHURCH

I see my people subjected to a system of violence which has flattened them. This conference can do well to debate the issues of a just war. I am not advocating violence, but I am warning that the spirit of violence will overtake the spirit of humility and brotherhood unless something dramatic is done. And unless the church witnesses and is prepared to suffer for truth as presented in the Gospel, violence will prevail.

Political and economic questions we face in this country are questions which relate to the possible dominance of violence. This conference must come to accept a movement away from an exploitative free enterprise system in which unbridled capitalism sows discontent and revolution. This conference must accept that there is an urgent and desperate need to abandon a political system which disenfranchises the majority of the members of its society. Until such time as there is meaningful power-sharing in this country, the spectre of revolution will live with us in everything we do. The time has come to accept that majority rule alone will stabilize our society and make possible an orderly change. The redistribution of political power and economic wealth, the creation of equality of opportunity, the re-establishment of the dignity of man in the rule of law, the re-emergence of a free press, the emergence of an impartial judiciary, the coming into being of a government which is obedient to the people, all depend upon a fundamental change of heart and a willingness to sacrifice far beyond the levels now in evidence. This is the Church's responsibility.

As I see it, our starting point is not with a neat constitutional plan, or with a neat alternative economic order. A blueprint approach is probably worthless. In this sense the imminent white election is absolutely irrelevant to us blacks vis-a-vis what is at stake in our South African society.

Our starting point should be with the experience of men and women. I am totally convinced that no blueprint, no matter how intricate it may be, and no matter how appealingly it is constituted, will persuade whites to sacrifice their privileges and to share what they have with the poor and the oppressed. We need a change of heart before we need a change of constitution. If we continue with our constitutional approaches, I can only foresee the increasing abuse of constitutional machinery, whether it be from the far right or from the far left. My own view is that the best employment of constitutions is in their preservation of that which is valuable in human experience. The Church could well be an important channel for discovery of these values.

If we, as Christians, come to recognise that we are faced with a very real situation of violence which by all signs and portents can only increase in severity and scope, and if we are faced with a possible situation in which the employment of violence on both sides in the struggle for liberation will become all-pervading and all-embracing, we have to consider, or perhaps reconsider, our strategy and our tactics. This reconsideration is essential even for those who cannot go as far as I go in my apprehension. All we need to do is to consider the possibility of this being true, and we will become obliged to re-examine our own positions and our own contribution to the emergence of a just society.

Circumstances, and in some cases necessary conditions for human existence, constrain thousands upon thousands of blacks to indulge in civil disobedience in our unjust society. Every black who has been arrested for a pass offence is being civilly disobedient. Every black wife who lives illegally with her husband in town is being civilly disobedient. Every black who speaks out against apartheid and is arrested exercises his right to be civilly disobedient. Black society already pays the price of civil disobedience. One of the political issues this conference could well consider is white involvement in civil disobedience. Whites as whites cannot love their black brothers while they stand in a position of protected privilege and watch their black brothers suffer under the yoke of apartheid.

Refusing to share in the consequences of living in apartheid society is a political issue. White civil disobedience may be the last opportunity we have of remaining relevant without a gun in our hand. The Church as a church needs seriously to question whether it is possible to discharge its Christian responsibility to society without involving itself in civil disobedience.

We have argued something like this:

1. South Africa is a society in which a minority privileged group maintains itself at the expense of the majority who are poor and oppressed.

2. Internal dissent and tensions make our society unstable.

3. Stabilizing forces keeping the status quo intact are primarily the employment of violence and the participation in the society by the oppressed masses because they are people with few alternatives.

4. A point has been reached in which the emergence of justice cannot be ensured by making existing institutions and practices more efficient.

5. The spectacle of violence as a dominant ingredient in the forces of social change may already be real.

6. Christian commitment to justice and truth identifies the Church with the power of the oppressed.

7. The Church has been impotent in its opposition to the growing ugliness of apartheid society. This impotence of the Church in real measure can be traced to its preoccupation with itself as an institution.

8. The prophetic voice of the Church needs to be awakened.

9. Christian love means demonstrable identity with the poor and the oppressed. Civil disobedience could be both such a demonstration and an effective check on the growth of draconian powers employed by men who are professional oppressors.

10. The real issue we face when looking at South Africa's political and economic questions is the issue of increasing opposition to injustice. This means more than pious churchiness.

Chapter **7**

MORE ON THE CHURCH

TO THE CANADIAN ANGLICAN NATIONAL EXCUTIVE COUNCIL

November 1975

I wish to take this earliest opportunity to thank His Grace, Archbishop Edward Scott, the Primate of Canada, for extending an invitation to me to be here at this time.

I was not given any particular subject to address at this National Executive Council meeting. I have come to realize that there are today many questions that the Church must face squarely. Some of these questions go right to the core of our faith, and they have brought the whole question of the relevance of the Christian Gospel to the world we live in to the forefront of these discussions.In this context I find that it is imperative for me, as a churchman in the South African situation, to look with you into the whole issue of whether the Church has any role to play in the liberation of the black man in that troubled land.

Recently, in Europe, I looked at this question of the relevance of the Church in the struggle for liberation. I wish to recall, as I did then, some of the words banon Burgess Carr, the Secretary of the All Africa Church Conference, used when he preached at a Thanksgiving service to mark the national independence of the People's Republic of Mozambique:

> I would be woefully guilty if I did not say how deeply we repent that we were so late in arriving at the realization that our alliance with the forces of oppression, racism and colonial exploitation were grevious sins against God. Because we sinned against God, we sinned also against you. Today, in this public manner, I make confession of the sins of the churches against the people of Mozambique, asking God, the Holy and Righteous Judge, to pardon us and to give us His grace to amend our ways and asking you, your government, its leaders and all the Mozambique people to forgive us.

As Canon Burgess Carr spoke on behalf of the Church, I wish as a churchman in Africa to identify with what he said. This means that in the "We were so late," the word "we" identifies those present with the churches, and as churches expressing indivisibility of the Church in its responsibility to the people of Mozambique. I am using the word "we" in the same sense. I identify myself as a Churchman with the task of the Church, the successes of the church and the failures of the church. I am aware that some of you may be troubled about my role as a churchman operating within the framework of the South African government's policy which is so abhorrent to all sane human beings.

There are those of you who might be tempted to judge me superficially, "as just one of the Vorster government's minions." From this distance, and owing to the influence of certain elements (who have taken it upon themselves to denigrate all of us who are serving our people in this way), we may be seen in this light. We are, however, individuals, even within the framework of those policies, and have different reasons for being so involved. Despite my royal birth, I see myself as a peasant who is forced by circumstances to carry the burden of leading his people in their struggle for liberation. This dual capacity, I am aware, might bother some people. It does not bother most of my people. They see no conflict in my two roles as their leader and a churchman. I am deeply concerned about the lot of my people as they now live their daily lives; I am even more concerned about the nature of their future circumstances. I am doing what I do in South Africa because I strongly believe that, notwithstanding the fact that South Africa is a society built on violence, the liberation of my people will come ultimately from their suffering and struggling through daily circumstances. Their real stake in the current circumstances, as far as I am concerned, is the opportunity to build a better society. What will prove to be a better society in decades to come and in centuries to come, only time will tell. I feel certain that many of you will be troubled by these assertions and perhaps ask the natural question, "How can one hope to achieve liberation of black people while working within a straitjacket?"

I think this necessitates my sharing with you what I understand by liberation. The word liberation tends to be equated with freedom. I consider liberation to be much more than just a process whereby we in South Africa gain freedom from want and injustice. To me it also means our involvement in a process whereby we gain a foothold in the process of reconstructing a new society in South Africa. So that in this sense, I see the word liberation as connoting both "freedom from" and "freedom *to*". Freedom from injustice, and freedom to enact justice and enshrine it in the institutions of our country. Social justice needs to be expressed in day-to-day activity. Liberation in this context means the destruction of apartheid and much more than that. It means the creation of a new society. To me, it means our realization with John Donne, that "no man is an island". The new society we seek to create will reconcile South Africa with southern Africa, with Africa, and with the whole world.

MORE ON THE CHURCH

To go back to Canon Carr's dramatic truth I quoted before, it must be said in fairness to the Church, that the Church has played a significant role in the liberation of man. It is important to observe here that despite the chequered history of the Church, the World Council of Churches has produced a turning point in the progression of Christianity. Its identity with the oppressed and the suffering must be applauded. We must applaud the boldness in the practicality of its love for the underprivileged of this world, as that love expressed itself in financial and other aid to a wide range of forces working for the betterment of the oppressed. No one can question the fact that behind its deliberations and debates there is genuine and deep love. Even within South Africa we have seen church leaders dedicated to the cause of liberation. We have seen in our lifetime men whose lives have stood out as beacons of light in that dreariness which is our South African way of life, as symbols of the triumph of the Church through her persecution. Names of the following servants of God come to mind: Bishop Huddlestone, Bishop Colin Winter, Bishop Wood, Canon French Beytagh, a number of pastors of the Lutheran Church in Namibia. It is fair to say that these are stalwarts who have bought time for the Church and who have prevented many blacks from rejecting the Church. Even now, as I am talking to you here, I think I say without any fear of contradiction that the spirit of Christian commitment is not dead in South Africa. It is alive in the witness of such Church leaders as Archbishop Denis Hurley, in Durban. Even our South African Council of Churches is only beginning to come face to face with issues such as conscientious objections to military service. But whilst all these things are evidence that the spirit of Christian committment is alive, it is still going to take a long time before that commitment is translated into effective politics.

Just look with me at a recent headline in one of the largest, white daily newspapers in South Africa, the JOHANNESBURG STAR — "White Man's Christ Kept Out of Politics." The sub-heading states: "The Christ Who Is Worshipped by Most of White South Africa Is No Politician." The report itselft states:

> The Star's latest opinion poll shows that 55 percent of white South Africans repudiate the idea that Christ had any involvement whatsoever in political affairs during life on earth.
>
> Nineteen percent are prepared to admit He had a partial involvement in politics, while only seven percent see Him as having been extensively involved.
>
> However, a hefty 19 percent either have no opinion on the subject or prefer not to say what their opinions are.
>
> The Afrikaans community is more opposed to the idea of Christ having had anything to do with politics than is the English-speaking sector.
>
> Sixty-one percent of Afrikaners say Christ was "not at all involved" compared to the 48 percent of English speakers who agree with them.

Twenty-three percent of English speakers see Christ as having been "partially involved." Fifteen percent of Afrikaners agree.

Women opt out of having an opinion on this subject in greater numbers than men. Twenty-two percent of them either have no opinion or refuse to answer compared to 16 percent of men.

Younger people are more likely to see Christ in political terms than their elders.

Thus 29 percent of the 16 to 24 age group see Christ as having been partially involved, while only 13 percent of those over 50 agree.

Surprisingly, the towns are more opposed to a political Christ than the villages — the figures for non-involvement are 69 percent and 62 percent respectively.

On a provincial basis the Cape and the Transvaal were most opposed to politicizing the Christian ideal, while the Free State has the largest number of don't knows — a hefty 31 percent. The survey is dated Thursday September 25, 1975."

I hope I have not bored you with this opinion poll on this subject. I think it is pertinent to quote it as fully as I have done to enable you to understand the problem the Church faces in our country.

When issues such as conscientious objectors to military service come up for discussion, much more heat than light is generated, even in Church circles. Whoever supports conscientious objection is immediately accused of supporting violence. This reasoning leaves me flummoxed as a black Christian, for it gives the Church scope to be hyperactive only in the corridors of power, with the result that it has no time to devote to those without power. And yet the Church is supposed to belong to no man and to no sectional interests. The Church should not even have to cross barriers built by human sectional interests, for it should have been present in human experience whereever that experience has begun. The peasant in me asks, why is it that the various denominations in South Africa second their ministers and priests to the army to supply chaplains for armed forces, but they have the greatest difficulty in debating conscientious objection. Why is it that they have not even found it possible to raise the question of pastoral care for the South Africans who have opposed the armed forces in the front lines of action.

As soon as one talks like this, one stands condemned, even if it is a person like myself who does not believe in violence as a means of resolving our problems in South Africa. One talks like this and one is immediately reminded of the fact that without the Church we blacks would not have had any education such as we have at present. This is true. It is also pointed out that it is the Church that has provided us with hospitals to meet the medical needs of our people. This is also very true. The schools were taken away from the churches by the present South African regime. But this did not have the effect of promoting black educational interests; in fact the converse is true. Recently the state has decided to take over the mission hospitals from the churches. All these things we deprecate and all these things we condemn. I sometimes think to myself that these very things we lament, done by the state against the Church, may be divinely ordained. I think

MORE ON THE CHURCH

this may be God's way of drawing to the attention of the Church the fact that the Church has more scope, and is called upon at this time to play a crucial role in the liberation struggle in South Africa. Without playing this role the Church in South Africa will be brought closer to equating might with right and sanctimoniously exercising its ministry under the umbrella of the powerful. The Church seems to me to be the only "white" institution (I use "white" with apologies) which can act as a midwife in bringing about the birth of meaningful change with any hope of a reconciliation.

The debate that the decision of the World Council of Churches programme to combat racism has stimulated in South Africa should never be allowed to get bogged down in the debate of whether the churches, by identifying with the suffering man, are supporting violence or not.

Before debating this issue of violence, I believe that those who wish to debate it impartially should ask themselves the question, "Who was the first to use violence?"

It is an indisputable truth that our whole society, with its assault on the dignity of the black man, is structured on violence. When we speak about the South African situation, we are in fact talking about the bondage of my people. There are many who assume that blacks in South Africa are too docile and are even too afraid "to fight for their freedom". The history of the now-banned liberatory organizations in South Africa such as the African National Congress and the Pan African Congress belie this spurious assumption. Africans did use arms to defend their human dignity in various wars. The last of these examples of armed struggle in South Africa was the Bambatha Rebellion or the Zulu Rebellion in 1906.

From the time Afrikaners and the British sealed their marriage of convenience, Africans soon learned that it pays to put up democratic opposition. They had seen the Afrikaners defeated by the British in the armed struggle, in which Afrikaners were pitted against the sophisticated armaments and warfare of the British. Eventually the Afrikaners worked into the British institutions and staged their democratic opposition from within those institutions.

In many ways the parallel with the black/white situation does not go very far. The Afrikaners who today rule us never suffered the amount of racial discrimination we suffer. The racist doctrine of apartheid has been institutionalized. To discriminate against a people in the manner that it is done in my country is one of the worst violent systems ever devised by man to keep others in subjugation. To deny blacks a share in decision-making, as in the case in South Africa, is violence. To deny blacks equal educational and employment opportunities available to their white countrymen is violence. To enforce a migratory system of labour, which denies husbands and wives the opportunity of exercising their conjugal rights for more than 11 months a year, is violence. To deny blacks a share in the wealth they participate in producing is violence. To hold people in solitary confinement, where they are beyond even the reach of any legal assistance, is violence. To arrest people for pass offences, of which hundreds of my people are victims every hour of the day, is violence.

Who can deny that it is a violent society where, despite the wealth of the country, one in three children born die before they reach the age of 18 months. Who can deny that it is only the result of the violent nature of our South African society that diseases caused by poverty maim and kill people.

Most of the churches in South Africa have always expressed moral indignation at this abhorrent system. But I think we have now reached a point when any self-righteous expression of moral indignation at what is happening in South Africa amounts to some form of violence. That is why the mere debate of conscientious objection to military service by the South African Council of Churches is such a heartening development. It indicates that the churches realize that we, as God's people, are called to be more directly involved in the struggle of the suffering man than with mere expressions of moral indignation. That is why the World Council of Churches in wrestling with the question of racism makes progress in Christian commitment. As someone who is not committed to violence, I believe that only the Church, the institution which by its very calling pursues the ideals of the Prince of Peace, can give any hope of reconciliation between the various peoples who at the moment are in conflict. Neither violence or non-violence are by themselves panaceas for all our ills. That is why I even deplore the use of non-violence in the negative sense of simply getting on with the South African way of life. There are many people in South Africa, and outside, who understand non-violence as merely the tactics of doing nothing to oppose the violence on which our South African society is structured and maintained. Those whose thinking goes along these lines are themselves guilty of participating in violence.

We must admit that although non-violence has not been effective in South Africa, neither has violence. Black people are still a bonded people who are without political or economic power. I am convinced that this is not the time when we should be engaged in debates on whether violence or non-violence is the answer. I believe that it is goals which are important. Whilst I do not believe in violence, for example, I well understand what drives those of my brothers who now resort to violence to do so. I respect their decision because quite clearly it must be a decision they have not reached lightheartedly. In the same way, my decision of struggling beside my people where they are is a decision which I have not taken lightheartedly. Nor was it decided in a bloody-minded way to score points against people who do not think as I do. I am engaged in the struggle of my people in the present situation because for me there is nothing else to do. My people are opposed to the hideousness of our South African circumstances. My people are not resigned to the wicked system. The very draconian measures which the white minority government extends every month, and every year, are evidence of my people's constant opposition to the system and of their resilience.

When people are cornered, as my people are, I believe that the Church has a role to get involved in the struggle for our liberation, even if this only amounts to determining with us our sense of direction.

The people must, despite their circumstances, be able to see their struggle towards fulfillment. In order to do this their children have to be educated. Africans who are the poorest section of the South African population lack a free and compulsory education. Africans have to battle against a very high illiteracy rate. In this struggle of the people the Church has a great part to play. The scope is unlimited.

My people are economically exploited because they are denied trade union rights which are exercised by all other race groups.

This brings me to the important question of economic justice for my people. The whole concern of the churches on the question of investments in South Africa is another proof of the progression of the Church's concern with the suffering man, and it deserves our encouragement.

The whole question of investment and disinvestment has become a current Church issue in this country, in the United States and in Europe.

I have stated over and over again, that it is simplistic to imagine that the mere destruction of the apartheid system automatically spells out the birth of a just society. I am concerned that a redistribution of wealth, power and opportunity takes place in a meaningfully short period of time. I am certain that even if skin colour ceased to be the decisive factor in our South African society there would be no guarantee that what I wish to see happen in South Africa would take place. It is quite conceivable that the gap between the "Haves" and the "Have-nots" might even widen. At the same time I am only too aware that there can be no guarantee that the productive capacity of the land and its industries could keep pace with the black population growth which at present is 3.1 percent in KwaZulu.

Any democratic opposition, however limited, within the existing institutions of South Africa must be encouraged and strengthened. It is this very experience which will form the fabric of the new society which we want to see emerge in South Africa. Our struggles aimed at the destruction of the present unjust society in South Africa would be pointless if they mean merely giving a few blacks the opportunity to join the few whites in their exploitation of the masses of our people. We need a new social direction in South Africa, which means the emergence of a better way of life that will radically change the existing direction in social, economic and political development.

The South African economy is both inefficient and deficient. It is my argument that no responsible leader of a poor and developing country or people can realistically aspire to lead his people to the heights of industrial development presently achieved by most affluent Western nations. If I seek, as I believe I do, to lead my people responsibly, I find that I cannot abandon the masses of my people in favour of a minority elite. This is impossible even with the hopes that new technological developments will speed economic growth so that a decent living could be had by all in the space of decades, rather than generations.

It is of no use for me to deny that industrial development is of utmost importance to South Africa. This necessitates investments on a large scale. As populations grow exponentially, we would lose much ground which we would never regain, if we delay investment, the very base from which economic growth takes place. If we did so it would mean that economic growth will be that much smaller for that much longer. My argument is that, if this situation were to take place, disinvestment would have an inevitable detrimental effect, increasing the poverty of my people perhaps for generations. There are those who will say if this happens it would be good; for will it not then hasten the bloody revolution, which some forces working for liberation in South Africa regard as a panacea for all our ills? Whether it would happen in this fashion is itself a highly debatable matter.

Let me go into depth with you on the role of foreign capital in the economic development of a country with the kind of problems which South Africa has. I hope you will not mind my making comparisons. Britain has been a classic example of an exporter of capital. British capital or British investment capital has played a major role in the development of British Commonwealth countries as well as in the United States of America and in the Argentine in South America. In India and Argentina, for example, British capital was responsible for the development of their national railways. In other former British colonies, British capital has been used for the development of their agriculture, mining industry and commerce banking, as well as their economic infrastructure, such as transport and communications.

In South Africa, British investments have played a major role in the development of mining, secondary industries, commerce, finance, banking, railways and harbours. Today, as you are aware, British investments are by far the largest, exceeding more than 4 billion. American investments are still just a fraction of those of the United Kingdom (1.6 billion), but they are growing amounts and of importance in the South African economy. These are followed by those from Switzerland, West Germany and Japan. It is also a fact that South Africa, despite her growing role in internal savings and funds, is still heavily dependent on foreign capital.

We all realize that external investments of the countries mentioned above have benefitted the foreign investor in the form of interest and dividends or profits, which have also enabled the economies of these countries to grow and develop, thus requiring a high level of technical know-how, management and supervision as well as varying labour skills. In South Africa foreign investment has created economic activity to provide employment and income for the people. Employment and income have not benefitted all racial groups to the same extent, owing to the South African population structure and unequal development of the different regions.

This leads us to examine the three serious disadvantaqes of foreign investments:

The first point is that foreign investments have been applied in a very selective manner. They have gone to the white-owned or white-occupied areas and bypassed areas designated as black "homelands," by white South Africa. These are areas we blacks were pushed into by the might of the white man's gun. They are in most cases a fraction of what comprised our countries as they were before our conquest by the British. White South Africa is now trying to balkanize South Africa. Various white minority governments, aided and abetted first by imperial colonial interests and later by self-interest, have used this tactic to entrench white monopolistic control over the major resources of South Africa and have thus gained for whites total control over the country's productive process. You must understand that we found ourselves confined to these poor areas long before the word "apartheid" ever was coined. As world opinion mounted against it, white South Africa was embarrassed by the plight of the millions of blacks, who were excluded from participating meaningfully in the development of South Africa's riches. This embarrassment led whites in South Africa to talk of these unused corners of their country's backyard as "homelands" for blacks, and as areas where their experiment in self-government could take place. We have no illusions about these political sleights-of-hand of our white countrymen. Having shaken our heads in wonderment at the dishonest brutality of our white countrymen, we have to remember that millions of people live there, and have lived there not merely when the present Nationalist regime acceded to power, but since our conquest.

We may be seen by some here as "puppets" of the white minority regime, but to those who think so, I say. "Lord, forgive them for they know not what they are talking about." It is important to note that black people were not consulted when the 1913 and 1936 Land Acts were passed to give these reserves the stamp of law as the only areas in which black people were to be confined. It is important also to note that a person like myself, who is a hereditary chief of my own tribe, and a traditional political leader of the Zulus, would have been involved in the present work for my people, whether there was separate development or not. In fact I was so engaged even before the white minority regime imposed separate development on KwaZulu. So my concerns for people have nothing to do with apartheid, which should indicate the difference between what motivates the white minority regime to want these areas developed and what motivates me in seeking human development of people confined in these regions of South Africa.

Maybe I have digressed a bit too much in stating the first disadvantage of foreign investment. The second disadvantage is that foreign invesments have been used by the whites in such a manner as to create inequalities among the population or racial groups. Whites have benefitted the most and Africans the least in terms of distribution of income and wealth. I believe that the Church's concern on this issue of investments gives scope for pressures to be brought to bear on multi-national corporations to eliminate these inequalities through these foreign investments.

The third disadvantage of foreign investments is the mere fact that they have made the country wealthy, which has meant more revenue to the government, thus increasing the size of the Consolidated Revenue Fund. Those who are against investment rightly point out that this enables the central government to finance programmes of separate development or apartheid. They further point out that this also enables the South African government to raise its military budget to the astronomical figure of R1 billion for the current financial year. The last point is stated as the main reason for campaigning for disinvestment. I cannot argue against those who argue from these premises. But I firmly believe that there is a limit to what outsiders can do to bring about a change in South Africa. In the final analysis it must be realized that whatever methods are ultimately used by blacks to throw away the yoke of oppression, they will be carried out by blacks themselves in South Africa.

I do not regard anyone involved in the struggle for black liberation in South Africa as my enemy. Anyone so engaged, even those who are committed to methods different from my own, are my brothers. I have pointed out many times that when I say I am committed to non-violence, I am not doing so as some kind of competition to what they are doing. For me, as someone who believes that Christianity offers the only possibility for a reconciliation, non-violence is my way. Apart from that, I do not believe that it would be responsible for me to undertake a course of action which pins its hopes on controlled mass violence and in the process turn my people into cannon fodder. So far, I am not convinced that I can be involved in liberating certain areas of South Africa through violence, in such a way that the machine of violence will be tightly disciplined. I look at the topography and ecology of South Africa and wonder about the success of any strategy and tactics which could be employed to ensure the success of violence. My knowledge of the Afrikaner and whites generally convinces me that the tactics of hot pursuit across borders will be used against marauding freedom fighters. From my point of view, large-scale violence as a planned strategy will not serve the interests of my people. I maintain that my non-violent strategy is the very fabric out of which a new society will be built with chances of reconciliation. I regard this as an essential ingredient in human relationships, and I believe that without it, those who have chosen a course of violent action will have nothing to build on. As much as it is their view that violence is necessary, my view is that non-violence is necessary. I realize that the banned liberation organizations, such as the African National Congress and the Pan African Congress, resorted to violence because there was nothing else to do. I wish to state that I have resorted to non-violence because for me there is nothing else to do. These liberation movements, whilst they operated from platforms inside South Africa, did not talk about violence as the only method of struggling for liberation. I have recently been attacked by the Prime Minister of South Africa for pointing out in a speech I made in Holland that the South African government threw down the gauntlet when they banned these organizations. I have pointed out that the whites, through institutionalized violence which is the very fabric of South African society, are the aggressors. It was they who, by banning these organizations, declared war and commenced the phase of the violent struggle. This led some of my brothers to conclude that violence was the only thing left at hand. About 20 million of my people have perforce to remain in South Africa and have perforce to employ non-violent means. Blind condemnation of non-violence means not taking cognisance of the consequences of violence to millions of people.

Estimates indicate that approximately 120,000 male African workers will enter the labour market in South Africa this year. It is further estimated that 60,000 workers will be absorbed through normal growth in the South African economy. Another 60,000 will have to be supplied with job opportunities in these so-called "homeland" areas each year within the next few years. The creation of 20,000 new industrial jobs will cost R160 million per year. I know that some of you are already saying, and rightly so, that the majority of black people still lie in abject poverty, even though they are employed, owing to the vicious system that is operating in my country. You will say that these people do not earn enough to enable them to enjoy proper and decent lives, that there is still unemployment and underemployment amongst black people. You will then wonder in what way investments can help black people to reach economic justice within the wicked system in which blacks find themselves?

There is another complication here as far as employment opportunities in the Republic of South Africa are concerned. There are thousands and thousands of citizens of the former British colonials who are employed in South Africa. I refer here to the citizens of Lesotho, Botswana, Swaziland and Malawi. In addition thousands of Mozambicans are employed in the South African mines, even after Mozambique attained freedom and independence. The fact that South Africa has this abhorrent apartheid system is not a deterrent to our brothers' coming from these countries to South Africa to earn a living. Nor is it possible at the moment for governments of these countries to stop their citizens from coming to seek work in the Republic of South Africa.

Most of these countries are unable to employ the majority of their own labour force. Only five percent of Lesotho and Botswana citizens find work at home. The situation in Botswana has improved with the discovery of diamonds and other mineral deposits. It is clear that the problem of absorption of the citizens of these neighbouring African states can have both economic and political pressures. In 1967 about 300,000 labourers from the former British protectorates worked in South Africa. During that year their income represented about 25 per cent of the gross national product of these three countries.

The question of investment in South Africa is much more than a South African problem: it is a southern African problem. The destiny of southern Africa is one, whether we like it or not. Any starvation and any bloodshed in any part of southern Africa is bound to send ripples through the rest of southern Africa.

Let me state that I do not believe that it is investment which is wrong. I have stated over and over again, in South Africa and in other countries, that I have at no time spoken for investments which exploit the poverty of my people and which drain the economy of a degree of its potential growth. I have stated over and over again that I am not unconditionally in favour of investments. I have no wish to invite or promote investments that would result in the exploitation of my people.

My people must have a stake in economic development. I have had discussions with investors and would-be investors in South Africa and in various countries on the basis of finding ways and means whereby such investments could be made both profitable and give my people a stake in the economic development of their own land while obtaining a sufficient degree of control over their own resources.

Some of my brothers who are with me in the liberation struggle of black people have been hypercritical of my views on investments in South Africa. Their criticisms have forced me to consider this question in greater depth. Each time I have done this, I have come to the same conclusion. If my people have to remain in South Africa, they must eat, they must buy clothes, they must educate their children. They need work. I am not speaking for white South Africa. But I do speak for black South Africa. Any drying up of the stream of foreign investments in a country still so dependent on them would impede economic growth of the country generally, injure those economic activities which have been the largest absorbers of foreign capital, such as the mines and secondary industries, and so cause a decline in the volume of employment. Black people, and Africans in particular, who are the only race group subject to the pass laws and influx control regulations, would suffer more than whites or other racial groups. White employment is protected by the government whereas the Africans are the first to be fired and always the last to be hired.

The whole campaign against investments can serve a useful purpose in influencing industrialists and commercial concerns, mining, etc., to improve their employment practices. This can be done in various ways — for example, by training and promoting black labour to occupy higher positions in the ladder of employment. It can be done through paying our people a living wage, paying them on the basis of the rate for the job and by ensuring social benefits for them.

The campaign for disinvestment is also useful in pressuring the government to give our people trade union rights enjoyed by all other race groups, as I have pointed out earlier in this speech. We are committed to seeking these rights for our people. Any trade union rights blacks may acquire in South Africa will be a great breakthrough in our whole campaign for economic justice for blacks.

As stated above, I am deeply concerned with the gap between the "Haves" and "Have-nots," and a new formula we have adopted seeks to make a compromise. Share capital is divided on a fifty-fifty basis. Fifty percent to be held by the investor, and the other fifty percent held for the people by the KwaZulu Development Corporation and by KwaZulu individuals who can afford to purchase shares. (This system has now been modified.) The KwaZulu Corporation can ensure that profits on the shares held for the people are ploughed back for the benefit of all the people and not in the interests of a new black elite replacing the white power elite. I believe in an African brotherhood which enables people as a whole to have a stake.

The aim in developing areas where Africans live and where it is legally possible for them to have a stake is part of the liberation struggle of black people. It is not geared towards just giving economic viability to a country, but towards enabling these backyard areas of South Africa to develop in order to give some economic teeth to the oppressed African masses.

I know of no independent country in Africa which is discouraging investments. Anything geared towards the weakening of the economic muscle of blacks will have the effect of retarding their liberation struggle. I wish to repeat, however, that we can do without any investment aimed at sheer exploitation. I would not mind the withdrawal of an industry falling into this category. But whatever efforts are made to bring pressure to bear on multi-national corporations, should not be done at the expense of black human development, without which I cannot see our struggle for freedom gaining momentum.

All these may not be what orthodox Christians would regard as Church things or issues. But I am convinced that through involvement in these issues the churches have a great role to play towards our liberation.

"I would be woefully guilty if I did not say how deeply we repent that we were so late in arriving at the realization that our alliance with the forces of oppression, racism, and colonial exploitation were grievous sins against God. Because we sinned against God, we sinned also against you."

Can anyone of us here predict just what kind of things will be said at Thanksgiving services to mark the liberation of South Africa when that day of liberation finally dawns? I believe that this will largely be determined by the role the Church will play in our liberation.

Chapter 8

STORM WARNINGS UNHEEDED

ONE YEAR AFTER

ULUNDI, March, 1977

Last year I stated that we were meeting in what I called "a watershed year in many ways." Looking back, I can now say that I am not happy about my predictions, but those who regard me as someone who is in the habit of making wild statements had better reflect the next time they feel like making this accusation. My judgment has been confirmed by this country's State President when he opened the present session of Parliament. He also described 1976 as a watershed year.

It is my unpleasant duty to remind not only members of this assembly but the whole country about the fact that my humble warnings about possible eruptions of violence which I stated to the Prime Minister, the Hon. Mr. B.J. Vorster, in the presence of all black leaders who were present in Capetown on January 22, 1975 when we spoke to him, have been shown not to have been the wild predictions they seemed then. It is sad that such tragic loss of life as has resulted from the recent unrest, has had no lessons for those who wield power. I realize that I am making a rather serious statement when I say this. When the first eruptions took place, I sent telegrams to the Prime Minister and to the Minister of Bantu Administration. Except for acknowledgment of receipt from the Honourable Commissioner-General there was no response to my telegrams. My telegraphic message was a plea for an urgent meeting with the Prime Minister and with all the other leaders. I sent copies of the telegrams to all the homeland leaders and asked them to support my plea for such an urgent meeting. Only two leaders supported my plea to the Prime Minister. The Chief Minister of Gazunkulu, Professor H.W. Ntsanwisi, and the Acting Chief Minister of the Ciskei, Mr. Sebe, were the only two leaders who did so. For all practical purposes my telegrams were disregarded by both the Prime Minister and the Minister of Bantu Administration. Such are the dynamics of real power in South Africa. Those who wield real power in South Africa, which comes only through the barrel of the gun, can treat with disdain and contempt any suggestions made to them by people like us, regardless of the fact that we are willy-nilly operating within the framework of their policy. This attitude was, of course, in keeping with the amount of violence that was used to quell the unrest. This is a warning to all of us that those who wield power prefer the unleashing of violence rather than surrender any real power or decision-making to us.

We ultimately met the Prime Minister and the Minister of Bantu Administration and Development and of Bantu Education on the 8th of October 1976. This was almost four months after the first exchange of bullets and stones in Soweto. Such is the worth of human life if one is not represented in the corridors of power where real decision-making takes place. Had white human life been destroyed to the extent to which black human life was destroyed, then hell would have been let loose. I realize that those are serious things to say, but they have to be said by someone, unequivocally, and I see this as my duty to do so.

The discussions in October between the Prime Minister and the Minister of Bantu Administration and ourselves were the biggest farce of the year. If one thinks of the Prime Minister's words to the effect that there was no crisis, at the height of the unrest, this was not at all surprising. The issue of unrest, which we regarded as a priority, was conveniently shelved on the pretext that we had to wait for the findings of the Cillie Commission. To me this was only partly valid because after all is said and done these discussions in the Prime Minister's Office were IN CAMERA. At this point, let me lay before this house the memorandum I read to the Honourable Prime Minister, Mr. B.J. Vorster.

> This meeting between the Honourable Prime Minister and South Africa's black leaders serving their people within the framework of policy is taking place in the midst of civil violence which has reached proportions unparalleled since the War of Independence fought by the Boers at the end of the last century.
>
> It is therefore right and proper that we turn our attention to fundamentals and do not only talk about what are primarily administrative matters within status quo politics.
>
> No matter how much we disagree with the methods adopted by tens of thousands of blacks of all shades, we must take cognisance of the mood of the people and the desperation of their actions. At a meeting such as this, it would be the height of irresponsibility to regard the country's present unrest as the result of a handful of agitators. In our last discussion with the Hon. Prime Minister, I in fact predicted that we might soon be faced with the option that has been taken by our people in the last three and a half months.
>
> We leaders who are serving our people within the framework of your policy hold the view that the unrest in the country was planned by nobody and that the first violent outburst, when it occurred, took all of us by surprise, despite the predictions I made to you in our discussion last year.
>
> Spontaneous civil violence of the proportions we have witnessed amounts to a breakdown of law and order and indicates the impoverishment of the South African Government's administration.

STORM WARNINGS UNHEEDED

Put bluntly, the present unrest is nothing other than a mass rejection of apartheid and white privilege. As such, the unrest must not be seen as a temporary and passing problem. It indicates a chronic state of affairs which has now become so acute that it lays claim to our most urgent attention at this meeting.

As leaders representing millions of our people we will be expected to face a politically impossible task unless this is productive—productive from the point of view of our people. They are aware of our meeting here today. Some may be expectant but many are skeptical. Those who are skeptical are not skeptical because they do not trust us; they are skeptical because we have always returned from this kind of conversation with the Hon. Prime Minister empty-handed.

At the outset, a general point must be made. Legislative assemblies which are located in the so-called homelands, cannot function for any length of time unless decisions in these assemblies are seen to be relevant to the interests of all blacks, including the interests of urban blacks, as determined by themselves. After all, these legislative assemblies were created on that assumption by the republican government.

The extent to which urban and rural blacks have common interests is the extent to which they will subject themselves to the same leadership. The common interest of all blacks is real fulfillment. Blacks do not see why they should have separate ethnic destinies when whites have one common destiny, which is not ethnic.

A situation in which urban blacks are controlled by riot police is not a situation which we can tolerate. Riot police were resorted to because white political control of urban blacks had failed. This failure is not simply to be laid at the door of Bantu Administration Boards or the Urban Bantu Councils. The failure is fundamental, and it is the failure of apartheid as such.

The numerous representations we have made about the grievances of blacks, particularly urban blacks, have not resulted in any meaningful changes. These changes were impossible within the grand design of apartheid, "separate development", call it what you will. The failure of the Honourable Prime Minister to introduce what are to blacks meaningful changes makes our task as leaders seeking a peaceful change, impossible. As blacks with the responsibility to lead blacks, we have no desire to resort to riot police administration.

We do not want to cover our failure with shows of strength. We stand rather condemned as politically impotent. This admission is not a comment on our leadership ability. It is rather a comment on apartheid. The institutions of apartheid are not instruments of nation-building, and it is not possible to exercise responsible political leadership within an apartheid framework. I am not indulging in sheer agitation when I speak as I do, I am merely being factual and constructive.

Whites as a minority group claim the right to make decisions for the country's black majority and claim the right to enforce those decisions. They have failed in that enforcement and they have failed because they have attempted what is politically impossible. This they should know from their own history.

The interests of the Afrikaner in South Africa have been self-determined. This process of determining what constitutes their interests has welded people of diverse origins and different languages into a coherent political body.

To a large extent it was the Afrikaner protest movement and the Afrikaner's involvement in liberation politics which turned a heterogeneous group into a VOLK — a people with a specific identity.

In achieving this distinctiveness, the Afrikaners acted outside the constitutional framework provided for them by their political opponents. They refused to recognise the laws of the land, staged a rebellion and fought a full-scale war.

The power advantages that were achieved by these tactics were consolidated by secret associations, the Church and various cultural organizations.

We blacks have the same rights of self-determination as did the Afrikaner whites. As the Afrikaners had the right to choose who would be regarded as eligible as VOLK and who would not, so do we blacks have the right to choose whom we regard as our people. As the Afrikaners involved themselves in nation-building among people of diverse origins, so too do we have that same right.

In point of fact, Afrikaner solidarity was the consequence of political ideals. Political ideals for the Afrikaner did not emerge from an ethnic group. The call to the struggle for liberation drew many different peoples together and the criteria for acceptability was involvement in that struggle.

Black solidarity is growing out of a similar call for liberation and the black man's acceptability is similiarly being determined by his or her involvement in the struggle for liberation.

We as black leaders are aware of these facts. We are aware of the fact that had the renowned Afrikaner leaders in the various phases of the struggle allowed themselves to be dictated to by their political opponents, their people would have abandoned them. Those of us who aspire to serve our people in leadership are aware of the fact that our people will reject us if we do not fulfill their desires for liberation. That is liberation as determined and understood by themselves.

Let us now call a halt to such talk as there has been about the National Party's policy of self-determination of the people for the people. Our people have not and never will desire self-determination within the framework laid down by the whites. To expect them to act differently is to expect them to do what the whites, and the Afrikaners in particular, never did during their own struggle.

Let us talk about how the irresistible urge for political expression which is now a fact of self determination can be made constructive. That the political process in this country has become destructive is plain for everybody to see. It is our responsibility to turn what is now destructive energy into a nation-building force.

STORM WARNINGS UNHEEDED

It must be obvious that political leadership in the white community as well as in the black community will face almost insurmountable obstacles in introducing constructive political changes. If we cannot even talk to each other about these difficulties, there is no hope for our country. Talking to each other is meaningless unless we also listen to each other. If one thinks realistically within what one can perhaps call "internal detente", one must not lay down preconditions. We do, however, find it necessary to point out that the definition of common ground which justifies detente is essential. Such a definition would, in our opinion, be advantageous beyond all measure.

Knowing the limits of white political creativity, we must ensure that the definition of common ground is not offensive to them. To this end we propose that the legitimacy or otherwise of political practices and political institutions as determined by the Western free world be accepted as limitations in our definition. If we cannot find common ground within these terms, more and more of our people will feel that violence is the only alternative left to the black people of South Africa. Here again let me stress that I am merely expressing the feelings of most of my people.

We are even prepared to go further than this. We are prepared to determine by consensus within the international Christian community what the minimal ethical standards in political matters are for Christian countries. Having done so we are prepared to make such standards part of our definition of common ground.

Having elected to initiate internal dialogue between black and white we need to make it possible for whites to accept our initiatives. This we have done by indicating acceptable parameters. We hope that the Honourable Prime Minister will accept the challenge of getting a mandate from his people to enable him to approach the difficult future in unity with us.

If we cannot talk to each other within these terms there is nothing left to talk about and there will be no joint venture into the future. I speak boldly about these things as they are issues of life and death for all of us. I am therefore being highly responsible when I talk as I do.

After reading this memorandum to the Prime Minister and presenting it to him, he did not react even to one single portion of it. The Prime Minister asked me whether this memorandum represented the views of the other leaders present. I told him that I authored it and that if other leaders disagreed with its contents they had a right to disagree with me. No one came forth to disagree or agree with the contents. I am not saying this in any spirit of condemnation as far as my colleagues are concerned. I am merely informing members of this assembly, as it is my duty to do. After my response to his question he did not deal with any aspect of my presentation to him.

On the question of holding a national convention he dismissed the idea by merely saying that he saw no merit in it, calling it the "baby" of the Progressive-Reform Party. I have no intention of going into the details of this conference. All I can say is that it was the worst of all the farces that these consultations or conferences with the Prime Minister have proved to be. The Prime Minister took exception to the fact that we had in our press release, after the meeting of black leaders we had by ourselves in August, stated that the Prime Minister had at these meetings treated us "shabbily." He wanted us to withdraw the word "shabbily" but we totally refused to do so.

The Chief Minister of the Ciskei, Mr. L.L. Sebe, was afterwards asked by the Chief Minister of Gazunkulu, Professor Ntsanwisi, as convener to pass a vote of thanks at the end of this farce. Quite frankly I was puzzled what the vote of thanks should be about after a conference that was to me a virtual non-starter. I was quite amazed to hear the Chief Minister of the Ciskei stating, in spite of this non-discussion, that the Prime Minister would go down in the annals of this country as a great statesman. I indicated that I wanted to respond to some of these remarks. The Prime Minister, however, ignored my hand, responded swiftly to the Chief Minister of the Ciskei's vote of thanks and left the room.

In the past he always stayed on for the preparation of a joint communique. He did not do so this time. The Minister of Bantu Administration had left earlier as he had to catch a plane. So one of his deputies, Mr. Cruywagen, presided over the preparation of a joint communique. The Deputy-Minister wanted Mr. Sebe's statement on the Prime Minister as a great statesman included. I told the Deputy-Minister that I disagreed with that view. The Deputy-Minister was angered by this, and accused me of having not had the guts to state my view in the presence of the Prime Minister. I told him that the Prime Minister had not given me a chance to respond to this when I indicated I wanted to speak. I was, fortunately, supported by the Chief Minister of QwaQwa, who backed my statement that although I wanted to speak, the Prime Minister had not given me the opportunity. There was a lot of unpleasantness. I wanted to indicate that since this remark of Mr. Sebe did not have the unanimous support of all the participants, it should not be part of the press release. In the past, when I objected to things during the preparation of the press release at the end of these meetings, Dr. Eschel Rhoodie, the Secretary of Information who normally is charged with the task of putting it in writing, has always respected my feelings, however grudgingly. The Deputy-Minister Mr. Cruywagen insisted on including Mr. Sebe's remark on the Prime Minister as a great statesman. However, in fairness to the Deputy-Minister, let me say that some of the leaders, led by the Chief Minister of QwaQwa, Mr. Mopele, insisted that my objection must be ignored, as I was the only one who objected.

I deal with this incident in detail, not because I intend on revealing what other leaders do at these meetings, but because I want you to know the difficulties I encounter. I am undecided now as to whether I should continue to attend these meetings at all, and I think you can advise me on whether I should attend any future meetings of this sort with the Prime Minister. These meetings compel me to conclude that they are made to give our people the impression that something concrete is going on. To the world, they appear like some kind of internal dialogue, which they are not in any sense. This is my problem. I allow the Prime Minister the credit that on peripheral issues like granting our people some security of tenure in the urban areas, he did promise us a lease. I must also say that he promised to scrap restrictions on African businessmen.

On fundamental changes that black people want to see in order to prevent bloodshed in this country, the Prime Minister is as hard as granite. You heard over your radios and you have seen in the press the government's determination to pursue their apartheid policies to their logical end, which is the dismemberment of our homeland, South Africa, into mini-states, which will for all practical purposes remain as client states of South Africa. The government has been encouraged by those leaders of these so-called homeland regions who have opted for so-called independence, to pursue their apartheid policy. This is the predicament which people like myself are in. We are, as a result of this development, tarred with the same brush as others who have opted for this empty fragmentation of our country. A lot of black political opportunists are joining hands in using all of us as political scapegoats.

Let us face it; all efforts to crush apartheid from within and from without have been unsuccessful. None of the forces for liberation have come anywhere near success. This does not mean that such success is beyond our reach. It is very much within our reach. The problem that bedevils the situation is the lack of black unity which has guaranteed the continuation of apartheid. Even if there have been lessons for thousands of blacks in the power of the stone and the match, these lessons, for those who believe in that strategy, are meaningless so long as blacks are as fragmented as they are at present. Even for those blacks who believe in pursuing a peaceful solution there can be no success if blacks continue to be as fragmented as they are and fail to have a common strategy. I have said before and I would like to repeat it here today, that those feelings which turn people into violent mobs cannot be conceptualized out of existence. These currents of stinging human anger which are the legitimate experience of people who are exploited and denied political self-expression cannot be conceptualised out of existence. It is only when conceptualization coincides with human reality that it becomes a productive factor in our response to political situations. Misconceptualization has dangerous political consequences. We have seen what these misconceptualizations have done to the Portugese colonists, and we have seen what it is doing to Zimbabwe. This is the danger point we have reached — the cross-roads. The difficult and painful choice is between a great future for all the people of this land and greed and violence which will consume all of us.

Last year I stated in this house that the Prime Minister had disregarded my warnings of 1975. I wanted to see violent confrontation, which has now occurred, prevented by the Prime Minister, but he reacts as if it has not occurred, and he has displayed even more determination to maintain apartheid society in South Africa. As he puts it: "Law and order will be maintained at all costs." The costs include human life, as we have seen. So the central government persists in its misconceptualization despite the costly warnings — costly in terms of human life, as we have witnessed in the past ten months.

The majority of whites seem persistent in wanting to be seen by most blacks not as our fellow countrymen, but as extractors of wealth at the expense of the black man's humanity. White colonists' vested interests determined that black savages must be dispossessed of their land, conquered and enslaved economically. Whilst encouraging noises are being made by various white groups, such as industrialists and individuals, that present whites should get away from this mentality, there is not the slightest evidence that the present regime wants to do more than sugarcoat the pill at the very most. This, of course, is the very height of political stupidity, which neither the whites nor we can survive if whites continue to bow before the political lunacy of the hardliners. There is every evidence that the present regime seems determined to do no more than superintend the lunacy of the hardcore of party hardliners.

The Inkatha Central Committee has just recently circulated a statement of beliefs to Inkatha branches. Even at this late hour, we are still hoping that there might be a slim chance that white political rationality may yet save South Africa from a future which Mr. Vorster has defined as "too ghastly to contemplate." In order that this slim chance might grow and prosper into everyday household attitudes, both blacks and whites have to take stock. What has emerged in the past ten months must be seen by all races as a last ditch attitude on the very brink of disaster. Both blacks and whites need a realism which will permit constructive political action. The mere getting together with whites to present a facade that there still exist whites who are reasonable is no longer good enough. The time for that is gone. We need to be involved in joint action that will ensure the emergence of a South Africa which all of us who are not chained by greed want to see. We have reached a point now when the mentality which believes that whites are God-chosen superbeings, or simply inately better than blacks, has produced superblacks and confrontationist politics. Jails and bannings, the deterrents of the sixties, are no longer deterrents. In the sixties whites believed that they could build jails as fast as they could arrest people. However, these attitudes have at last produced black preparedness to go to those jails with ever increasing willingness. That is where we are now.

It seems to me that there is a need for a basis of belief endorsed by all the people who do not want to see a race war here. I realize that there are many people who hate my guts for daring even to grope for a peaceful solution after the violence that has been unleashed against blacks in the past ten months. I am not ashamed to do whatever is within the realm of the possible to prevent bloodshed. I am not so naive as to be over-optimistic about any successes in that direction. I, however, do not think, even at this late hour, that it is good enough for me to wait, biting my nails and hoping that the holocaust will come to solve our problems. I accept its possibility as something that we are drifting towards because of present attitudes. I know what this will mean for my people. People should not think that I am naive when I still talk of a black-white future for this country. It is the acceptance of this fact that makes me think it is worthwhile to try until the last moment to prevent a race war, which for all practical purposes will be suicidal. I am not even afraid to die. I would, in fact, thank the Almighty if my death or that of my people meant fulfillment for our new generation. I do not believe, however, in seeking martyrdom for the sake of it. Nor do I want to be misunderstood as implying that those of my brothers who see the armed struggle as the only solution are doing it for the sake of any martrydom. I am on record as saying that, whilst I am committed to a peaceful solution, I very well understand what compels them to resort to violence.

Neither those of us who believe in a peaceful solution nor those who believe in a violent solution have succeeded in solving our problems so far. It is therefore too early to condemn each other, and it is indeed a fruitless exercise. There is much that can be done by each force for liberation and it amazes me that energy should be wasted quarrelling among ourselves. That is why I welcome the emergence of the Black Unity Front, in whose launching I participated. I am committed to the nurturing of it. I see in it a future basis for a black common strategy. I see it as our only hope for the avoidance of a black civil war in this country either during the course of the struggle for liberation or during the post-liberation era.

Some people have tried to read double-talk into my commitment to black unity and to the black/white joint action strategy. With brain-washing through the racist mass-media, it would surprise me if there were no people who felt this way. Whilst there are whites who still regard themselves as the only true patriots, this is inevitable. These are the people who debase the concept of patriotism and who will suffer the eventual fate of all political traitors. On the other hand, there has emerged as a direct result of this white political lunacy, a group of blacks whose definition of patriotism excludes whites.

Let me re-state that we are one people in one land. No amount of political histrionics by white or black hardliners can alter this fact. Blacks and whites have been thrown by fate together. They must therefore learn to live together, eat, love and work together. I see no alternatives without holocaust. Those who do not want to live together must live elsewhere. This country, it must be emphasized, is no place for race supremacists of whatever hue. A new constitution is the only political alternative we have.

It is, therefore, absolute stupidity to accuse me of trying to play the game of ganging-up with whites against the government. It would be politically naive for me to think it could succeed. I see that strategy as one or two steps short of our complete and utter destruction. My strategy, therefore, can only involve all willing South Africans in this last hour of crisis to prevent the escalation of the violence, the foretaste of which we have all experienced in the last ten months.

This is also the very last opportunity that South Africa's friends have to help us get to the conference table. I therefore welcome anything, short of bloodshed, that South Africa's friends do to force us to that conference table. I believe it would be in the interests of all South Africans if our problems were resolved by South Africans themselves. In other words, I am saying that there is a limit to what friends can do for us. If efforts by friends or foes go beyond getting us to a conference table, it will be something we can lay squarely on the shoulders of those who wield power and who continue to refuse to share such power with us. As long as we are pariahs in our country, we blacks will not die to perpetuate apartheid.

This is no time for ambiguities. That is why I am taking all the trouble to deal with fundamental issues at such great length. This is the time for people of all persuasions to be counted so that it can be known on which side they stand.

I want to make it clear that people must not be mistaken and think that merely because the violence did not escalate in this province, that we are not on the side of our people. We are one hundred per cent on the side of our people. We may differ on tactics as a people, but we are all struggling for one liberation and one freedom. I want to warn white South Africa as far as this is concerned that they should not make the mistake of thinking that a couple of swallows make a summer. The majority of blacks are solidly behind me in what I am saying here. No amount of propaganda over the pro-apartheid mass media can ever alter black thinking on this issue. No amount of wishful thinking by the pro-apartheid mass media can ever alter black thinking on this issue. I want to state this over and over again, for who knows? this may be my last chance to do so. I want no one in South Africa, white or black, to have any illusions about where I stand. For this is where I stand whatever the consequences may be. So you will forgive me if I tend to be repetitive. There are so many forces arrayed against me that I regard it as a duty to you and myself to be as lucid as I can be on these issues at this moment in our history. I have spurned popularity among some blacks and some whites for daring to offer cooperation of any sort with whites. At the same time I have also spurned popularity among whites by offering to cooperate with blacks.

Let me repeat what I have said so many times before for the consumption of whites, that blacks are my brothers and sisters in the struggle for liberation. This is so regardless of the fact that the white government has seen fit to maim and kill some of them. It does not matter one jot that the instruments of the government have forced some of them to flee the country. It does not matter even if some of them have become so demoralized that they are being used as informers and saboteurs of our struggle for liberation by the present regime. Let us get this clear once and for all: we, they and us, are the blacks of South Africa. We are, at the same time, fellow citizens with the whites of South Africa.

That is why I have always deplored the political idiocy of some blacks who assist the government in its divisionist tactics by attacking other blacks. Some of my brothers who indulge in these extravagances have even threatened my life for my views.

On the other side of the coin let me state that to me South African whites are not expendable expatriates. South Africa is their land of birth and they have a right to be here just like the white Americans in the United States or the Australians in Australia.

If this is accepted, then it is clear to me that there can be no political solution in this country in which whites are not active partners. Whether we like it or not, we have got to admit that we are all South Africans together with them. We can, however, only survive together if we share one sense of patriotism. It is only if we feel partly committed to a common destiny with them that there will be no race war through our, or their, political lunacy.

Homeland politics are a pipedream. The whole idea that we blacks can be declared foreigners in any part of our land by our countrymen, who are descended from foreigners, causes such revulsion that its enforcement can only mean ultimate war. The violence of the last ten months proved beyond any doubt that apartheid can never be fully implemented.

STORM WARNINGS UNHEEDED

I have no hatred in my heart for any section of our population. I accept that we are all South Africans before we are Zulus, Jews, Afrikaners, Sothos, Indians, Coloured, etc. Certain sections of the Afrikaans press have tried to portray me as someone who hates whites, and to be more specific, my Afrikaner countrymen. As for the press, one can do nothing with them. But I was quite amazed when no less a person than the Honourable Prime Minister attacked me at Ladybrand in the Orange Free State and accused me of wanting to push the Afrikaners out of Africa! The following are his words:

> Now the leader of the Zulus is quoted as saying: "Afrikanerdom and the Afrikaans culture was not likely to survive in South Africa," Chief Gatsha Buthelezi said here last night. Just fancy, and I think I must now tell Chief Buthelezi very clearly that: "You are the leader of the Zulus; it is time that you confined yourself to your work."

(Applause)

> "The future," so he goes on, "the future is a black future and we blacks want our future to begin now. We know there will be whites in that future, but they will not be the determinants and the oppressors. They will be liberated whites adapting to a black man's world in a black self-conscious continent." There have been greater men than this chief who have wanted to push us out of Africa. They discovered their mistakes.

Nothing amazes me more than the way the Prime Minister has misunderstood my remarks about the Afrikaners. The Afrikaners wield power in South Africa, comprising as they do, more than sixty percent of the white population of our country. The Nationalist Party which is in power today in Parliament in Capetown, got into power on the apartheid ticket during the 1948 election and at subsequent elections. Most of the things the present regime does are understood by our people to be representative of Afrikanerdom. The imposition of Afrikaans on our children in the urban areas sparked the recent unrest. The imposition of Afrikaans was done in complete disregard of the representations we made to the Prime Minister and the Minister of Bantu Administration and Development and of Bantu Education. All the things done by the present regime are, therefore, done in the name of Afrikanerdom and apartheid. So I merely warned that, if they were not careful and if they persisted in ramming their apartheid policies down the throats of the majority of the population, they might find that by so doing they have committed group suicide. Afrikaans is one of the indigenous languages of our land. But clearly, judging by the events of the past ten months, there has been a revulsion against it throughout the black community. This is not the way to ensure the continued use of Afrikaans by the majority of the people in the first place.

In my speech I had warned that if the Afrikaners are not careful, through the acts of those who govern us they may commit group suicide. I said that nobody will begrudge the Afrikaner his heritage if it is no threat to the heritage and freedom of other people.

It must be remembered that the imposition of Afrikaans as a medium of instruction caused last year's unrest. So at the Witwatersrand University Law Students dinner, I stated that the heritage of the Afrikaner has become a threat. I warned that it lives on exploitation and shores up its foundationless walls with draconian powers. I warned that the heritage of the Afrikaaner will be doomed if, in order to retain its identity, it continues to dominate and to divide and rule. It was what the rulers conveyed to us in the name of Afrikanerdom which made me issue these warnings. That is what the imposition of the Afrikaans medium on black children, for example, conveyed to blacks. The resultant violence speaks volumes in this respect. The Afrikaners should know this from experience. Catherine Taylor, a former member of Parliament, quotes the following in her biography, entitled IF COURAGE GOES.

> One day in May 1959, more than 2,000 boys and girls from six schools in the Parow-Tiervlei area (adjacent to that controlled by the Cape School Board) marched along Voortrekker Road to attend a celebration at the Civic Centre to mark "Die Wonder Van Afrikaans."
> Children from each school recited poems and prose that traced the history of Afrikaans, and all took part in the singing. The function had been organized by the Parow Committee of the Federasie van Afrikaans Kultuurvereenigings as part of a language festival taking place throughout South Africa. Among verses recited was one in early Afrikaans by C.P. Hoogenhout. Translated it read:
>
> "English! English! English! English
> which you see and hear;
> In our Schools, in our churches, our mother-tongue
> is murdered.
> Oh, how our people are being bastardized, our teachers
> helping to this end. Dutch still in certain schools
> it is fraud, simply a name!
> Who refuses to let himself be anglicized, is abused
> and suppressed."

That is what I mean then when I state that the Afrikaners should understand what impositions of another culture and heritage meant to them and how they resented it. They must therefore appreciate more than anyone the resentment that came to a head in June 1976 in Soweto and other parts of South Africa.

I must report also on Inkatha (The National Cultural Liberation Movement) whose constitution was passed by this assembly. Inkatha's growth is phenomenal. The people everywhere want members of the central committee to come and set up branches. As a political constituency Inkatha has no parallel in black South Africa. It will continue to grow in strength and influence by leaps and bounds. I acknowledge that it will do so before it is an epitome of democracy. Inkatha has direction and it has the will to achieve that which it sets its mind to achieve. It has moved resolutely, paused to consolidate its position and moved forward again. Its strength is not derived from political extravagances on the one hand, or KIERRIE or PANGA (weapons) on the other.

We seek no favours from anyone, and we are not in this business to get pats on the back from white small town politicians of VOLKER ilk. But we believe in truth, in justice and in fair play. We are a liberation movement, and oppressors of the VOLKER type cannot help throwing mud at us because they know that ours is a just cause.

We accept that, like all liberation movements before us, we are infiltrated by all kinds of agents. We stand on the justice of our cause and on the principles and objectives so clearly set out in our constitution.

There is a wave of intimidation which is being carried out by members of the security branch, and other agents against Inkatha. Whilst this does not surprise me, it amazes me that such methods should be used to try and break down a national movement of this nature, whose constitution was approved by this assembly. As if this was not enough, the very first bulletin of Inkatha was banned by the publications board. I will lay a copy of its contents in this house for the information of members of this assembly. The central committee decided to appeal against the banning order. To our amazement the publications board, in its reply to our submissions, made wild and apocryphal charges against Inkatha. When you see the almost eighteen page submission, you will understand why the security police and other government agents in Natal and the Transvaal are conducting such a concerted campaign of molestation against Inkatha members. Some of you may have read the outburst by Mr. Le Grange, the Deputy Minister of the Department of Information, who accused me and Inkatha of all sorts of things at a political meeting at Mooi River towards the end of last year. It is not a coincidence that it should have been a Deputy-Minister of the Department of Information who made these snide remarks against me and our national movement. This assembly is only too aware that ever since there was a KwaZulu assembly, the Department of Information of the republican government has always been in the forefront of this central government campaign to denigrate me and to hatch up artificial opposition politics in KwaZulu. So this was no surprise after the Roodts of the world, the Paul Zulus, the Elses, the Joseph Madlalas and the Van der Watts in London. And to crown it all the support the Honourable Minister of Information gave Mr. Van der Watt after the latter's scurrilous attacks on me from the South African embassy in London is worth mentioning. We are not whining about it. My information from impeccable sources is that attempts are being made to make preparations for the rigging of elections by some of these agents. The struggle is very much on.

As a hereditary chief I am concerned about allegations made against the chiefs. The chief is a chief because of the people. It is therefore highly dangerous for chiefs to be seen to be ranging themselves against the people. The results of this kind of conduct during the Banbatha Rebellion of 1906 are well known to most of us. The fate of chiefs who did so was not a pleasant one. On the other hand, I am aware that the agents who frighten the chiefs mislead them into believing that Pretoria still has the final word on chieftainships. This is not the case. They are told that Pretoria is against Inkatha and that if they are active in Inkatha they will lose their positions as chiefs. It is this government that is fully in charge of chieftainships. We have no intention of using that position to threaten anyone. The biggest threat against the chiefs who do not cooperate is not the government of KwaZulu but their own people. It is for these chiefs to clearly define now whether they are on the side of the people or on the side of the oppressors. That is the clear choice before them. The whole institution of chieftainship is at stake here. Its whole future is at stake depending on what the chiefs decide to do.

As one of the chiefs, I warn you that your people are your safest bet. No crumbs from agents can be compensation for the alienation and disenchantment you are likely to find among your tribesman if you continue with your anti-Inkatha stance taken at the instance of these agents-provocateurs. We know how Mr. Fouche of the Bureau for State Security a few years ago opened up an account at the Wuikere Bank for one chief in this assembly, with the intention of creating divisions among us as an insurance for our perpetual subjugator. More than any other white group in South Africa, the Afrikaners know and understand what unity really means. They know what Afrikaner unity did for them.

Since the last sitting of this house, I have had a few trips abroad.

Namibia: In September, I was invited to Namibia to address a symposium. I was quite interested to attend a discussion of several hours in Windhoek on the Turn Halle Conference. Whatever the demerits of the Turn Halle Conference, I was impressed to know how people of all race groups are groping together to find a formula acceptable to most people. It is not even the result I am concerned with for the purposes of my remarks today. Efforts by any people to seek joint absolution are plausible by any standard. Imposition of formulae by one group on others is despicable and deserves only condemnation. That is why our country is the polecat of the world. It is because it operates on that basis.

Nigeria: In October I received an invitation from the Nigerial Institute for International Affairs to deliver a lecture in Lagos. I submit the press release I made at the time, as my report to this assembly on that trip.

The United States: In November 1976, I was also invited by the President, students and faculty at the Washington Technical Institute. I will also submit my press release as my report to members of this assembly.

The United States and the United Republic of Tanzania: Last year I was invited to give lectures at Willamette University in the State of Oregon and also at the World Affairs Council in Los Angeles. I could not go because of unrest in our country. My press releases on these trips will also be submitted by me as my reports to this assembly on those trips.

It is fortunate that, as poor as we are, we are offered these trips, which in each and every case were financed by my hosts. I stressed once before how important it is that we should be in touch ourselves with the international community. White South Africa, like most countries in the world, is represented in most countries and cities of the world by embassies and consulates. Since the government in Pretoria represents only whites, it is quite clear that blacks need to represent their own interests as well on an international diplomatic level. To be quite honest, these few trips abroad are not sufficient at all when one takes into account the fact that other people have full-time staffs who represent their interests from day to day in practically every country of the free world. We are also disadvantaged by the fact that certain of our brothers who are permanently represented abroad are not always well disposed towards us.

I am not surprised when there is hostility expressed by certain people in South Africa against these trips. We blacks are supposed to be on our own. It follows that even internationally we must do our own thing. People in power abroad know what goes on in South Africa and make up their own minds about stances they adopt towards us in South Africa. They are not as stupid as certain pro-apartheid mass-media would like us to believe. Remarks on my meeting with President Jimmy Carter by one Aida Parker of THE CITIZEN must be seen in this light. In the issue of this newspaper dated March 8, 1977, Aida Parker writes:

> Does President Carter's surprise 15 minute interview on Saturday with Chief Gatsha Buthelezi constitute American recognition of South Africa's controversial homeland policy? That question is being asked in diplomatic circles in Washington and Pretoria after Chief Buthelezi pulled off what for a South African must be regarded as the biggest protocol scoop of the year.

Let me state that I met the President on Sunday the 6th of March and not on Saturday just for the sake of the record. The President's meeting with me had nothing to do with the recognition of the homeland policy. The President is committed to human rights and he has demonstrated his commitment to human rights by meeting even Russian dissidents. So he met me as a victim of apartheid who rejects homeland policies as a solution for South Africa's problems. The President is not a nut like Aida Parker; he knows that my leadership here is not a creation of the homelands. The President, unlike Aida Parker and her friends in the diplomatic circles of Pretoria and Washington, is a humble Christian leader and not a hypocrite. Apartheid is the step-child of the West.

Britain was instrumental in giving South Africa shape and form by accepting the Act of Union and the Statute of Westminster. From that time white South Africa has been sustained by the West. In trade and diplomacy the West has continued to give credibility to apartheid. That is why even the present tokenism of not giving Transkei independence recognition has been severely criticized by some, as the same nations have diplomatic and trade ties with the white minority power elite in Pretoria. In other words, in both trade and diplomacy the West has continued to give credibility to apartheid. We, the victims of apartheid, have been used by many Western countries to buy respectability for themselves. They have attempted to use us, the poor victims of apartheid, to salvage their image which is tainted with the blood of our suffering because of their diplomatic links with white South Africa, by ignoring our existence. President Carter takes his Christianity seriously enough not to join the camp of Uriah Heeps, which the West's vested interests have always represented in the black/white struggle in South Africa.

The West, for far too long, has indulged in this neocolonial diplomacy which makes us virtually the political skivvies to Western vested interests. President Carter knows that a new southern Africa, which the West will have to live with, is fast emerging.

Aida Parker, apartheid's megaphone, goes on in her article to write:

> By granting the leader of the KwaZulu executive an audience only six weeks after assuming the Presidency, Mr. Carter has — again — from a protocol point of view — pushed Chief Buthelezi into the very front rank of foreign visitors. There has been no suggestion that Prime Minister Vorster meet Mr. Carter. And when Mr. Pik Botha, the retiring South African Ambassador to the US, and South African Minister-designate, was summoned to the White House to meet the President, he stood in line with 150 ambassadors from all parts of the world. Chief Buthelezi even beat Israeli Prime Minister Yitzhak Rabin to the gun. Mr. Rabin will not be received at the White House till this week.
>
> The query now is: Was Mr. Carter badly advised on Chief Buthelezi's political importance? Or is there a much deeper political significance behind this meeting?
>
> By refusing to grant diplomatic recognition to the new State of Transkei, the U.S. Congress has formally rejected recognition of the homeland philosophy. Most of the American media dismiss homeland leaders as puppets of the South African government, claiming that the true black leaders of South Africa are Nelson Mandela and Robert Sobukwe.
>
> Mr. Carter's audience with Chief Buthelezi would appear to upset all that, or is there something deeper behind the meeting? Said one Pretoria analyst: "The Americans have now given Chief Buthelezi some sort of role, not yet defined but clearly one of paramount importance."
>
> It has been known for some years that the American Embassy, in particular through the U S. Consulate Offices in Durban, has played an extremely active role in grooming Chief Buthelezi as a sort of political "Crown Prince", but the full purpose behind this has never been made clear.
>
> Nor is this the only strange role the American mission has played in South Africa. It is known that the U S. Information Service, based in Johannesburg, opened a branch library in Soweto shortly before the riots — and that included in the literature made available to this library were several works on revolutionary warfare.

This is typical of Aida Parker. She has been specializing in writing scurrilous rubbish about me for pro-apartheid newspapers for quite a few years. I have known her since the time she was a reporter for THE DAILY NEWS in Durban. Her writings always remind me of that famous saying that: "Hell hath no fury like a woman scorned." I have had the misfortune of being the object of her frustrations, of whatever nature, for quite some time. I have nothing against English-speaking South Africans becoming nationalists. This is not my business. I, however, lament the fact that each time English-speaking nationalists operate, they always try to be more nationalist than Afrikaner-nationalists. A typical example of trying to "out-Herod-Herod." They become more acid in the venom they spit in the direction of apartheid's victims, as evidenced by Aida Parker's article.

President Jimmy Carter, as a committed Christian, will always be misunderstood by hypocrites of Aida Parker's ilk. Pharisees always blamed Christ for making no distinction between people. In particular they always voiced objections when Christ shared meals and mixed with those they despised. He was for this reason Himself despised.

President Carter knows that the majority of black people reject apartheid and do not accept the idea of being made foreigners in 87 percent of their own land. He stated to me that he had heard some good things about me. Although he did not define them, I assumed that he was referring to what President William Tolbert of Liberia referred to as my "constant and consistent" rejection of apartheid. He was not seeing me as a leader of a homeland. He is well aware that my leadership at local level is not a creation of the homelands. He knows that when Africans carry passes, they have no choice. He knows that when Africans reside in these rural slums such as kwaZulu and urban ghettoes like Soweto, and travel in separate buses, taxis and trams, they do so out of no choice.

Unlike Aida Parker, I know that the President was seeing me as a victim from an area where human rights are violated. He also knows that I represent millions of black people in South Africa. The people, in whose area I am, reject homelands independence. They are five million and would be in the majority in South Africa even if, for arguments sake, all the homelands followed the Transkei and Bophuthatswana. The President knows that I share common borders with Mozambique and Swaziland, which are independent African States. He knows that Inkatha, the liberation movement I lead, has more than 70,000 paid members. If all that is unimportant to Aida Parker and if all this makes me unimportant, that is her business. She can live in that fool's paradise,if that soothes her nerves and makes her frustration problems better.

Many people in Africa and in the world know who I am in presentday South Africa. The two-and-a half hour meeting which I had with the President of the United Republic of Tanzania, Julius Nyerere on the 7 March is significant in underlining this fact. He is the primus of frontline presidents and he has never seen me as a puppet, and this was our second meeting.

There was nothing more than that to my meeting with President Carter. There is no special role assigned to me by Americans, even the President's words to me were that it was people like myself who had to guide him on how he should conduct his human rights commitment. He did not single me out.

It is so much nonsensical gibberish for Aida Parker to suggest that the U.S. Consulate Offices play any part in "grooming" me. My family, on both my father's and mother's side, have been leaders here for about 200 years. It is therefore so much silly nonsense for Aida Parker to suggest that I need grooming by Americans or any other foreigners. Nor do I need homelands policies to groom me. I have never seen myself as a political Crown Prince of South Africa. I think Aida Parker needs to see her psychiatrist as her hallucinations are dangerous for someone who writes material for the perusal of thousands of people. Black people of South Africa have never seen me as a puppet, not even in Umtata (Transkei). The headline of Aida Parker's article is in itself an insult to the American President:

"Is President Carter wooing Buthelezi?"

Wooing me? What for? Have the men who have wooed her in her private life, done it the same way as I met with the President? It must have been very dull and no wonder she exudes so much frustration and bitterness.

For the record, let me state that I met a number of our brothers in exile. Amongst these it is important for the sake of the record, to report to this assembly that I met also Mr. Potlako Leballo the President of PAC in exile in Dar-Es-Salaam. He had heard about the report made to this house last year to the effect that allegations were made that I would be the first target of his military trainees if and when they returned to South Africa. This he denied and in fact stated in front of a top Tanzanian official that he respected me as both a traditional leader and for the things I do in South Africa.

An essential element of the KwaZulu government's economic policy is to attract industries into Zulu areas. At present Isithebe is the only industrial growth point but other areas are being actively investigated. The industrial estate at Isithebe is being enlarged with facilities owing to the increase in the number of industries already established there, which now number nearly 16. This is very slow progress, but it is progress nevertheless. If one thinks of pressures that are constantly being brought to bear on would-be investors, it is surprising that there are investors at all who want to come to KwaZulu.

Since the assembly last met, five white industrialists have made application to the KwaZulu government to establish industries at Isithebe. The BIC is already conducting negotiations with the firms concerned. It is the belief of the KwaZulu government that industries in suitable growth points of KwaZulu will increase employment and earned income, and diversify production, and so raise the standard of living of the KwaZulu people. It is also the intention of the KwaZulu government to encourage such agro-industries as sugar mills, maize mills, leather tanneries, fruit canning enterprises and farm factories for the production of dairy products. It is realized, of course, that these things will only come about when agriculture in KwaZulu is more developed. In connection with the establishment of the industries in KwaZulu growth points, there are four policy matters which members would do well to bear in mind. I am at this time deeply concerned about our producing enough food to eat.

Investments in South Africa have become a very serious and controversial issue abroad since June 1976 when unrest and violence were unleashed in South Africa. There is no place one visits abroad without being asked what one thinks on this question of investments. As a result, whatever one says is seized upon and bandied about by .various factions abroad for their own ends. It is true that for a century and a half investors have had great rewards from their investments here, which were based largely on the exploitation of the blacks. Looking at the question impartially and trying to be analytical, one must also admit that the other side of that coin whose one side is exploitation, is that human endeavor in taming an undeveloped land brought some economic progress. So, however grudgingly, one has to admit that even through exploitation there was some progress, even for victims of that exploitation. Today South Africa is the economic giant of Africa. The only country in Africa which may soon surpass South Africa, because of its potential, population, and training is Nigeria. Nigeria has oil and this is the most sought-after of all assets in the world. It also has other resources.

The development of southern Africa must be dependent on how the development of South Africa is used for all the people of southern Africa. Southern Africa is one economic region. Were it not for the political problems of southern Africa, this region would be the economic giant of Africa with all its assets and population.

The question of investment is always seen by me in the context of southern Africa. It does seem to me that for the sake of southern Africa and the future stability of the region development must continue. The question is, how does one continue in a political climate which is so explosive?

I have always stated my pragmatic stance in this assembly. It has always seemed to me that change which destroys the base of future development of southern Africa would be self-defeating. At the same time, I am only too aware of the fact that black people have been abused to beyond the point of human endurance. Blacks can no longer tolerate their insufferable position. The last ten months have demonstrated this all too clearly. I am aware all the time that my leadership here and in the black community of South Africa will cease to mean anything to the blacks of South Africa if they cannot receive tangible results from it. What is more, I love my people and share their suffering. These are not academic issues for me, they are life and death issues we face from day to day. While I must continue to espouse my non-violent stance, I find that it would make my statements unbalanced if I did not add that I also want to stress, as a historian, that when nothing is left but to fight a just war, people all over the world throughout the centures have done just that. Black people, it must be remembered, also belong to the species HOMO SAPIENS, and they should not be expected to behave differently when challenged by history to take steps which other humans have taken since the beginning of time. There is, however, too much lighthearted talk about violence. When I speak as I do, I am not doing so lightheartedly because I am only too aware of what such moments of history will mean, if we ever have such a tryst with history as an unarmed people.

In these circumstance, therefore, the role of the foreign investor is a crucial one in South Africa. I still cling to the hope that, even at this time, it may not be too late for a peaceful solution to dominate over a violent solution. I intend to cling to that hope as long as this is possible.

I cannot dispute the fact that injections of foreign capital do keep the South African economy going. I am only too conscious of the dilemma which this fact poses to me. It is this very strength of the South African economy which props up the white military might, which is used by our white countrymen to maintain the status quo. The reliance on military might by itself can never be a decisive factor, because of our interdependence, particularly as the scales in numbers are weighed against whites.

I have, for both pragmatic and moral reasons, stuck to the hope for a non-violent solution in spite of the fact that the owners of capital in South Africa have not sustained me in that hope. They have played the white government game within the rules dictated by that government for far too long. I am hoping that, with the awakening of white industry which seems to be starting at this time, this wicked partnership between capital and repressive legislation may be drawing to a close. But more than that, it is important for South African investors, as well as foreign investors, to realize that the people will conquer capital if capital opposes the will of the people. Despite the severe warnings by the Prime Minister that businessmen must keep out of politics, let me stress what I have said before. Investment in South Africa now must take sides in the central political struggle—between apartheid on the one hand, and the full participation in the government of the country by the majority of the country. Capital must therefore not continue to side with the forces that seek to maintain the status quo. This is a political issue which can be thrashed out in one and only one forum and that is the political arena.

We have now reached the era of what I call the melting pot. Apartheid, white political dominance, white technological advantages over their black countrymen, a virulent black consciousness, white and black trade unionism, the black work force, the tribal land tenure system, white rights to freehold property, all these are already ingredients in this melting pot. Quite clearly none of these will emerge from this melting pot untouched. Investors have therefore to look ahead into the future.

The issue of investment has therefore become an issue of a very fundamental nature. That is why I suggested a conference of black organizations when I delivered my majority rule speech in Soweto on 14 March 1976. That meeting has not taken place because of the unrest we experienced last year—in particular because of the detention of many leaders under the preventive detention legislation. The unrest has further compounded our problems in South Africa. The present world economic climate is bleak. In addition to this, the unrest has made the issue of investments in South Africa much more critical to the economy of South Africa. There is a failure of South Africa to cope with its balance of payments. Added to this is inflation and the fluctuating gold price which has at times reached its lowest ebb in the history of the metal. This has resulted in worsening unemployment, particularly in our black community. There is a lie which white employers, particularly the pro-apartheid employers, have been spreading about me. On the Reef several Zulus have gone to offices of the Principal Urban Representative (KwaZulu representative in urban areas) when they were sacked from employment. They are told to come to me, because I supposedly suggested that they should be sacked. There have been several distortions of my statements on the issue of investments. I have been abused abroad and in South Africa for not advocating disinvestment. At the same time I have stated over and over again that I cannot deal with the question of investment in academic and esoteric terms, because I belong to my people. I have their ears and their hearts. I have a serious dilemma which is thrown up by the realities of our South African situation which neither you nor I can escape. I cannot afford the luxury of theoreticians and armchair critics. I have rejected unfettered capitalism and have stated that we need a redistribution of wealth. I have said so because I am frightened by extremes of wealth and poverty; I know from my study of history where such polarization will lead us. I have not gone beyond those statements so far. If I had, what would have been the purpose of my calling for a national convention, if I had already made up my mind? More and more of our people are unemployed. As I have indicated hundreds of thousands of people are already swelling the ranks of the unemployed blacks. It has been estimated that the number of unemployed blacks will be a million by July of this year. The land our people farm is overcrowded by both man and beast. Our children are badly clothed and we are badly housed. Our children receive a second or third grade education. I cannot, in these circumstances, take an ideological puritan's stand on this issue of investments. I cannot afford to be insensitive to my people's needs by adopting strategies which are careless of humanity. The reality is that, whether we like it or not, we are in an exploitative capitalist system, and it is exploitative because a minority vested interest wields power and authority which should be transferred to a non-racial majority. I believe that in the final analysis the economic order of the future will emerge as a product of the way liberation is achieved.

I believe that members of this house must face up to this issue of investments. I was most interested when President Jimmy Carter and Ambassador William Schaufele, the Under Secretary for Africa, both mentioned to me the announcement by the Rev. Leon Sullivan of a set of principles aimed at promoting fair employment practices and the preservation of human dignity, which certain U.S. companies supported in their operations in South Africa. The following is the statement:

Principles of U.S. Firms with Affiliates in the Republic of South Africa:

1. Non-segregation of races in all eating, comfort and work facilities.

2. Equal and fair employment practices for all employees.

3. Equal pay for all employees doing equal or comparable work for the same period of time.

4. Initiation of and development of training programmes that will prepare, in substantial numbers, blacks and other non-whites for supervisory, administrative, clerical and technical jobs.

5. Increasing the number of blacks and other non-whites in management and supervisory positions.

6. Improving the quality of employees' lives outside the work environment in such areas as housing, transportation, schooling, recreation and health facilities.

We agree to further implement these principles. Where implementation requires a modification of existing South African working conditions, we will seek such modification through appropriate channels.

We believe that the implementation of the foregoing principles is consistent with respect for human dignity and will contribute greatly to the general economic welfare of all the people of the Republic of South Africa.

The following companies have announced their support of the Statement of Principles as of today:

American Cyanamide
Caltex Petroleum Corporation
Citicorp
Ford Motor Company
General Motors Corporation
International Business Machines
International Harvester
Mobil
Otis Elevator
Union Carbide
Burroughs

There are those who have criticized this statement as "too little, too late". They think only withdrawal of these investments will be good enough. I will be interested to know what members think of this view in the present hot debate of whether "to invest or disinvest" which vexes the minds of many people in the West today.

Chapter 9
BUILDING ALLIANCES

THE TRIPARTITE MEETING

Ondini, 11 January 1978

My first task is to welcome you all to Ondini in the name of Inkatha yeNkululeko yeSizwe, our National Cultural Liberation Movement.

I think it is important for me to lay bare my whole thinking on how I see today's event in order to counter some of the interpretations of our motivation that have been made. I want to make it quite clear that I realize that mass media have a right to speculate on political events as much as they want to. This is their prerogative. At the same time, however, speculations sometimes cloud issues and create misunderstanding. That is the last thing we would like to see happen to these plausible initiatives which have been taken by the leaders of the organizations represented here today.

I think the most important point that we are making by gathering is that South Afica is one country, and that we are all, regardless of our cultural affiliations, one people in one land. We realize that the racist regime which is at the helm of our affairs in South Africa thinks differently.

For several generations we have been separated deliberately in a calculated manner, by various white governments and not just the Nationalists (i.e. the British) in order to divide and rule. It is quite incredible that the Afrikaners, who suffered so much injustice at the hands of British colonial rulers, should also assume the status of a colonial power over us. Because of this separation we have been indoctrinated into seeing ourselves as different people who must stay separate from each other.

The net result of this brainwashing by the oppressors is that we have accepted the political fallacy that our interests are not only different but that they are also unrelated. But the truth of the matter is that not only do we have common interests as black groups, but they are also intertwined with the interests of the rest of the South African population, who repudiate a common nationhood with us as fellow South Africans.

We have all, at different times, called for a national convention which should map out our common future as South Africans and this suggestion each time has been totally rejected by the Prime Minister, Mr. Vorster. The whites have arrogated to themselves the right to dictate to the rest of us a future which makes us chattels and pariahs in the land of our birth.

Chief Minister Buthelezi and King Zwelethini Goodwill, Constitutional Monarch of the Zulus

Various black political leaders have worked on the basis that whites can see reason and mend their ways. But what we have seen in the past few years is that whites are not prepared to change. For any of us who are still hoping that whites will follow reason and change, the last election if we see it as an expression of white solidarity, demonstrated beyond doubt that nothing short of a miracle can make most whites of South Africa change on the basis of any rationality. I am not by any means making a call to you, or to our people, to abandon all hope. Not by any means. I am just trying to be analytical. Whilst one cannot always claim to be doing the dissection of these problems with surgical precision, one must try to be as coldly analytical as possible. I think it is important, from the very outset, for us to understand exactly where we are. I think it is of no use for us to try and live in the world of make-believe. I think the tendency to believe our own daydreams of the past, has caused us to fall short of finding the correct paths to our solutions. What we do is often based on a misanalysis of the problems we face in this land of suffering and death for the powerless.

BUILDING ALLIANCES

For quite some time now there has been talk by all of us on black solidarity not accompanied by any meaningful action to accomplish it. I would like to congratulate those of my brothers on whose initiative we meet today. They deserve our thanks and the thanks of our people for taking the bull by the horns. One of the main causes of past failure has been the fact that, in southern African black politics, we are still very susceptible to the tragic political game of one-upmanship. Whilst the present initiatives are applauded, we will end up as one more failure to add on to our past failures if we do not avoid these tragic mistakes. Black unity cannot just be based on judging each other's sincerity on the basis of who shouts "black" loudest. In the past we have seen that we have tended to fall into this trap of judging the authenticity of black patriotism on that basis. The infighting which has flowed from this has opened our ranks for our enemies. They have taken advantage of these divisions which we have opened up ourselves.

The call for black unity is not our invention. Great patriots of the past, such as Dr. Abdurahman, worked for this throughout their lives. I may recall in this connection the first meeting Dr. Abdurahman called in June 1927 in Kimberley. One writer states that that important conference did not achieve much apart from what he called "elaborate oratory".

During my own youth, when I was a member of the African National Congress Youth League, we admired the political cooperation that existed between black organizations under the leadership of such leaders as Dr. Xuma, Dr. Dadoo and Dr. Monty Naicker, and this alliance was at its zenith during the Presidency of the late Chief Luthuli. The alliance, which was so much a reality at the top level of these organizations' leadership, was clamped on when the organizations concerned were banned. But even if they were not banned, the main flaw of these alliances was the fact that unity at top level did not filter through to the grass-roots level of the people that the leadership represented.

I mention these things because we dare not fall into the same pit. It is important to understand where we are and where we are going. It is also important to learn from our past mistakes.

Before I go on to explain the viewpoint of Inkatha on these matters, I want to deal briefly with our detractors. There has been a cacophony of voices that have sniped at us for thinking in terms of meeting like this in order to work out a common strategy. I find it most interesting that the apartheid mass media have been used so extensively to expound the viewpoint of our detractors and of their mentors. We all know the mentors of some of them. We know that they are their masters' voices.

I find it interesting that Dr. W.J. Bergins should be the leading light amongst these voices. Among other things Dr. Bergins stated that the alliance with Inkatha showed "the bankruptcy and dilemma of the party's political leadership". I would like to say that the converse is true. Dr. Bergins' criticism reflects his own political bankruptcy, and the dilemma he is facing through that bankruptcy in wanting the coloured people to accept a glossed-up sweeper's role in the all-white parliament. The coloured people are not foreigners to South Africa; they are as indigenous to our soil as anyone of us who are here. I think Dr.

Bergins' statement as quoted by the RAND DAILY MAIL of the 4th January is most interesting:

> The acceptance by the Labour Party bosses of Dr. S.M.E. Bengu's call to form a strong front against the whites in South Africa witnesses to the political peasantry, bankruptcy and the dilemma of having no perspective in which the leadership of the Labour Party strangely finds itself. They are evidently not able by themselves to find practical and directional solutions for the problems of the country. Instead, they now leave it to the Inkatha organization, which in any case is not representative of or has never been elected by the Zulu people to represent their interests, to formulate the Labour Party's policy for them. My party and I acknowledge our immovable solidarity with the interests of the coloured people of this country. We will not allow ourselves and our people under any circumstances to be taken in tow by anyone or by any organization. We firmly believe that there is room for everyone in this country and that the leadership of the Federal Party is completely capable to accept the challenges of our time and that it is not necessary to fall back on others to serve the interests of the coloured people.

I think you will agree with me that this is a scurrilous statement based on both racial prejudice and ignorance. We in Inkatha do not apologize to Dr. Bergins and his cohorts for being in the main, a mass movement of black peasants and workers. We represent the majority of our people, who fall into those categories. We do not pretend to be an elitist organization and we accept that there is no future for elitism in the new southern Africa that is now unfolding. Neither the Labour party nor Inkatha movement apologize for being representative of the mass of our people. So the snide remarks on peasantry reflect only the political idiocy from which Dr. Bergins seems to be suffering and his pathetic attempts at bending backwards to placate his masters at our expense.

For the record, I want to state most clearly that Inkatha has no intention of taking over any other black organization. We regard the peoples of South Africa as one people in one land. We will therefore talk to anybody who wants to talk to us about mapping out our joint future regardless of race. That is why we have had an ongoing dialogue with the Progressive Federal Party for a period of more than a year. We do not necessarily agree with all details of their policies. But it is not necessary to have such agreement on details between organizations before we talk to each other. If we cannot talk to each other, we will be accepting that the one thing left for us to do is to kill each other. We agree with the Progressive Federal Party that the future we face in South Africa is a non-racial one. We agree with them that all the people of this land must participate in decision-making exercised in one parliament. It is therefore not necessary to agree on every detail of their policies or that they should agree on every detail of our policies before we can relate to each other politically. Dr. Bergins seems to be asleep like Rip Van Winkle who slept throughout a revolution. We would not deny him his political snooze if it were not so divisive of our people. By such stupid fulminations he hampers the struggle for the liberation of South Africa.

BUILDING ALLIANCES

To my great disappointment Dr. Bergins was backed in this negative attitude by no less a person than Professor R.E. van der Ross, the rector of the University of Western Cape. He did worse, for he states that he won't comment on the issue after he has already done so. In this way he thinks he has kept his place in the ivory towers, from which he has descended into the mud, which he flings at us so mercilessly. He was quoted by The RAND DAILY MAIL, saying that there was a great deal of uncertainty as to what Inkatha stood for. In other words, in his professorial arrogance he implies that the Labour Party leadership have not the comprehension to understand what we stand for since he, with his academic background, chooses not to understand what we stand for. We have a constitution which is printed and which is available. After delivering that insulting blow, Dr. van der Ross goes on to state, "My view is that it's a cultural organization which supports the Buthelezi Administration. I don't know its political aims and so I won't comment."

That is the ultimate insult. If Dr. van der Ross does not know that we stand for the liberation of South Africa, then I am afraid his professorial mental aberrations are dangerous for someone in charge of a university during this volatile era in southern Africa. What beats me is that Dr. van der Ross finds no problems in relating to the nationalists who stand for black oppression. Like him, I have always believed in having dialogue with anyone. That, I thought was the reason why we both belonged to the synthesis group, which has members of all kinds of political persuasions. Dr. van der Ross goes on in his comment to state that he hopes that the Labour Party Congress at Oudtshoorn was fully informed about the whole matter and that it was aware of the implications. This is a threat of sorts. By implication, we are depicted through this remark as a menace, and I take strong exception to Dr. van der Ross' hardly veiled innuendo. By his snide remarks against Inkatha he has indicated where he stands. He would rather embrace nationalists than have anything to do with his African compatriots. Dr. van der Ross has come a long way from the man who wrote such fiery articles for publications like DRUM a few years ago when he advocated the same unity we are looking for with the now-banned African National Congress. Is it the perks of office which have done that amount of damage to his political thinking?

Prominent leaders of liberation movements, such as Amilcar Cabral, had a lot to say about the role of culture in the liberation struggle. He seems to think of culture in the context of our movement in too simplistic terms. Amongst our detractors in the Indian community is one Dr. Farook Meer. I would not waste your time with any comment on him were it not for his playing quite a dangerous ball game through the snide remarks which he has made it his special business to make about me and Inkatha. It just amazes me that he should pretend to speak for the Indian people when I publicly challenged him in October last year to reveal the membership of the Natal Indian Congress and he never did. His remarks are dangerous in that they sow seeds of conflict amongst us as the oppressed of this land. He is not even consistent. Only about a year ago, the Natal Indian Congress leadership, including the Meer family, found no problem in relating to me politically. They seem to have thought, in their political myopia during unrest in the country, that they should back what they considered to be winners in what they saw as the final revolution in South Africa. I do not say that revolution is not coming to this land. But what is happening is not the ultimate revolution. It marks the birth of the revolutionary spirit, not the beginning of the revolution itself.

Since our brother Mr. Rajbansi dealt with Dr. Meer in newspaper articles, I would rather not try to get too involved in my response to his snide remarks when he described our proposed alliance as "an alliance of rubber stamps".

I apologize for having been rather lengthy in my responses to what our detractors state. I wish now to concentrate on the Inkatha view of today's meeting, what we think can be done and what we think that can accomplish. I applaud our getting together as people who are all involved in constituency politics. That is why we who have constituencies cannot really afford the extravagances of aspirant politicians and political analysts who have no real constituencies. That is why their thrust is drum beating and self-acclaimed ideological purity rather than the constituency building in which all of us here are seriously engaged.

We are here today because we know that we need every man, woman and child, black, brown and even white to bring about a change that will ensure a redistribution of political power in South Africa. We are here because we reject Mr. Vorster's future, which he described as "too ghastly to contemplate". His policies, I am afraid, offer us only that kind of future. And his policies offer us nothing else apart from a race war. Unless a radical change can be brought about, there is nothing we face as an alternative. We are here not because we can confidently express a hope that such a radical change in our country can happen peacefully, but we all think that to chase after peace is a noble cause, regardless of whether one accomplishes peace or not. At the very worst, when the chips are down, none of us will not be proud of our efforts to attempt a peaceful change. Even if we are faced with a race war, our efforts will not have been in vain, if the scale of violence is at least reduced.

We are here because we are tired of the schisms and the disunity of the past. We blacks have a clean record because we have always recognized as a fact that whites are not expendable expatriates. We realize that they have every right to be here, because over so many generations they have also become indigenous. It is ironic that our white countrymen should, instead of appreciating our reasonableness, threaten us instead with political destitution and foreign status in the land of our forefathers.

Time for talking is past. We need to be involved in concrete political actions aimed at producing a just society in South Africa. We as blacks need not use all our time and energy mourning the fact that whites spurn our hand of friendship. Let us unite in our efforts to eliminate all the things that our constituents abhor. Our people abhor apartheid. Whites are going further and further on the road to suicide. Let us refuse to sign a suicide pact with them. Whites in general refuse to share thoughts with us on our common future. Let us, as black groups, have our own think tank which will serve as a pool into which all our different thoughts on the future will gravitate.

110

BUILDING ALLIANCES

Much of what has been written implied that when we talk about unity we mean organic unity in the near future. Politics is based on reality and not on fantasy. We know that we would love to merge into one political body today. We know that this is not possible within the time range we have at present. There is, however, nothing to prevent us from having hot lines to each other and of getting together on the various issues we face in order to share our collective wisdom. It is no longer good enough just to support each other in press statements at six-months' intervals. Our strength as blacks also lies in our unity of purpose. I would like to squelch once and for all the mischievous speculations that we have plans for merging the organizations we represent. We would love to do this but it is not politic to do this in the immediate future. But let us be realists and refuse to act stupidly in political terms. There are many people, black and white, who would love to see this happen. Let us be aware of this fact. "Once bitten, twice shy," is nothing more than just common sense.

We are not afraid to face the music that should come as the logical consequence of our political stands. Despite our determination to refuse to be racially divided as fellow countrymen, we will not, because of this fact, deliberately create a situation which will make our people lose hope and confidence in themselves by making our enemies clamp on us. They do so in any case for no reason. Let them not get from us a reason for doing it.

I do not want to go into details of what I see as concrete steps that we need to take to move away from this old mountain of empty rhetoric on black unity without taking one single step to achieve it. I think this is a matter which we should look at together IN CAMERA, and there are many suggestions that can be made. I think it is silly to lay bare details of our strategy because we will in this way be playing into the hands of our enemies, as forewarned is forearmed. We do not intend indulging in acts which can so easily fall into the category of acts that are defined as subversion. We will not seek martyrdom for the sake of it. But we will not run away from it when those who wield power over us chase us with it.

The racist regime loves to state that the separation of races is God-ordained. It must be clear, therefore, that they are likely to leave no stone unturned in order to foil our efforts. Let us not make that task easy for them. We know pretty well that we are infiltrated and that they will get hold of our plans through their secret police and their agents. Let them pay for it as usual. They have more than R12 million at their disposal to do it. This knowledge can be no excuse for handing over our plans to our enemies on a platter.

I have rambled a lot and at this point I plead for your forgiveness for doing this. I, however, regard today's meeting as something more than just an occasion for a few press headlines, which will in a couple of weeks' time die a natural death. We know that we have a lot of steam to let off. We have every reason to be angry about a million wrongs in South Africa. But this is not an occasion just for letting off steam. The millions of people who support us expect direction from us. This is the task we must sit down and do something about. There is no reason why we should not plan a series of consultations on a wider basis than today. This should be by planned action and it needs to be charted. Whether this is preceded by meetings of the kind we are having today is a matter that you can decide about today. We are not here to gang up against anyone. We are here only to gang up against apartheid. We have every right to dismantle it, whatever this may cost.

I want at this point to state that our task has been made difficult by the action taken by the Minister of Justice on the 19th of October. I am sure, although we did express our condemnation of this ruthless action, that when we are here together we need to repeat our condemnation of bannings, detentions and actions against certain publications. I further want to put on record that speaking for myself and Inkatha, we are determined wherever possible to speak to our brothers who are in exile and those who are banned and detained. Their being out of political circulation in South Africa makes the whole task of finding solutions to our problems extremely difficult. We miss their courage and contributions in the struggle. We applaud the contributions of those of them who are at large.

Chapter 10
VICTIMS TWICE OVER

INANDA SEMINARY ADDRESS

Inanda, 14 February 1978

The Principal of Inanda Seminary Mr. Lewis, and members of staff, Mr. and Mrs. Hubner and other VIP's from IBM, students and other distinguished guests.

The whole black community of South Africa appreciates the role such an institution as Inanda has played in the development of our community and of South Africa. Inanda, having been founded by missionaries from the United States, stands today as a monument to all missionary endeavor in this part of Africa. Most of us who went through missionary institutions are often overwhelmed when we visit here by a nostalgia which is often too difficult to bear. We are therefore most grateful that Inanda has, in spite of her difficulties, been able to continue to operate. We are aware that this would have been impossible if we were not so fortunate as to have a few benefactors who have made it possible for Inanda to survive, such as our friends from IBM. We are very conscious of the significant contributions that IBM in particular has made in this regard. We are also equally conscious of other contributions by other American corporations such as, for example, the Mobil Oil Company.

Apartheid raises the hackles of the world community and rightly so. It is an ideology which does not only rob the black person of his or her dignity, but whose application and effects on people of colour are demeaning.

The proponents of apartheid have been at the helm of power in South Africa for the last 30 years. There is no evidence so far that anything is going to change them from operating within the repugnant, narrow perimeters of their abhorrent ideology. The results of the November 1977 white election makes this all too clear to us. This does not mean that they are invincible or that apartheid society can survive in Africa. All it means is that we have a very heavy task and responsibility to perform as blacks to liberate ourselves. This struggle is not new. It has been going on for more than a century, ever since white domination saw the light of day in these parts. We are not discouraged by the fact that the struggle for liberation has been so long, and that it is still going on. After all, slavery here and in the United States went on for quite a long time, but it never lasted.

In the past few years we have seen the triumph of the liberation over oppression in southern Africa, with the liberation of Mozambique and Angola. The struggle in Zimbabwe and Namibia has also gained momentum, to the extent that we all know that the question is no longer whether they will also be liberated, but when it will happen. That is all.

The effect of these events on young people has been very deep. We have seen the determination of young people in the past two years in Soweto and many parts of our troubled land.

The outside world has taken note of these events as well. The agitation against South Africa as a result of the apartheid policies pursued in this land has heightened black expectations.

As a result of this situation the campaign waged against apartheid has heated up in such a way that many people in the world want to be helpful. As a result of this campaign there are those who are so conscience-stricken about any involvement in South Africa, that they want to have very little to do with South Africa. We as black people appreciate the wrath of the world which apartheid has unleashed. We are, however, very unhappy about the fact that many good people get so carried away, that some of the things aimed at white South Africa hit at the blacks hardest. We are quite conscious of the fact that we as blacks have also to sacrifice for our liberation struggle. We realize that we must be prepared to suffer. That we must be prepared even to die for our liberation. Our common sense however, tells us that this struggle is still going to go on for a while.

This does not mean that we are scaling down our efforts in the liberation struggle. All it means is that white resistance is going to increase, as we have seen in Zimbabwe in the past twelve years. So we blacks must survive in order to see our struggle through to the finish. We dare not allow white racists to destroy us. This survival can only happen if we prepare ourselves for this long ordeal ahead of us. Education, to me, is one of those important preparations that all those who are confident that South Africa will certainly be liberated dare not ignore. When South Africa is liberated we hope this will mean a just society. You cannot have a just society in the midst of chaos and ingovernability. So institutions like Inanda are playing a very significant role in this preparation we need. Inanda is unique in this respect. By the nature of its non-racial staff, it already gives us a taste, even if only a minor one, of a non-racial South Africa, which all men of goodwill in South Africa and outside are seeking. We are aware that the principal wants this cosmopolitan nature of the staff of this institution to ultimately spread out to students as well. It is most difficult for me to speak about how we in KwaZulu see that, as Inanda is not under us, at present. But I can say that this does not conflict with our policy in KwaZulu and with the policy of Inkatha which envisages a non-racial society in this land, as the ultimate goal of our efforts in the liberation struggle.

It is, therefore, very important for the international community to assist us in all sorts of ways in the area of education. There is too much play with words here, when it comes to some of the greatest opponents of apartheid abroad. Some seek ideological cleanliness at the expense of black people, the very people they

114

claim they want to assist. When, for instance, people overseas say that they cannot help blacks in education because the South African government can do it, I am often in a great dilemma as to their sincerity. The South African government should do it, yes, and a big yes, at that. But the South African government is not doing it. Must we, the victims of apartheid, suffer because the racist regime does not do it for us? Must we be deprived of whatever valuable assistance is available, in order that people may aim for ideological puritanism? I cannot understand how anyone can be tainted by any assistance to black victims of apartheid to get better educated. It is worse with an institution like Inanda which operates on the non-racial principle even as far as pay for its teachers is concerned. When people refuse to assist such an institution as Inanda to enable it to survive, I question their commitment to black people. To refuse to assist in any area of black education does not help blacks in their struggle. To refuse to do so even in the case of an institution like Inanda savours of hypocrisy.

Black people know that this is their struggle. Black people know that no one can fight that struggle for them, except themselves. Black people know that the struggle is still going to be long and costly in terms of human life. Black people understand that there is a limit to what any outsider can do for them in their struggle. Black people expect those who have genuine concern for them and their suffering to contribute indirectly in their struggle by strengthening their own efforts. Education is certainly one of the most non-controversial areas in which there is absolutely no limit to what concerned people overseas can do. Black people pay for school buildings themselves. People of other race groups do not have to pay; the government does it. Black people pay fees for their education. People of other race groups do not have to pay; the government does that. Black people have to pay for salaries of hundreds of privately paid teachers. No member of any other race group has to do that. Black people have to pay for furniture in their schools. No member of any other race group has to do that. Black people are paid on a disparity scale, which includes even professional blacks. Black people do not get the standard pay for the job. These factors make their financial burdens heavier than those of any member of any of the other race groups. No, good people, we are now getting just a bit tired of futile stances that have no meaning in the struggle for liberation in all its totality. There is no limit to what all the people who are indignant about the dehumanizing system of apartheid, can do to assist us. This is a non-controversial area. I cannot see how such assistance to blacks can contaminate the donors.

To you students I want to say that as a young child I used to sing a little song, "Count Your Blessings, name them one by one." I have children too, some were educated here, and there is one who has been here only for a couple of days. One thing that strikes me more and more each day is that very few of our children who are at school, let alone in a school like Inanda, appreciate this fact as a blessing. It is a blessing. When you see thousands of your people who have never entered the gates of any educational institution, remember to say, "There goes me, had I not been blessed by God with the opportunity to get education, and to be here."

We need people in our struggle to know what they are doing. We need people who know that man's inhumanity to man is as old as man. One can only appreciate this through education. It is by studying man's performance on earth that you will really appreciate that regimes like the Pretoria racist regime are not something new. Man has oppressed man throughout the centuries but the spirit of liberty which God planted into all human beings enables oppressed people to triumph.

We need you in the field of preparation that black people need in order to consolidate for the final onslaught against apartheid and oppression. This you can only do efficiently if you bear your difficulties for a few years, in order to acquire your education. Do remember that we form the majority of the poor in South Africa. Do therefore remember the sacrifices of your parents. A person who has no sense of appreciation for such sacrifices cannot talk about the liberation struggle to me with any credibility.

I thank you all for your patience, kindness and tolerance.

Chapter 11

HEARTACHE AND TREACHERY

THE FUNERAL OF ROBERT SOBUKWE

Johannesburg, 9 April 1978

My brothers, my sisters, daughters and sons of Mother Africa, I greet you in the name of freedom. Each one of us whether we be men, women, or children, is involved in this great quest for freedom. Each black person in this part of Africa yearns for a taste of what freedom tastes like.

We, the descendants of great warriors, cannot afford to be oversimplistic about our struggle for liberation. We know just how much blood has been shed since the last century in defense of our birthright as sons and daughters of Africa, whom God placed on this tip of this great continent for a purpose. We are men amongst men, and we have been given the greatest challenge that any black men have ever been faced with in Africa, in being called upon to break and smash the granite wall of apartheid. Yes, we are called upon to remove from our necks this millstone of apartheid which debases not only our dignity as human beings, but which insults God Himself our Creator, in whose image we believe we are also made.

As a historian I always feel that we have a great duty to acknowledge that the struggle for our liberation commenced long ago. We have to pay tribute to the many sacrifices which were made by those who resisted this ruthless administration which is jackboot in its nature, long before we were born. We must remember that thousands of black lives have been lost in this same struggle in which we ourselves are engaged. The fact that so many lives have been lost and so many other sacrifices have been made without our grasping with our hands the phantom of freedom should not discourage us. Not for one moment should anyone of us feel that we are on a wild goose chase. On the contrary, we should be inspired to play our part whatever price we are called upon to pay in order to reach the top of the hill, which is our fulfillment as human beings in our own land.

The spirit which inspires us to gather around here in our thousands, to proclaim these truths, that like all men created by God, we blacks of this country must also be free, is itself the product of sacrifices made by many African patriots of yesteryear. The forces of darkness which have kept us oppressed for so long would have snuffed out any resistance to oppression, which each one of us feels so strongly in our very sinews. We should never see the sacrifices of our ascendants as failures. The contributions they have made before us over several generations, even with their very lives, should be seen as the very measure of success they achieved to keep the spirit of the struggle alive in order to enable us to take up the struggle from where they left off.

We owe them a great debt and none of us has a right to sleep peacefully at night until we have discharged our duty to our forebears and to our future generations, by playing our parts in full in the on-going struggle for freedom. None of us dares to fold arms by avoiding to soil his or her hands, as we are determined to fight apartheid, even within the structures that the regime foists on us as the oppressed of this land. We are not involved in what is a purely ideological struggle. We are involved in the struggle for our right to be human. For several generations we have been penalized for being our parents' children, in that the racist evaluation of a person has been a determinant of a person's place in life. None of us except those who have sold their souls, accepts that only these urban ghettoes such as Soweto and that only these rural ghettoes called "homelands" are what constitute the land of our forefathers. This we have made very clear, often. We want a stake in the whole country, which is South Africa our homeland. We want to be joint rulers of our country.

Ten weeks ago I had the privilege to stand here before you, just a few weeks, then, before the KwaZulu elections. We have made it clear and anyone who knows history knows that in KwaZulu we were once the mightiest nation in the whole of southern Africa. King Moshoeshe of Lesotho and King Shaka of KwaZulu were brothers. When I was in Maseru a few years ago with Mrs. Luthuli who was to receive the late Chief Luthuli's OAU posthumous award, the Prime Minister of Lesotho, Dr. Leabua Jonathan recalled that King Moshoeshe and King Shaka maintained cordial relations. He recalled that King Moshoeshe periodically sent beautiful feathers to King Shaka, to maintain these cordial relations, and from these he got also some protection. The KwaZulu King Cetshwayo was provoked into an unjust war by Sir Bartle Frere, whose aim was to "break the Zulu power once and for all". The ultimate end of these evil designs was that the Zulu nation of the last century lost its sovereignty with its conquest by the British in 1879. From 1910 when whites, by imperial edict, hoarded citizenship rights for themselves, we threw in our lot with all our African brothers in the one black struggle for freedom. The culmination of our throwing our lot together as blacks with other blacks was the founding of the now-banned African National Congress in 1912. It is ironic that although the African liberation idiom was born here, through the African National Congress, we are still not free in this part of Africa.

There are many people here and abroad who simplistically think that we are not free because we have not tried hard enough to free ourselves from these chains of bondage. Most of our problems in this struggle are a product of this mis-analysis by arrogant people here and abroad who cannot understand what blacks of South Africa face in this struggle.

A few weeks ago I stated right here, that our KwaZulu election manifesto was the rejection of the Pretoria-type independence. I want today to thank those who voted in the KwaZulu elections for rejecting this pseudo-independence so unequivocally. The new Minister of Plural Relations, Dr. Mulder, has been quoted as saying that we will not be forced into the Pretoria-type independence, after it has been so clearly rejected with 100 per cent of the seats won on the basis of this rejection. This was something quite unique in the history of both white and black politics in this land. One of the reasons for my coming up to this Thanksgiving rally and prayer meeting is to thank you and all the black people of KwaZulu for vindicating my clear stand against homelands independence, dating back more than 27 years ago. As your faithful servant I thank you.

I am most grateful that I have received this mandate to go on with the South African Black Alliance, which I have been given by the black people of KwaZulu through the support I have been given during the recent election. I also thank Inkatha, whose central Committee endorses the Alliance. I realize that in our strategy we have earned for ourselves enemies on both the left and the right, and amongst both blacks and whites. This is mainly caused by the fact that we present a concrete challenge to status quo politics. It also emanates from quite a pathetic mis-analysis of the political situation we face as blacks, and of the odds that are stacked against us.

I warned the Prime Minister about the violence we faced in this country in 1976 and 1977. My warnings were unheeded. I would like Mr. Vorster to know that when I state these facts, I do so only for the sake of the record. I do not do it as some kind of gloating over what has happened. After all, it is we, the blacks, who have suffered more than whites through the violence that has erupted. We are no longer at the stage when we merely prognosticated that apartheid would fail, because it had already failed. In March 1976, I warned that the apartheid society, nurtured with a plethora of discriminatory laws for more than a quarter of a century, had already been overtaken by history. The violence we witnessed merely underlined this fact.

I want to return to the South African Black Alliance meeting in Capetown on the 13th of March. The South African Black Alliance aims at creating a just society in South Africa, based on the statement of belief which I presented to you at this very amphitheatre on the 29th of January 1978. The South African Black Alliance accepts as a fact of history that black unity is a phantom we have been chasing after for several generations without success. The South African Black Alliance knows that there is the divide-and-conquer policy of the imperialists and colonialists which has created divisions between us. We realize that we have not much time and we therefore start from where we are, by allowing black organizations, which exist, to join us to create the kind of groundwork which alone can force the whites to come and sit with us around the conference table. This is the only alternative we have, unless we choose the one which Mr. Vorster's policy offers us, which he himself described as "too ghastly to contemplate."

We worked out a constitution for the South African Black Alliance. We are not deluding ourselves into thinking that we are untouchable as far as the government is concerned. We have tried not to play into their hands by deliberately making it easier for them to take action against us. If we sought martyrdom for the sake of it, we would not worry about this. We do not mean that the government has any rationale for frustrating its opponents. But we believe that as far as martyrs are concerned, we have now enough martyrs and to spare, some amongst the dead and some amongst the living. We do not want to appear as if we deliberately seek to swell the ranks of black martyrs.

We have been criticized for what some people have unjustifiably called "our exclusiveness". And yet one of the aims of the Alliance is liaison between the constituent members of the Alliance and other organizations, and one of the main objectives is to arrange to hold a national convention, in which people of all races and different political persuasions will be represented. We as constituent members, for example as Inkatha, and the Labour Party, Dikwakwentle Party, etc., relate politically to those organizations that want to relate to us. To pretend that amongst black groups all is well, is a dangerous oversimplification of the situation. As black groups we need time and energy to put our own house in order. We cannot expect whites to take us seriously if we are not united even as black groups. There is a lot of work that needs to be done in this respect.

We of the South African Black Alliance realize that we have very little time at our disposal. If one takes into account the imminent collapse of white domination in Namibia and Zimbabwe, one realizes that the world community will soon find that all their attention must now be paid to the South African situation. The political conflicts can only be defused by a formula which can only be produced around a conference table. We will need machinery fairly soon for speaking as blacks with one voice. We have seen just what complications the fragmentation of forces for change have caused in many parts of southern Africa. We should be sufficiently intelligent to learn from these events.

The South African Black Alliance meeting was a great success, and we mean business and we intend keeping this new thrust a success whatever this may cost us. The garbled and distorted reports which some of our political opponents filtered through to some newspapers, would be laughable if one did not realize that the tragedy of these distortions is fragmentation of the black forces for liberation. There are many political idiots with black faces who are tools of oppressors, who unwittingly sow seeds of division without realizing the extent to which this retards our liberation struggle as blacks. Some are in the payroll of the secret police. Several poison-pen pamphlets are being sent to several African, coloured, and Indian people by the secret police in rather shabby attempts to denigrate me. They are hoping to undermine the Alliance through these puerile poison-pen pamphlets which they hope will undermine my leadership. This is a compliment to us, because it means that the oppressors realize the potential for bringing about change in South Africa which the Black Alliance has. So they are forced to take us seriously as a threat to the status quo.

We believe that if this is not done we are all in the republic going to drift willy-nilly into a situation where black and white will soon be locked in violent confrontations, and, if we do not strengthen the Alliance, black will also kill black in fratricidal and self-destructive civil conflict of proportions yet unseen in the continent of Africa.

The only way of avoiding that situation is to move towards reaching a consensus on the ultimate goals. We intend, as the South African Black Alliance, to mobilize internal opinion, which alone can create a crescendo of demands for a national convention to work out a new constitution for South Africa.

This is the era of initiatives. If we as blacks leave initiatives to whites only, we will be committing suicide, as white political creativity is very limited. It is the all-white perspectives, and it is the all-white initiatives which have brought this country to the brink of disaster, where we are now.

I would like to pay tribute to one of our great sons who died recently in the person of Robert Mangaliso Sobukwe. The political bankruptcy of a coterie of political thugs who abused the funeral of this great patriot at Graaf Reinet recently [An attempt was made on Chief Buthelezi's life. - ED.] underlines what I have just said. I want to thank many black and white South Africans who sent me messages of goodwill and support after the BPC-SASO grouping at Graaf Reinet misused the funeral of Robert Sobukwe to give the impression of having a constituency which they do not have. I have been informed that the plans for abusing me were worked out here in Soweto at Regina Mundi. This is why I think it is right and proper for me to mention this matter right here.

I spent two years at Fort Hare University with the late Robert Sobukwe. We were both members of the African National Congress Youth League under the Chairmanship of Mr. Godfrey Pitje. Amongst other members were other patriots such as the late Duma Nokwe, Denis Siwisa, Sally Motlana, John Pokela, Joe Matthews, Tsepo Letlaka and several others. When Sobukwe left the African National Congress, he founded the Pan African Congress in 1959. Even when he broke away from the African National Congress, the feelings of great warmth and affection between us never changed. When we met by accident here in Johannesburg four years ago he encouraged me in the work I am doing and said to me in Zulu, "Uyabashaya mfondini . . . bashaye!" Some of you saw our photograph together in THE RAND DAILY MAIL. When the PAC in London, asked me to attend the funeral, I felt that it was a duty that I could not shirk. When I reached Capetown, I spoke to Bishop Patrick Matolengwe who told me the exact time and date of the funeral. He later on phoned and asked me on behalf of Bishop Ernest Sobukwe, the Suffragana Bishop of St. John's Diocese, and the only surviving brother of Robert Sobukwe, to speak at the funeral. Inkatha chartered a plane for me as we felt that this amount was worth spending for the sake of going to pay our last respects to a great leader and patriot.

I do not intend going into details of what happened. Many garbled versions of what happened were published here and abroad. Many of you saw the whole ugly scene on television. This was also seen abroad. I gave my version to THE CAPE TIMES whose report of the incident, I must confess, was the most balanced I have seen so far. The most surprising thing to me was the extent to which adult Africans had the funeral of so prominent a leader snatched out of their hands by the youth, as one journalist put it to me, when I arrived at the show grounds where the funeral service was to take place. The first thing that convinced me that there was something wrong was the kind of songs which no one would expect could be sung over the mortal remains of anyone, let alone someone that most of us had respected so much for his sacrifices and sufferings. Robert Sobukwe had great gifts of leadership. He clearly would have gone very far had he been given a chance to use his great gifts. His greatness therefore came out not from what he did, because apart from the Sharpeville tragedy, he was not given a chance thereafter. His greatness came out of what he suffered, the prosecutions he stood and the incarceration he suffered at the hands of the government. The greatest tribute that has ever been paid to him is that paid as a backhanded compliment by Mr. Vorster who, when he was Minister of Justice, described him as a "man of magnetic personality". It is quite clear that it is only in a sick society like ours that a man can be persecuted and not given a chance to serve his country because he has a "magnetic personality". We pay tribute to a great son of Africa and he lives although dead in flesh as a symbol of the unbroken spirit of a true patriot, I am sure you will agree with me that we need to pay this tribute to him. We pay tribute to his family who suffered so much just because they were members of his family. If there is any evidence of how dehumanizing apartheid is, the treatment of Robert Sobukwe is evidence of just that. The ruthlessness of white oppression was seen in his treatment in its naked callousness.

As we stood there with other mourners, I heard some of the songs in which I was called a "traitor". It amazed me, particularly after the KwaZulu blacks had demonstrated so convincingly our rejection of "homelands independence," that I was lumped together with Chiefs Matanzima and Mangope, who have opted for the so-called independence. As if this were not enough, the young people, some of whom did not look sober, converged around the dais, where Sobukwe's body was lying and where the bereaved and other mourners were and chanted songs in which the foulest expletives were flung at me. I decided to remain quite cool. There seemed to be no one in charge, as not one person attempted even once to ask this bunch of thugs to behave at such a solemn occasion. They were just allowed to do as they pleased. To my greatest surprise, one clergyman moved towards me and said these thugs were demanding that I should leave immediately. I told him and others who were with him that I was not going to leave even if remaining there meant death for me. I asked them why they did not tell the thugs to behave. I went on speaking to the mourners and expressed my sympathies to Mrs. Veronica Sobukwe and her children. When I saw my former colleague's children near his coffin, I felt a lump in my throat and wept. Fr. John Dumezweni of the Church of Ascension, Cradock, agreed with me that I should not go because of this intimidation by thugs. Just then I was approached by Bishop Desmond Tutu, the Secretary of the South African Council of Churches, who I had been told would be in charge of the funeral service. I had seen him before the whole row started, and we had exchanged greetings. He now asked me whether I should not reconsider my decision as the funeral was clearly not proceeding. I reflected and thought maybe I should stop Sobukwe's funeral from degenerating into a worse shambles than it already was, on my account. I decided to go, but pointed out to Bishop Tutu that there was no way of getting out at that time as these characters had completely surrounded the platform where we were and their foul songs were deafening. Bishop Tutu undertook to make way for me to leave. As we stepped out of the platform the thugs surged forward towards me shouting insults, calling me all sorts of names and saying "Makabulawe!" In a few moments Bishop Tutu was a distance from me. I could not understand what they wanted from me at that point in time, since I had voluntarily decided to go, to spare the widow and family further misery of seeing their loved one's funeral changed into a political circus. My secretary, Mr. Eric Ngubane, stopped one of them from stabbing me at the back as I left. Just then a stone hit me on the leg and I heard a shot and all the thugs together with Bishop Tutu and others ran as fast as their legs could carry them. I did not know at the time where the shot came from, and a second shot sounded, and it was only because of these two shots that I am alive today. The only people with me then were Fr. Rakale, my aides, Rev. Ngidi of the Methodist Church in Nyanga who had flown up with me and Mr. James Africa. Fr. Rakale walked with me right through until I reached the outskirts of the show grounds where the Rev. Nicholas Bengu of the Assemblies of God had his car ready to take me to the hotel. From the hotel I was taken to the airstrip where my plane was and I then flew back to Capetown.

You will recall that on the 29th January, at this very amphitheatre, and on March 14, 1976, I warned those amongst us who thrive on thumping the drums of division amongst us against this habit. I mentioned the categories into which these characters fall. I stated that some do their drum beating on the basis of ideology. I went on to say that some did this on the basis of ethnicity and that some did this on the basis of rural and urban entities. I mentioned that the white establishment also had their fingers in this pie, particularly certain white liberals in the mass media. It seems to me that both the white right wing and sections of the left wing have a stake in black disunity. About this I have not the slightest doubt.

You have just seen what I meant by this. I was saddened by what I saw at Robert Sobukwe's funeral. But the hurt was inflicted into my heart by Bishop Tutu's remarks to the press. Bishop Tutu is the man who should have restored order at the funeral. But instead of doing so, he asked me to reconsider a decision I had already made to stay and asked me to leave. It is absolutely untrue that he had asked me to leave for my own sake and for the sake of Robert Sobukwe as reported in the press. I refused to be evicted. Bishop Tutu asked me to leave. I never suspected his motives. It was only later that his true motives were revealed when he described the thugs who misconducted themselves at the funeral as "a new breed of blacks who," Bishop Tutu said, "have iron in their souls." He called them a significant group of blacks who are totally opposed to separate development. He described them in THE SUNDAY EXPRESS of March 19 as follows: "They are not afraid of things that used to be bogies to many of us. It's no use trying to frighten them by telling them about police, about jail and about death."

I am most astounded that a cleric who holds the position Bishop Tutu holds should ask me to leave merely to give political credibility to a bunch of political thugs who abused, instead of honoured, the memory of Sobukwe. I also do not understand whether it is his position as the Secretary of the Council of Churches which allows what he says at the funeral of Sobukwe to supercede the interests of the PAC in London who requested me to go the funeral, and those of Bishop Sobukwe who had asked me to speak. Robert Sobukwe's widow did not regard my presence as harming the funeral service of her husband, but she thanked me instead for what she called, "coming to comfort us". Both as a churchman that I am and as a political leader, I would be interested in how the South African Council of Churches look at this behaviour by their General-Secretary. Quite clearly the Bishop was playing the role of an ideologue who admired the group of thugs who tried to stab me, who threw stones at me, who tried to trip me and who spat at me. He is on record describing them as young blacks "with iron in their souls". Should I comprehend this to mean a stamp of approval for all the things they did to me from the General-Secretary of the Council of Churches? I did not blame him for running away and leaving me behind as I had not asked for or expected any protection from him. I thought that he, being in charge, would appeal to the horde of political thugs to make way for me to leave as I had agreed on his request to leave.

As if this was not enough, Bishop Tutu's South African Council of Churches' newspaper, THE VOICE, has added insult to injury with a first page article under the heading: "Tutu Saved Gatsha's Life". I have already explained how the Bishop conducted himself. If that is how he saves lives, then God help others from such a saviour. The whole issue of the South African Council of Churches' newspaper THE VOICE has gone out of its way to denigrate me, even with a cartoon which depicts me following Chiefs Matanzima and Mangope in waiting in the queue for independence soup. This, despite my rejection, and the KwaZulu voters' rejection, of homelands independence, just a few weeks ago. This further elucidated the motives of Bishop Tutu in the first place, when he asked me to leave. Many clergymen even amongst those who were his colleagues at the seminary thought of the Graaf Reinet incident as a ghastly incident.

So, tragically, what I spoke to you about both in 1976 and only a few weeks ago right here about those who thrive on beating the drums of division in the black community is already very much with us. In my warning on this kind of characters, I stated that some of these folks do the drum thumping on the basis of ideology and some on the basis of ethnicity. The Graaf Reinet incident as interpreted by Bishop Tutu has clearly got those two elements about it. I want to appeal to members of Inkatha and the black people of KwaZulu not to allow themselves to deviate from the path of black unity which I have followed throughout my whole political career, just because of the cheap ambitions of the kind of soapbox orators we have seen after the Sobukwe funeral incident. It is not ethnicity under the guise of ideological purity which will liberate black people from white oppression. This kind of soapbox oratory is clearly spun for the consumption and entertainment of the left wing here and abroad which is the key to our liberation as blacks. I would like to emphasize that it is high time we realize that we are part of the southern African problem. We must learn to take constructive initiatives. At no time in our history has black unity been more urgent than it is now. If we do not realize this and isolate soapbox orators and those who indulge in empty ideological purity we will be caught flat-footed even after the Nimibian and Zimbabwen people have achieved their freedom.

I have admired and applauded, for example, the constructive initiatives of Dr. Nthato Motlana and his Committee of Ten on getting municipal autonomy for Soweto, their concern for the sufferings of people from day to day without abandoning national goals. That is why members of Inkatha who had made a pact concerninq participation in the Community Council elections dared not break their agreement with the Ten while our brother Dr. Nthato Motlana was in jail. I was delighted to learn of his release and those of his colleagues who have been released. I am equally distressed that other members of the Committee of Ten are still incarcerated. I realize the political problem he has about participating in the elections while some members of his Ten are still in prison. When I talked to Dr. Mulder on Dr. Motlana's release in February, I made it clear that even if Dr. Motlana does not feel like participating in the elections, it was his democratic right to do so and that if he felt like agitating against the elections he must be released to do so if he feels that way. I want to repeat that Inkatha as a movement is not participating in the elections.

In the meantime, however, I have read with disquiet a certain report entitled "Inkatha Gets Outwitted" in a Durban newspaper (THE SUNDAY TRIBUNE, April 2, 1978). I am convinced of one thing and I want today to convey this conclusion to all members of Inkatha. My conviction is that we must accept that in the eyes of certain white liberal journalists and in the eyes of certain drumbeaters of division within the black community, the Inkatha movement can never do anything right. I do not know if our brother Dr. Motlana was quoted correctly in the article. The article reported on how Dr. Motlana was brought to Dr. Nyembezi, the Chairman of the Soweto Region of Inkatha, on his release. Then the report stated:

> But both Dr. Motlana and Ishmael Mkhabela, the Chairman of the Soweto Action Committee feel Inkatha has been outwitted by the government. "This is something the press has not published." Dr. Motlana said, "When the Committee of Ten first voiced their opposition to Community Council elections, we were supported by Inkatha. They supported us on the basis that Soweto would be given full local authority. We did not accept any transfer of powers or phases of powers which were to be added on because our experience has shown that the added on powers never materialize. Inkatha accepted this and supported us, I think that was in August 1977. During our detention, Chief Buthelezi opposed the elections. But he did it on the basis of saying, 'No vote,' while the Committee of Ten was in detention and not on the basis of our original stand. This was followed by my release and the events culminating in the statement by Dr. Nyembezi that Inkatha would take part in the elections. I agree that Inkatha has been outmanoeuvred very badly," Dr. Motlana said.

I wish to recall that when I spoke at this very podium on January 29, this year, I stated quite clearly that the question of acceptance or non-acceptance of Community Councils was a matter for the people of Soweto. Inkatha as a national movement was concerned merely with the members of Inkatha who had reached agreement with Dr. Motlana and his Committee of Ten, keeping their side of the bargain just as I have made this point quite clear. It was the Committee of Ten who approached the Soweto Region of Inkatha. When members of the Soweto Region made the pact with Dr. Motlana, I was informed as president of the movement. This did not mean that this was a decision of Inkatha at the highest level, either through the Central Committee or the National Council. Dr. Motlana is right when he states that my stand therefore was only on the vote while the Committee of Ten was in detention. I regarded this as treachery in the light of an agreement between them.

I think it is grossly unfair of those who comment that Inkatha, as a national movement, has betrayed their brothers and sisters of the Ten in any way. Inkatha, through the Central Committee, has decided last weekend not to participate in the elections. The whole question of individual participation on the basis of acceptance or non-acceptance of the handing over of full authority in phases or at once, is again the question that the Soweto people must resolve. It is a question which Dr. Motlana and Dr. Nyembezi and their Committees in Soweto must sort out between themselves. This is a question of detail rather than of principle. It is not for us as Inkatha to pontificate on it for the residents of Soweto. It is a local issue that deserves attention at local level.

I want also to state that I only learnt afterwards about the release of Dr. Motlana and some of his Committee members. Inkatha has no plans for a Soweto takeover as reported in the article. It is a gross distortion and a blatant lie for the writer of the article to state that there is any money that Inkatha will be spending at all in the Community Council elections. There is no behind-the-scenes support for any candidate by Inkatha as a national movement.

There is an interesting expression of a common attitude between officials of the Department of Plural Relations and people such as Ishmael Mkhabela about me and Inkatha. An official of that department is quoted as saying, "I wonder what Chief Gatsha Buthelezi thinks of all this?" "Inkatha's enthusiastic interest in elections for the Community Councils can be construed as a rather sudden and very significant turnaround in its attitude to the government's handling of the urban black issue," one official said this week. He said that Chief Buthelezi had in the past restricted Inkatha's activities to KwaZulu and had not taken interest in elections outside his territory, except to advise voters in Soweto not to vote while Dr. Motlana and his Committee were in prison. I wonder if Dr. Motlana, the Minister of Plural Relations approves of the kind of strictures directed at me by his officials. But what interests me are the common interests of these officials and the Ishmael Mkhabelas at having a dig at me, to the extent of deliberately distorting facts on Inkatha and the Soweto Community Council elections, just because they are motivated all the time by trying to put me and Inkatha in a bad light by attacking my integrity on the basis of distortions rather than facts.

HEARTACHE AND TREACHERY

I hope my brother Dr. Motlana was misquoted. As far as Ishmael Mkhabela and his cohorts are concerned, I expect anything to come out of his mouth as has been demonstrated by him in recent times.

I want Inkatha members to accept that we must learn to do things because they are right and not for the sake of placating this Charlie or that one. We must learn to accept that Inkatha, having grown to the giant black organization that it is today, has both white and black enemies, quite naturally. I was at university with Dr. Motlana and Mrs. Motlana. At one time we were all university students at Fort Hare. We all belonged to the African National Congress Youth League. We have never had problems between us after 30 years, as brothers. Last year we had a joint press conference right here in Johannesburg with him at his request. Our stand on issues is not new. I hope that he should keep out of the drum-beaters' path, whose sole purpose in life is to sow seeds of division which can only lead to internecine strife between us as black brothers. Whose interests they serve by doing this is quite obvious. I want just to repeat that my respect and affection for Dr. Motlana is something that has happened not overnight, but out of knowing each other in the field of politics in the last thirty years. It is not opportunistic or based on which way the wind blows at any given time. It is based on a common commitment to the liberation of people.

The Graaf Reinet incident must not delude these elements into thinking that just because Inkatha is a non-violent liberation movement, our non-violence stance precludes self-defense. I want to warn them that in spite of our commitment to non-violence, we will defend ourselves with all the might at our command from any violence they unleash against us. I think it is high time black people of South Africa say to these elements, "Thus far and no further." We cannot take these insults and acts of violence lying down. The black people of South Africa suffer enough intimidation from whites practically at every turn and just about every day of the year. We cannot bow down before a coterie of cowards, who have no defined strategy for the liberation of South Africa, just because they indulge in intimidation. We of Inkatha know who our enemies are. We do not regard other blacks as enemies. Those who differ from us on the basis of debates about what strategies to adopt in the liberation struggle are not our enemies, because we are committed to the same goals.

Those who are not resorting to violence which they unleashed against other blacks in the past two years clearly want to set back our struggle for liberation by several generations. We must say "No!" to this bunch of political hooligans who have no constituency and who think they can bully their way into black leadership through acts of intimidation against other blacks. I pray Dr. Motlana and those of our brothers and sisters we respect even if we may differ on strategy, to keep a safe distance from these political thugs, so that we can deal with them as such, without harming innocent people in any way, when we meet these thugs in their own game and on their ground.

I want to emphasize the urgent need for us to bury the hatchet of petty political bickering on peripheral issues. We need black unity more than anything else now. This is urgent.

The issue which I want to leave with the people of Soweto to consider is whether we are going to go very far in our struggle on the basis of black intimidation of black. I think it is suicidal to base one's leadership on the formula of, "Do this or else I will set your house on fire tonight." This kind of formula is fraught with grave dangers of cruel self-lacerating civil wars between us which would, of course, please some people. We never want to see another Mzimhlophe type of internicine strife. We cannot afford this kind of setback at this moment in our struggle. Those amongst whites who may be enjoying this kind of phenomena of blacks murdering and indulging in cruel, self-multilating civil wars, should not delude themselves into thinking that as long as blacks confine it to blacks, that they are safe. An example of whites who indulge in fanning the flames of violence and disunity amongst blacks was an article by Mr. Patrick Laurence of THE RAND DAILY MAIL, in which he indulged in the usual cliches of bankrupt soapbox politicians we have become familiar with since June 16, 1976. Mr. Laurence attempted, just like Bishop Tutu, to justify what was done to me by parroting threadbare cliches about "system blacks." He went quite far and even accused me of political opportunism for going to bury my black brother, Robert Sobukwe. I loved and respected Robert Sobukwe very much. But my own leadership stands on its own merits and does not need even the shadow of as revered a brother as Robert Sobukwe to prop it up. Nothing was going to rub off onto me if I had stayed on for the funeral. I did not stand to gain anything politically by being present. I questioned this when Mr. Laurence spoke to me by telephone last week and he said to me that he was only saying things the Soweto Action Committee said to him. I asked him why these insults were not attributed to their authors. So you can see just how imperative it is that we should not allow whites who, after all, have a stake in white domination lasting as long as possible, to play us off against each other. Not that it is bad only for blacks, but also for whites, for it is only by hastening the black/white future that we can avoid the alternative which was described as, "too ghastly to contemplate," which apartheid and white racism offers us.

The interesting feature of the Graaf Reinet press reaction is that which was seen in the apartheid mass media such as THE CITIZEN and DIE TRANSVALER. They gloated over the incident as can be expected. All the venom aimed at "white pigs" and "Boers are dogs" which this bunch exuded was relegated to the background, because of the joy derived from what political thugs did to me, their political enemy, as if the colour of any thugs matters. If it matters it would have been just as silly for us blacks to gloat over the stabbing death of Dr. Verwoerd in 1966 by a thug whose skin was as white as his own.

I think we should realize that the solidarity we have demonstrated during the elections in KwaZulu and the kind of political achievement the South African Black Alliance has been, both spell trouble for us. For they challenge the status quo. We must not be daunted by taunts of the dying monster, Oppression. If white unity is strength, then for us as blacks, black unity in the same way spells strength. When we shout, "Strength!" or, "Power is ours!" let us ponder over these words.

128

Chapter 12

WHAT FOREIGNERS MUST KNOW

TO THE TIME MAGAZINE NEWS TOUR

Johannesburg, 20 March 1978

It is difficult to do justice in a talk of this nature to all the socio-political questions and economic questions which we face in South Africa. There is no real scope on these questions for blacks to play a meaningful role except in response to oppression. This flows from the fact that blacks on the whole, and by and large, are denied human rights in South Africa. South Africa, like the United States, has its skeletons dating back to the days of slavery in South Africa. Your country however, has already taken big strides in the area of human rights as far as men of colour are concerned. That is hardly the case here as you well know. In economic terms we are far from facing the realities of the situation when we are still talking about economic development in terms of border industry growth, on-the job training, and increasing employment for blacks in the central economy. Nor are we facing the reality of the situation when talk is confined just to how to make homelands governments work, or giving greater power to Urban Community Councils.

However, since we live in what is a fundamentally unjust society, we have to accept the realism of talking in these terms. We blacks face an avalanche of human needs as a result of the deprivations entailed in living in such an unjust society. I cannot escape the reality of coming face-to-face on a day-to-day basis, for instance, with the needs and sufferings of my people. I cannot escape being faced with the hungry, and the necessity to get them job opportunities. Facing the reality of our being administered by an alien white clenched fist does not, however, mean that I by choice define the fundamental problems of South Africa only in terms of this kind of issue.

I realize that the trauma of Soweto has reverberated throughout the world. I realize that this marked a watershed in the history of South Africa, not only for South Africa, but for all members of the world community who have dealings with South Africa.

When the Soweto unrest erupted, I sent telegrams urging an urgent meeting with the Prime Minister and black leaders. I felt at the time that the Prime Minister was going to realize that we needed to share our collective wisdom in the light of the tragic loss of life mainly in Soweto and in other

With President Carter at the White House

parts of South Africa. The Prime Minister did not even have courtesy to ask his secretary to acknowledge receipt of my telegram. Nor did his Minister of Bantu Administration, Mr. M. C. Botha, to whom I had also sent a similar telegram act differently from his Prime Minister.

Ultimately he agreed, through Professor Ntsanwisi of Gazunkulu, to see us on the 8th of October, 1976. The unrest had erupted on the 16th of June. Knowing how adept the Prime Minister can be at making one waste time on peripheral issues rather than on the burning issues of the day, I prepared a certain memorandum to present to the Prime Minister my view of things after the Soweto bloodbath. The memorandum reads:

> The meeting between the Honourable Prime Minister and South Africa's black leaders serving their people within the framework of policy is taking place in the midst of civil violence which has reached proportions unparalleled since the War of Independence fought by the Boers at the end of the last century.
>
> It is therefore right and proper that we turn our attention to fundamentals and do not only talk about what are primarily administrative matters within status quo politics.
>
> No matter how much we disagree with the methods adopted by tens of thousands of blacks of all shades, we must take cognizance of the mood of the people and the desperation of their actions. At a meeting such as this, it would be the height of irresponsibility to

130

regard the country's present unrest as the result of a handful of agitators. In our last discussion with the Hon. Prime Minister I in fact predicted that we might soon be faced with the option that has been taken by our people in the last three and a half months.

We leaders who are serving our people within the framework of your policy, hold the view that the unrest in the country was planned by nobody, and that the first violent outburst, when it occurred, took all of us by surprise, even despite the predictions I made to you in our discussion last year.

Spontaneous civil violence of the proportions we have witnessed amounts to a breakdown of law and order and indicates the impoverishment of the South African Government's administration.

Put bluntly, the present unrest is nothing other than a mass rejection of apartheid and white privilege. As such the unrest must not be seen as a temporary and passing problem. It indicates a chronic state of affairs which has now become so acute that it lays claim to our most urgent attention at this meeting.

As leaders representing millions of our people we will be expected to face a politically impossible task unless this is productive productive from the point of view of our people. They are aware of our meeting here today. Some may be expectant, but many are skeptical. Those who are skeptical are not skeptical because they do not trust us, they are skeptical because we have always returned from this kind of conversations with the Hon. Prime Minister emptyhanded.

At the outset a general point must be made. Legislative assemblies which are located in the so-called homelands cannot function for any length of time unless decisions in these assemblies are seen to be relevant to the interests of urban blacks, as determined by they themselves. After all, these legislative assemblies were created on that assumption by the Republican Government.

The extent to which urban and rural blacks have common interests is the extent to which they will subject themselves to the same leadership. The common interest of all blacks is real fulfillment. Blacks do not see why they should have separate ethnic destinies when whites have a one common destiny, which is not ethnic.

A situation in which urban blacks are controlled by riot police is not a situation which we can tolerate. But police were resorted to because white political control of urban blacks had failed. This failure is not simply to be laid at the door of Bantu Administration Boards or the Urban Bantu Councils. The failure is fundamental and it is the failure of apartheid as such.

The numerous representations we have made about the grievances of blacks, particulary urban blacks, have nor resulted in any meaningful changes. These changes were impossible within the grand design of apartheid, "separate development," call it what you will. The failure of the Honourable Prime Minister to introduce what are to blacks meaningful changes makes our task as leaders seeking a peaceful change, impossible. As blacks with the responsibility to lead blacks, we have no desire to resort to riot police administration. We do not want to cover our failure with shows of strength. We stand rather condemned as politically impotent. This admission is not a comment on leadership ability. It is rather a comment on apartheid. The institutions of apartheid are not instruments of nation-building, and it is not possible to exercise responsible political leadership within an apartheid framework. I am not indulging in sheer agitation when I speak as I do, I am merely being factual and constructive.

Whites as a minority group claim the right to make decisions for the country's black majority and claim the right to enforce these decisions. They have failed in that enforcement and they have failed because they have attempted the politically impossible. This they should know from their own history.

The interests of the Afrikaner in South Africa have been self-determined. This process of determining what constitutes their interests has welded people of diverse origins and different languages into a coherent political body.

To a large extent it was the Afrikaner protest movement and the Afrikaners acted outside the constitutional framework provided for them by their group into a people with a specific identity. In achieving this distinctiveness, the Afrikaner acted outside the constitutional framework provided for them by their political opponents. They refused to recognise the laws of the land, staged a rebellion and fought a full-scale war.

The power advantages that were achieved by these tactics were consolidated by secret associations, the Church, and various cultural organizations.

We blacks have the same rights of self-determination as did the Afrikaner whites. As the Afrikaner had the right to choose who would be regarded as eligible as VOLK and who would not, so do we blacks have the right to choose whom we regard as our people. As the Afrikaners involved themselves in nation-building among people of diverse origins, so too do we have that same right.

In point of fact, Afrikaner solidarity was the consequence of political ideals. Political ideals for the Afrikaner did not emerge for an ethnic group. The call to the struggle for liberation drew many different peoples together and the criterion for acceptability was involvement in the struggle for liberation.

We as black leaders are aware of these facts. We are aware of the fact that had the renowned Afrikaner leaders in the various phases of the struggle allowed themselves to be dictated to by their political opponents, their people would have abandoned them. Those of us who aspire to serve our people in leadership are aware of the fact that our people will reject us if we do not fulfill their desires for liberation, that is, liberation as determined and understood by themselves.

Let us now call a halt to such talk as there has been out the National Party's policy of self-determination of the people for the people. Our people have not and

132

never will desire self-determination within the framework laid down by the whites. To expect them to act differently is to expect them to do what the whites, and the Afrikaners in particular, never did during their own struggle.

Let us talk about how the irresistible urge for political expression which is now a fact of self-determination can be made constructive. That the political process in this country has become destructive is plain for everybody to see. It is our responsibility to turn what is now destructive energy into a nation-building force.

It must be obvious that political leadership both in the white community as well as in the black community will face almost insurmountable obstacles in introducing constructive political changes. If we cannot even talk to each other about these difficulties, there is no hope for our country. Talking to each other is meaningless unless we also listen to each other.

If one thinks realistically within what one can perhaps call "internal detente", one must not lay down preconditions. We do, however, find it necessary to point out that the definition of common ground which justified detente is essential. Such a definition would in our opinion be advantageous beyond all measure.

It is quite clear that the Afrikaner is not prepared to change unless he is forced by some pressures to change. The majority of black people reject the proposed division of South Africa into mini-States. The events in southern Africa have awakened the black masses and they are determined to put an end to inequality.

Whites from various parts of the world settled in South Africa and seized land by imperial edict, supported by military superiority. In their present intransigence they are again relying entirely on their military strength. Whites, as you know, did not fight only with blacks, but they also squabbled among themselves for a whole century before coming together in the Act of Union in 1910. This was mainly done in order to consolidate their white interests. While they themselves are heterogeneous, coming as they do from different cultural backgrounds, it suited their scheme of white domination to declare themselves to be one white nation, while blacks are conveniently being divided into mini-nations on the basis that they have different cultural backgrounds.

Before 1910, and in preparation for their union of the four South African provinces, a number of commissions were appointed to study the situation.

In 1913 the Native Land Act (by British rulers) was passed, which set aside the so-called scheduled areas in which we blacks were allowed to live. The 1913 Act was merely a formalization of a position which was already in existence. In the various colonies and republics which came together as the four provinces which constituted the Union, blacks had already been forced to live in restricted areas and were kept there at the point of the gun. These areas, such as KwaZulu for instance, were remnants of what was our country before white conquest. They were not created by whites, except in their present form, as remnants of our former territories. Blacks never accepted this position and in fact did try through a series of wars and rebellions to break out of the system and to recover their whole territories as they were before conquest. This they failed to do and this is the position up to now.

After the 1913 Land Act, blacks in some areas still had residential rights to purchase land outside their so-called reserves, as they were then called. This residential right was acted against with the 1936 Native Land and Trust Act [Again, British rules. — Ed.] This Act was an arbitrary division of land between blacks and whites, by whites in order to promote white self-interest. It excluded blacks from having any land rights in all the economically developed areas and all known mineral deposits were included in the so-called white areas.

Blacks were not consulted at the various times colonies were proclaimed and republics established. We blacks were not consulted when the 1913 and the 1936 Acts were passed. We were not consulted when the Bantu Authorities Act of 1951 was passed and we were not consulted when the Promotion of Bantu Self-Government Act of 1959 was also passed. We were not consulted and we do not feel morally bound by these acts of white self-interest. These white Acts certainly did not create a feeling of common loyalty in South Africa as a whole. To me, these are seeds of revolution, which whites have sown blindly as a moat around their besieged self-interest.

These Acts of exploitation were given a veneer of moral respectability by playing with words. The "reserves" were now called "homelands" in order to cover up naked white BAASKAP. The fact that we live in these so-called homelands, is not a creation of the present regime alone. We do live in them because the gun the white man has always relied on has given us no choice. That does not mean that we have been fooled by the application of this veneer on white domination. The whole callous game of playing with words in this fashion has not made any real difference to our position. To seal our doom as the oppressed of this land, it has been made necessary by law for us to have bits of paper from white bureaucrats if we want to be in the so-called white areas for any reason. To work in the industrial centres blacks need bits of paper and even to move from one area to another blacks need these bits of paper from white officials. As a result thousands of black people get prosecuted every year for contraventions of these regulations. They have now been assisted in this foolhardiness by some of the leaders who agreed that calling passes "travel documents" disposes of them.

It must be acknowledged that the whole process of exploiting blacks was strongly sustained by colonial economic interests. This means in practical terms that investors have for over a century and a half had great rewards for participating with whites in South Africa in their exploitation of blacks. I do not imply that this was a choice that investors made in each and every case. It was a willynilly situation for some, because of the wicked economic system which is in operation in South Africa.

In dealing with this question in depth, it must on the other hand be acknowledged that investments can also be seen as a human endeavor in taming untamed land and as a process of ensuring economic progress. This means that while we must acknowledge the fact of black exploitation, we have to concede at the same time that there was, however, progress even through that very exploitation. South Africa today is the economic giant of Africa. One must see this development in the context of the whole of southern Africa. Therefore for the sake of the poor not only in South Africa, but also for the sake of the development of the whole of southern Africa, that development must continue. The southern African countries such as Lesotho, Swaziland, Botswana, Malawi and Mozambique, still depend on the South African economy for thousands and thousands of jobs that they would otherwise not be able to give to their people. They all abhor apartheid as we all do. But this makes the issue of investment in South Africa much more than just a South African issue.

In spite of the failure of communicating meaningfully with Mr. Vorster, I have still for moral and for Christian and pragmatic reasons chosen the path of peaceful change. The chances of a peaceful change have since the sporadic uprisings in the country, seemed more and more remote, in the face of Mr. Vorster's clear intransigence. So it is quite possible that there can well be a holocaust, if Mr. Vorster persistently refuses to exploit opportunities for effecting such a peaceful change . Mr. Vorster, as I said earlier, is boasting about the Transkei and Bophuthatswans so-called independence. He received a large majority of white votes in November 1977 which he himself described gloatingly as "an avalanche".

The whole election was fought on the alleged interference by the United States. It worked wonders for Mr. Vorster. Even the so-called liberals were lured into making statements which endorsed Mr. Vorster's ploy in presenting the United States as a threat to peace in South Africa.

We blacks highly appreciate the American clear stand on the issue of human rights in South Africa. We do still have some heartburn about the fact that what was done in the past by America, was not done in the interests of blacks but in the interests of the United States. But in spite of this situation and Mr. Vorster's intransigence, we cannot afford voluntarily to precipitate a holocaust in this country. We are not afraid to die for our freedom, but we cannot assist the racist regime to make our unarmed people cannon fodder. This they desire to do more than anything. Mr. Kruger, the Minister Justice, has told me more than once that whites are now prepared to have a go at us. Maybe this will happen some day. Sooner or later, I do not know. Then you may ask the question, "Why should one support investment under these circumstances?" I must make it clear, speaking for myself, that I am afraid of change which destroys the base of future development. I believe that such change would be self-defeating. This does not mean that I am not conscious of the fact that my people have been abused beyond the point of human endurance. So I must also be pragmatic in another sense. My people can no longer tolerate their insufferable position. My leadership will cease to mean anything to my people if they cannot receive tangible results from it. Above all this, I want to emphasize that I love my people and share their suffering. So that when there is nothing left but to fight a just war, people all over the world, right down through the centuries of history have done just that, not least amongst these the founding fathers of the United States. We black

South Africans are people among the rest of humanity. My people's options are my own options. We realize that we have reached a stage in which white intransigence is playing brinkmanship with total disaster.

Even so, I still hope that it is not too late for a peaceful solution to dominate over a violent one. I find myself, knowing the circumstances of my people as I do, that I must cling to this hope as long as this is possible.

The role of the foreign investor in South Africa is a crucial one. Injections of foreign capital are vital for the survival not only of the South African economy, but of my people, in order to be able to continue their struggle for liberation. It is clear to me that the struggle is going to be long and hard. I am quite aware of the dilemma posed by the fact that it is the very strength of this economy which props up the white military might which is used to keep me and my people in oppression.

While I have not been able so far to support disinvestment as such, I must concede that investments which are made to prop up an increasingly white-only cash earning, are likely to be lost in the chaos which may ultimately arise. While military power can postpone such chaos for a very long time, military might alone can never be a decisive factor. This I say because in the interdependence that exists between whites and blacks, blacks outnumber whites by millions of people. This factor seems to be ultimately the only balance of power which, with more unity, blacks can use effectively.

There is, however, an urgent need if investments in South Africa can play a meaningful role, for a partnership to exist between labour and management. Unless the investor enters into partnership with blacks our whole political and economic order is threatened. In dealing with this question of investment and the role of investments in South Africa we have to acknowledge certain facts, which to recap, I will restate once again:)

—Blacks were not consulted when South Africa laid the foundations for a "Have/Have-not" society in which we blacks have become the "Have-nots".

— Blacks were not consulted when the land was so divided so as to give 14 percent of the population which is white, 87 percent of the land.

—Blacks were not consulted when the structures of apartheid limited the black man's participation in economic development to supplying so-called cheap labour.

—Blacks were never and are not now consulted on how the national wealth should be spent, despite the fact that the economy is by now entirely dependent on black labour.

—Blacks were not consulted when their ability to voice objections and protest peacefully and democratically against the political, social and economic injustices they suffer was whittled down step by step, by one obnoxious piece of repressive legislation after another.

136

WHAT FOREIGNERS MUST KNOW

I know the truth of these statements, not just from observation at a distance, but from my practical everyday experiences as a black man who has lived in South Africa for nearly fifty years. It is for pragmatic reasons as well as moral reasons that I have so far clung to the hopes of non-violent solutions. I must, however, make the point that the owners of capital in South Africa have so far not sustained me in that hope. This is because they have so far mostly played the white government's game. There is an urgency for measures to terminate this partnership between capital and repressive legislation.

It doesn't seem to be fully realized that in South Africa people will conquer capital if capital opposes the will of the people. Investment at this point in time in South Africa must take sides in the central political struggle, between apartheid and the right to participate fully in the government by the majority of the people of this country. So far we have only seen capital siding with the forces which maintain the status quo. This is, therefore, a political factor which must take its chances in the open political arena. It must be admitted openly that the neutrality which capital has always claimed is absolutely fictional.

At this moment in the history of South Africa everything is sliding willy-nilly into a melting pot. Apartheid, white political dominance, white technological advantages over black counterparts, a virulent black consciousness, the Westminster-type political model, white and black trade unionism, the black work force, the tribal land tenure systems, white rights to freehold property. All these are ingredients in the melting pot and none will emerge out of this pot untouched.

It is therefore absolutely foolhardy in the extreme to discuss investment in South Africa as though the past will continue into the future. It is equally foolhardy to say that the existing economic order will not undergo radical changes. The free enterprise capitalist system as it operates in South Africa at present, excludes the majority of the population, who participate only as pawns who operate in the promotion of white self-interest, and not in the interests of the entire population.

There are a lot of utterances in South Africa lately to the effect that only a fool cannot see that change is going to take place in South Africa. Those who say this to me do so in an attempt to move my political stance backwards by several years.

My stance was that apartheid would fail. My stance today is that apartheid has failed. My stance was that homeland development would suffer from lack of white sincerity. My stance now is that it has suffered irreparably from white insincerity.

Everyone is agreed that change will come in South Africa. But as more and more people talk this kind of language, it has become clear that change means different things to different people. There are those who say that I am becoming too hasty in taking this line. Those who take this line are invariably those who think of change only in terms of making the bitter apartheid pill more palatable by naively sugarcoating it.

The change I want with millions of blacks in this country is the scrapping of apartheid and the so-called homeland policy. I have become impatient with those who are building up a conflict situation in South Africa which will result in a conflagration.

Whatever we mean by "change", we start from a given point in reality. We will have black rural-residential and peasant farming areas for the foreseeable future. We will not have them merely because whites in this country want it that way. We will have them because for the foreseeable future the cash economy will not be able to transform peasant society into farming and industrial society for a considerable time to come.

Any hope, however, that the economically poor will remain politically disenfranchised is a misplaced hope. Any hope that the elite will not have to involve themselves in a radical redistribution of wealth is also wishful thinking. This can never take place as long as there is such gross unfairness in the distribution of land. After all, land throughout the world still remains the most tangible form of investment. This is a political issue which needs a new political dispensation to resolve.

Despite the draconian powers the government exercises in South Africa to limit political action, the dynamic force of politics in this country is the black man's will to fight for equality of opportunity, not only in their uban ghettoes nor in their impoverished reserves called "homelands", but in the suburbs, streets and market places of the cities. Blacks realize that outside political power there is no equality of opportunity.

In thinking about investment in South Africa, I find myself involved ever increasingly in a conflict of a very fundamental nature. On the one hand, I cannot bring myself to say to the poor and the suffering of this country that I am working for the cessation of foreign investment in South Africa. Investment means increased prosperity and it means jobs for the unemployed, clothes for the naked, and food for the hungry. On the 29th of January this year, I had a political rally in Soweto attended by about 20,000 blacks. I posed the question to them whether I should support investment or disinvestment. The people themselves in a chorus stated that they needed jobs. I pointed out to them that they must be prepared to sacrifice for their liberation. They stated that they were not yet ready for that sacrifice at this point in time. This question I realize has become more and more a very burning issue throughout the world.

Let me state that some kind of pressures rather than just persuasion may move the Afrikaner to think about change. It is very difficult to know just what kind of pressures can produce these results. It is of no use to put on pressures that are counter-productive. I think it is in consultation with blacks themselves that this question of the kind of pressures which need to be brought to bear on this regime can be resolved. There has been far too much speaking on behalf of blacks which has been going on. In March 1976 I stated that I intended calling a convention of black organizations to discuss this issue of investment and disinvestment. Most unfortunately the unrest erupted in June that year. Blacks should not be regarded as a monolith, which has complete accord on all issues.

WHAT FOREIGNERS MUST KNOW

But there is need for black unity more than ever before. It has always been considered my view that white oppression exists for so long because of the borrowed time which black disunity gives it. Attempts to forge the black unity front in 1976 failed to take off, mainly for the same reasons as the failure of the black convention. In January this year, the Labour Party, the Reform Party (an Indian party) and Inkatha(my movement) have launched an alliance. What will come of it, I cannot state categorically at this stage, but I consider it as a very important beginning in the continuing quest for black unity without which we will not be able to use our economic power as blacks to force whites to get to the conference table with us, to work out a political dispensation, to save this country from a holocaust.

On the other hand, I want to emphasize that I cannot bring myself to support an economic order within a political system which creates those poor and hungry I have mentioned. Investment has to convince us blacks that it has no supportive role within status quo politics. We are aware of the fact that big business has negotiated concessions from government departments in the areas of training, manpower utilization and housing. However, real political developments are forging so far ahead that these concessions and the negotiations which led to them will sooner or later become indictments rather than anything else.

Homeland development and the future of the homelands as such are bound up with these considerations. Investment, whether in the cash economy or in the peasant economy, is an investment in one integrated socio-economic and political system. I therefore cannot separate investment issues in the cash economy. My dilemma there remains a dilemma. I must pause to emphasize that the dilemma I talk about here is not self-inflicted. It is not a product of any ideological stand, or even simply a political stance I may have adopted. The dilemma is thrown up by reality in South Africa — a reality which none of us, you, myself nor my people — can escape. It is not possible to talk it out of existence.

Frequently those who are most ardent in their defense of the capitalist free enterprise system are the greatest enemies of that system. If ever there is any demise of capitalism here, white capitalists will fully share in the blame. It must be a matter of common sense that if, as is the case at present, the majority of the people, who are black, are not participants in the capitalist free enterprise system, it cannot survive in the southern Africa that is now unfolding. The South Africa we have known is bound to crumble in the face of the new southern Africa that is coming into being. It is, however, not too late to do something to ensure a continuing democracy within which a responsible free enterprise system can evolve. It is, however, important to emphasize that it is now too late to perpetuate the status quo.

Faced with inevitable changes in the future and the present situation in a state of flux, it is not possible to reduce the question of investment to a simple ABC formula. There are, however, some things which must be stated about the acceptability of foreign investment in South Africa. The first is that whereas my people at present still give approval to foreign investment, this is not a blanket approval, based only on the sole grounds of job creation and no more. Job creation is a very important reason for a particular investment being regarded as acceptable if a number of other acceptable criteria are met simultaneously. A view is often expressed these days that black support for any kind of investment simply on the basis that it offers jobs, can be interpreted in certain circumstances as amounting to blacks participating in their own exploitation.

We must realize that it is no longer sufficient to say to blacks, "You must welcome investment; it is good for you." The call has gone out in some black circles for disinvestment. This has made the question of whether or not to invest a contentious political issue.

There have been gross acts of exploitation under the guise of investment for the sake of developing the economy. How investors can be responsible in the totality of the South African situation has yet to be explored. It is clear that this responsibility cannot be explored by the dialectical use of words and concepts in theoretical debates. We need to develop a framework within which the explanation of investor responsibility could take place. The following two areas of responsibility would have to be included:

—Responsibility in Partnership between Labour and Management.

There can be no responsible investment which does not lead to a partnership between the owners of capital and labour. That partnership cannot now exist because the Industrial Conciliation Act excludes blacks in the definition used for an employee. This alone does not make trade unions illegal. A consequence of this exclusion in the definition is that there is no possibility of disputes between labour and management being settled by arbitration. The government imposed the Works Committee system. The Works Committee system is no substitute for a free trade union movement.

—Responsibility in Partnership between Community and Investor.

There will be a strong tendency for investment to be exploitative if investment is not mutually beneficial to both the community in which it takes place and the investor himself. Investors must by now realize that if things are not put right there will be a danger that as blacks realize how much economic power they wield; they might grab any exploitative investment and do with it what they like. If and when that kind of thing takes place, everybody will be losers. To avoid that situation, investors ought to start thinking about that situation now.

I hold the view that some form of a free enterprise system in which the private sector is permitted to play a creative role would be the best option for South Africa. But I would argue, on the other hand, against unrestrained capitalism in which the dependency of the South African economy would be perpetuated.

Such restraints as would be imposed should be determined by:

—the needs of self-sufficiency in the economy

—the developmental role the South African economy should play in the southern African context.

I wish further to argue that development should:

—be based on the home market

—encompass a wide range of industries

—not be reliant on foreign finance except where such finance is subjected to local control

—bring about independent technological progress.

Home Market: There will be no economic progress in South Africa unless there is political stability. That stability depends upon the people's involvement in the economy and their gains from it. The majority of black South Africans do not feel that they have benefitted from South Africa's economic development. There must be further and rapid expansion of the home market if people are to feel that their new political dispensation has any meaning for them.

Industrial diversification: A growing economy, drawing in an ever increasing percentage of the peasant community, can only come about by maximizing diversification. The development of the home market must go hand in hand with diversification if the growing peasant population's dependency on rapidly depleting resources is to be minimized. Free enterprise can make a significant contribution to the development of the home market and the diversification of industry.

Foreign Finance: It is not the origin of money which creates problems for a developing economy. Foreign capital brings with it managerial skill and technological expertise which every developing economy requires. The control over foreign funds is, however, problematic. If one looks at the Zambian experience, one realizes the extent to which foreign funds in the hands of expatriates were not employed to the best advantage of the indigenous population until there was forced Africanization.

Independent Technological Progress: Independent technological progress is an essential requirement of real grass roots economic development. Blacks in South Africa have now been excluded from full participation in technological development. Only now that there are too few whites for certain skilled jobs are blacks being trained in the various trades. Even today whites are still protected by legislation from black competition. Investors have so far participated in this exploitation of economic opportunity to the enhancement of white privilege and to the detriment of black workers.

Private enterprise, I believe, can play a significant role in the progress of independent technological development. This development can best take place on the factory floor. Training and human development does cost money but it also makes money. Making money out of people without exploiting them is possible.

If commodity production is important in the development of the home market and the diversification of industry, and if free enterprise is involved in those developments, it should also be involved in the development of independent technology.

Let me, before concluding this address, restate some of the points I have made. South Africa and its economy have up to now been exploitative. The black sections of the population have been used and abused to the point where they have been pushed to the edge of human endurance.

In the explosive South African situation, it is still possible that peaceful solutions may prevail, and it is still possible to continue South Africa's economic growth to become a significant developmental factor in the whole of southern Africa. That cooperation can now only be got by intentions of radical change in which blacks will fully participate in the government of the country.

Investors, who have been party to oppression in the past, must now be party to change in the future. I venture to say that doing reparation work on this score is much better than withdrawal at this point in time. A partnership with blacks is an absolute urgency. It must be developed. A Kissinger/Vorster partnership which excluded blacks was resented by us. We could only see a final conflagration which would, if it occurred, destoy the base from which progress can continue. We hope Americans in particular will note this most decisive factor.

Investor responsibility must go beyond palliatives and must involve the investor in confrontation with authority. Unless this takes place, and unless change results, and unless after change partnership between labour and capital is established; and unless there is rapid economic growth which decreases South Africa's dependency on capitalism as we now know it, it will pass from the South African scene forever.

The West did not assist the banned African National Congress and the Pan-Africanist Congress when they left the country to operate from outside, except for some continued assistance from the Scandinavian countries. Western countries refuse to be involved in supplying arms to those liberation movements that have opted for the armed struggle. I am not being judgmental in mentioning this or questioning the right of Western countries not to support violence. But the truth of the matter is that only now has there been a clear stand on the arms embargo against South Africa. But prior to this South Africa armed herself to the teeth through armaments supplied by the West. I find myself frustrated about coming to speak to audiences like this. I am finding it difficult to accept overseas invitations for talks of this sort. The West has not assisted the liberation movements in their armed struggle. This is the prerogative of the West. The West talks about apartheid and its elimination, and yet no Western countries assist forces for change that are operating within South Africa. Except for churches in a couple of European countries, no assistance has been forthcoming which is in any way commensurate with the amount of anger expressed by Western countries about our apartheid society. I, for example, serve my people where they are. But because this has now been done within what the government calls "homeland", I find quite often that I am abused by Western countries as an object of their self-righteousness. It is so easy to say that in supporting people who have no choice about living in the so-called homelands that one gives credibility to the homelands policy. I realize the difficulties caused by the so-called independence of Bophuthatswana and the Transkei. Mr. Vorster has predicted in Parliament that all the so-called homelands will be independent in five years time, except us in KwaZulu. This he said because of our clear rejection of homelands independence. And yet people, in spite of that, will use us, the victims of apartheid, to earn false respectability by saying that they do not want to support us lest they be misunderstood to be supporting the homelands policy. We blacks see this as a continuation of our betrayal by the West which commenced about sixty-five years ago, when the Union was formed.

There are many things that can be done to assist our cause. There is no limit to what can be done in the area of education, for example. Blacks build their own schools, they furnish their own schools, and they pay for books and privately paid teachers. Black universities need scholarships for black students. Trust funds for the erection of black schools have been launched in this country, and need support. Black academics need scholarships in order to do post-graduate studies in countries which are English-speaking, such as the United States, Britian, Canada, Australia, and New Zealand. Scholarships can be set up in African states as well for South African students to study at these universities.

It is heartening to see that the United States is prodding her conscience to the extent that some of her leading citizens, such as Clyde Ferguson and William Cotter have put down as they have done in the January issue of FOREIGN AFFAIRS some of the steps that need to be considered by the Carter Administration.

I do not think it is my job to tell Americans what to do in this area. I found most of their diplomatic options interesting and feasible. I do not think most blacks will find any problems about supporting their military options.

I find no problem with the implementation of their options with respect to refugees and non-military support for liberation movements and African states.

I have already dealt in depth with the issue of economic sanctions and I have nothing more to add. We approve the Sullivan principles as meaningful.

It must be remembered that the struggle for liberation will be decided within the borders of South Africa. It is equally important to recognize that there are forces within South Africa working for change. There is, therefore, a limit to what the friends of the oppressed in South Africa can do. For us, most of these are not academic questions. For us these are not ideological questions. These, to us, are people's questions. They are questions of humanity's response to suffering in an oppressive society. Suffering will determine the future of South Africa, and not the external requirements of an existing industrial setup, banking institutions or organized labour. The real issues facing us do not arise out of the need to protect an existing order, an existing set of privileges, an existing advantage of man over man at the expense of man. The real questions facing us are not how to preserve a South African way of life as it has evolved to the present point. The real issues facing South Africa relate rather to a people's force at work demanding the demolition of the instruments of injustice and oppression.

South Africa has for so long masqueraded as an appendage of the West.

South Africa is part of Africa and we must realize that her future has to be Afrocentric. This can only happen if all the assistance is geared towards making the black majority take their place with their fellow white compatriots to determine that future.

Chapter 13

1978 POLICY SPEECH

TO THE KWAZULU LEGISLATIVE ASSEMBLY

Ulandi, 20 April 1978

The struggle for liberation in Southern Africa is still on in a big way. I pointed out last year that it had narrowed to Zimbabwe and South Africa.

Since we last met here certain events have occurred which serve to underline the crucial era we in Southern Africa are passing through. In Zimbabwe we see a development which should have lessons for us in this part of Africa. The development I refer to here is the agreement we are told has been reached between the Zimbabwen factions plus the unacceptability of that agreement to the frontline presidents and the OAU (and also to the world community, which takes its cue in dealing with these issues from the frontline Presidents and the OAU). I think it would be presumptuous of me to sit in judgement of the parties concerned. In short, the settlement reached will not be recognized unless the Patriotic Front is involved. Chances of the Patriotic Front being involved look more remote every day. The Patriotic Front views the settlement as a sell-out. Those involved in the settlement view this attitude as arrogance on the part of the Patriotic Front, and they regard African countries and the international community as presumptuous in supporting the Patriotic Front or in taking the attitude that there can be no settlement without the Patriotic Front.

It was exactly a month after our meeting with the Minister on the 19th of October, that other black organizations, individuals, and certain publications were banned, and some locked in jail under preventive detention. These detained included Dr. Nthato Motlana and his Committee of Ten, and also Mr. Percy Queboza, editor of THE WORLD, which was also banned. I joined many people here and abroad in registering our protest at these drastic measures by the Minister. We felt these steps were completely unwarranted. What is more, some of these people were politically of no consequence, but by this kind of action they were martyred.

Thus Inkatha has that sword of Damocles hanging over its head, if I may summarize the Minister's threats. It is quite extraordinary that although Inkatha has today a membership of about 150,000, the largest black organization of its type ever to be set up in South Africa, we still have Inkatha's enemies who try to denigrate us, particularly in certain circles both abroad and in South Africa. But this is not in the least surprising. To be powerful politically causes enmity. Indeed, if you are strong whether in politics or in any other sphere, you soon have enemies. The enemies of Inkatha cover a most interesting range of people from the right and left. Some are black and some are white. In spite of this, the caravan still moves on. Although the Minister's attitude towards us should have vindicated our stand as a liberation movement, we have detractors who criticize us for not being banned. The strange thing is that the people who talk this kind of language belong to the recently banned black political organizations and their surrogates, both here and abroad. And yet none of us ever attempted to discredit their organizations merely because the main South African black liberation movements, the banned African National Congress and the Pan-Africanist Congress, were banned 18 years ago. These organizations include BPC and SADO. There is nothing Inkatha can do which is right in their eyes. Although through Inkatha we have halted the Pretoria-type of independence for KwaZulu, this is not good enough for them. And yet none of their own leaders attempted to block this type of "independence" in their own areas of origin. I am a black man whose perspectives are black perspectives, and yet I must for the record remark that the most vociferous of these critics in these organizations came from areas where the black man's birthright as a South African has been sold for an empty independence. To draw away attention from the shame of not having succeeded in opposing "homelands independence" they reserve the worst condemnation for us, rather than for the racist regime which keeps all of us oppressed. These people are tools of the enemies of black unity. By reserving all their energies for attacks on us, they help the only people who have a stake in black disunity, the white privileged minority, whose subjects we all are through the power they wield which comes from the barrel of the gun. The Minister of Justice did a grave injustice in banning some of these rootless organizations. By banning them he martyred their leaders, and certain white liberal journalists have attempted to move heaven and earth to portray them as more important than they really are. They had no constituency worth talking about. They had no grass-roots support. Their sole thrust was pretending that they were more patriotic than all other organizations such as the African National Congress and the Pan-Africanist Congress. The recent development where some of them have, after leaving the country, started to align themselves with some of these liberation movements is a new development. They exist in several factions, proving that it is political one-upmanship which makes them all want to be leaders. That is what motivates them. We have in the past bent backwards to have our relations with them patched up for the sake of black unity, all in vain. We are no longer prepared to do so.

That is why this political grouping was behind the shabby attempts to denigrate and kill me at Robert Sobukwe's funeral. They now want to give the impression that they and the Pan-Africanist Congress are one and the same thing. This funeral incident illustrates, more than any other factor, that they are not the same thing as the PAC despite all pretensions at masquerading. The fact

146

that I was invited to attend the late Robert Sobukwe's funeral by PAC, and these groups in turn organized a bunch of political thugs to do what they tried to do to me, illustrates this point. It was a clumsy attempt at highjacking a liberation movement such as the PAC, which has international credibility, by a bunch of political upstarts.

They have a lot of friends who use certain publications to give a false picture, as if these political thugs were representative of the black people of South Africa. Strangely, some are even clerics, who seem laudatory in their praise of what was done to me at Graaff Reinet.

The manner in which most newspapers rejoiced about the Graaff Reinet incident and the extent to which they garbled reports of the incident, to give the world the impression that it was black people of South Africa who did what these political thugs did to me, is an example of what I am talking about. The most startling aspect of this development was statements by people who have been my friends in the white community for so long and yet who unwittingly succumbed to baiting by the press in their attempts at trying to make sensationalism.

The Department of Information had a special issue of THE SOUTH AFRICAN NEWS DIGEST for overseas consumption which, not surprisingly, quoted these friends to show the world my so-called rejection by the blacks of South Africa.

I have come to one conclusion, that most whites seem to resent the growth of any black indigenous political initiative which is selfreliant, such as Inkatha. Most want to control whatever efforts we make as blacks. I do not know what motivates them in wanting to do so. They just do not seem to trust us to be able to do the right thing if we stand on our own as we do in Inkatha.

One of the gruesome things which happened since we last met was the deaths in detention of several people, who included the late Steve Biko.

Another feature which has come to stay in southern African politics is political assasination, in Zimbabwe, Namibia and in South Africa.

The last white election last November indicated that whites in South Africa are not prepared to share power with blacks, that is, at least the majority. It is quite clear to me that they do not mind even if this means the destruction of all we have built up together with them. Earlier I indicated to you that various peoples of South Africa do want to share decision-making. The homelands administrations are not the framework for such meaningful communication between the oppressed and the government. The homelands administrations are bases for local administration, at the very most.

In this respect I would like to welcome the role of the South African Black People's Alliance. I hope you will have made available to you copies of my inauguration address. Both the left and the right within the white community are against us in the Alliance. We have been accused of many things. Whites who have exclusive white rights are now accusing us of being exclusive, whereas this has been their game since 1910. There were scurrilous things which the apartheid mass media wrote about the Alliance, condemning the whole thing as my attempts at establishing a Zulu imperium. Strangely enough the Nationalists, who have fragmented South Africa into mini-states in order to have one giant white colonizer state in order to dominate the black mini-states, should accuse me of imperial designs!

As I have already stated, we as blacks must build up a platform on which we can meet the white rulers of this country and be able to speak to them with one voice. "Time waits for no man," as the saying goes. Let us stop being childish by pretending that all is well in the black community. These bridges that we are building between us as black groups are absolutely essential if we expect whites to take us seriously at the negotiating table. There are many idiots who want people to believe that all is well between black cultural and national groups amongst blacks. We can shout until we are breathless about the fact of our blackness, but black unity will never come by magic, but only through hard work on the ground.

Over many decades we have been divided and we live in different worlds even as blacks. This is not just the fault of the Nationalist Party. All white racist regimes are responsible for this, even those which were in power before 1948. We should be grateful to the Almighty who has given light to our brothers of Asian and coloured extraction at this time, just when they are being lured into the plot of not sharing a common South Africanism with us, on the basis of the so-called three-tier government which Mr. Vorster is offering them. Human beings prefer short cuts, and are often blinded by ephemeral advantages on the basis of not caring for the morrow, because the morrow must care for itself. It therefore says a lot for our brothers of this Alliance for refusing to be blinded by short term advantages, which can so easily result in self-lacerating civil wars between us. I want the government of the Republic to understand that when they approached me, I found it a national duty to respond positively. It should make it easier for them not to approach us as fragments but as one body that should speak for all blacks, or at least for the majority of them. After our rejection of independence, it should be evident that the voters of KwaZulu have indicated very clearly their reluctance to abandon their birthright as South Africans.

We offer a hand of reconciliation to our white countrymen and we want change through non-violence, in spite of the outbreak of violence even right here in our midst. Only meaningful change on fundamentals can ward off its escalation.

We still offer our Ubuntu ideas as the answer to the problem of the wrong evaluation of a person, which is the cause of all our problems.

There is a growing tendency in certain black circles to inculcate the spirit that we as black cultural groups should be ashamed of our different ethnic backgrounds. Acknowledging the fact of our different ethnic backgrounds does not make us less patriotic than those who would like to pretend that such ethnicity as history has created, can be wished away by repetitive: "We are black, we are black!" Of course we are black, but we are also proud of our distinct cultural backgrounds which are a product of traditions accumulated over years of history. There is no doubt about that. The fact that the Nationalist regime uses

148

our ethnicity to divide us, should not make us go to the other extreme, and pretend that there is no Xhosa, Sotho, Venda, Shangaan, Pedi, Tswana or Zulu languages and such cultures. Last year, I made this quite clear — our ethnic backgrounds are not necessarily contrary to the promotion of the larger Bunto-Botho ideal. In fact their cross-pollination makes our black culture rich.

There has been too much caution shown by such bodies as the OAU and the United Nations in dealing with us. I would like to hope that the South African Black Alliance will help to remove some of their problems vis-a-vis how to deal with the internal forces for change. It is essential for the Security Council of the United Nations to convene at some point a southern African treaty conference to enable us to work out a formula for peaceful co-existence. If white South Africa refused to participate we would all feel that they had by so doing endorsed only violence as the only method to bring about change.

Economic sanctions will pale into insignificance if compared with the extent to which we can hurt each other here as different population groups, once we are all convinced that peaceful change cannot take place. Our numbers as blacks are our biggest asset, which if used on the basis of white dependence on black labour will destroy overnight the economy of South Africa. We should be quite frank and make it clear that it is not as if we are unaware of the options which are open to us. We will all suffer if such strategies ultimately remain the only alternatives for those of us who are oppressed and who live within South Africa. One can only hope that common sense will prevail before we are forced to consider such alternatives. Such a UN-sponsored Conference as I am proposing should be the last offer by the international community to South Africa.

In all these strategies we need some disciplined machine to order to carry out these initiatives. That is why Inkatha is such an important factor in all this. Inkatha has continued to grow phenomenally; that is why it is hated and feared by all enemies of black liberation within the white minority power elite. Today we have membership of more than 150,000. Inkatha has just recently demonstrated its strength at the recent KwaZulu elections. That is why, as I indicated the other day, the SABC tried to move heaven and earth to distort facts about our effectiveness. Their role (that is the SABC) was so blatantly anti-Inkatha that the cabinet seriously considered asking them to leave Ondini. There was a highpowered delegation which was sent by the SABC to discuss the problem with the cabinet. It was a frank discussion. From what their representative has done after that meeting, it is quite clear that far from disappearing, their animosity towards Inkatha is growing, and that we can accept it as permanent.

The government can never take seriously our demands for a constitutional conference as long as we as blacks are in disarray. What is more, it is always easier to deal with an undisciplined rabble than it is to deal with a disciplined organization. Inkatha is hated today because people realize that our strength lies in our being a disciplined organization with a recognizable following.

The Financial and Economic Aspects of Our Policy:

After the events of the past year there have even been more pressures on multi-national corporations to disinvest from South Africa. I know what this Assembly decided on this issue last year. I think that the matter is of so much importance today that I think the mind of this Assembly must be known as of now. I have been involved in these arguments for and against disinvestment. I will not go into details. The only fly in the ointment has been the advertisement by the Department of Information which has been used in Canada, the United States, France, Germany and Britian, without my permission, to support investments. You will recall that I raised this matter in this house when I expressed my vote of thanks to the Minister of Plural Relations and Development and of Information, Dr. C.P. Mulder. His department hates me as I indicated on that day. Their use of my name in this manner has not been without malice. All the apartheid mass media at their command are used overseas to project a negative picture about me. After the Graaff Reinet incident the following are samples of the apartheid-supporting newspapers, which the Department of Information republished for overseas consumption. Even before republishing the editorials for the apartheid mass media their very headlines are an indication and extent of their being jaundiced against me:

Screaming Mob Ejects Zulu Leader

That was one of the most misleading headlines. Then they go on in reporting the Graaff Reinet incident:

> Three people were shot, several were injured by stones and part of a 5,000 strong crowd of mourners forced KwaZulu's Chief Gatsha Buthelezi and his bodyguard from the stadium at Graaff Reinet at the weekend during the funeral of Mr. Robert Sobukwe, founder president of the Pan-Africanist Congress.

They went on to use all the cartoons from the apartheid press which ridiculed me for the humiliation I suffered at the funeral, such as from DIE VADERLAND (in the cartoon I am depicted seated with the Minister of Justice, the Hon. J. Kruger — with injuries on my head (which they would have loved to see) and with Mr. Kruger saying to me: "Never mind Gatsha — they like me even less." In addition you have these three gloating editorials reproduced by the Department of Information for overseas consumption.

In the Newspaper *Die Transvaler* an article entitled "Lesson For Buthelezi" states:

> The treatment meted out to Chief Minister Gatsha Buthelezi, and Mr. Sonny Leon and the Rev. Alan Hendrickse of the Coloured Representative Council, at the Sobukwe funeral reflects extensively the

thorny political situation in the country.

The black radicals regard Chief Minister Buthelezi and Mssrs. Leon and Hendrickse as puppets, despite their vehement criticism of the government and their leftism.

These radicals are not interested in the multinational nature of the country and are determined only to gain power — much after the pattern of the Patriotic Front and Mr. Sam Mujoma's SWAPO.

It is to be hoped that the eyes of Chief Minister Buthelezi and the coloured leaders will be opened in this regard. They must realize that the choice lies between a radical black power takeover, or the creation of a meaningful governmental structure which in the widest possible measure will provide for self-determination by the various nations and population groups, with as much liaison as possible on community matters

Rather than move along a road of confrontation with the government which, as has now been shown, will only earn them and white liberalists derision and contempt from the radical side — they could profitably play a positive role in the extension of a governmental structure which provides for the various population groups.

In the newspaper THE CITIZEN an article entitled "Lesson For Chief Buthelezi" states:

Chief Gatsha Buthelezi rather fancies himself as the leader of all the blacks — and as the first black Prime Minister of Azania should South Africa ever fall into black hands and be re-named.

But he learnt the lesson of Africa at the funeral of Robert Sobukwe on Saturday.

It is that blacks are not beautiful in the eyes of other blacks simply because they are black.

That black does not mean that all blacks have the same allegiance or the same philosophies or the same aims.

That tribal and other differences cause more divisions among blacks than language, culture and political arguments do among whites.

That there is no black nation as such.

QED: There is no good in pretending there is one.

It is a lesson that Jimmy Carter, Andy Young and other Western would-be-do-gooders should also learn.

As they see it, the battle in southern Africa is between the whites and the blacks.

The whites are all against the blacks; the blacks are all against the whites.

Which is nonsense.

What makes the whole thing more fallacious — and dangerous — is that the Western ignoramuses lump all the blacks together — Zulus, Tswanas, Xhosas and the others — as one nation.

They are not.

And the sooner the West understands this the better for all concerned.

Chief Buthelelezi, we may add, is not a Mangope or a Sebe, nor will these and other black homeland leaders accept this dominance over them.

Nor will blacks forget their tribal and other allegiances, as the faction fighting on the mines and the tribal murders in towns have shown.

As for a Zulu dictatorship over South Africa, it would be no more acceptable to the rest of the blacks than it would be to the whites.

Chief Buthelezi is leader of Inkatha, which claims to be a Zulu cultural movement and is trying to spread its influence among non-Zulus, but he is not a leader of the ANC, or the PAC, or the Black People's Convention or the Black Consciousness movement, or Black Power, or a member of the Communist Party.

He may make angry noises about Pretoria, and he may be the most difficult of the homeland leaders, but he is not acceptable to the black radicals, the militants and the underground.

If and when the men with the guns attack South Africa, Chief Buthelezi will be as much a potential victim as anyone else.

That is the tragedy of Africa.

Some black leaders who can play a part in achieving a just and peaceful settlement of their country's problems seldom realize — until it is too late — that they are not radical enough for the radicals and not moderate enough to influence the rulers.

Gatsha Buthelezi is one of these unfortunates.

His ejection from the Sobukwe funeral, together with Mr. Sonny Leon, the coloured leader, shows that neither is accepted by the black militants, nor is their new Inkatha Alliance.

Mr. Alan Paton, former leader of the defunct Liberal Party, is correct when he says that the demonstration at the Sobukwe funeral is an important political event which can mean the end of Chief Buthelezi's aspirations as the leader of the new political grouping, and that it puts the whole future of the Inkatha movement in question.

Mrs. Helen Suzman is also right when she says that the incident clearly shows that young black militants are in direct conflict with the homeland leaders.

It may be too early to expect Chief Buthelezi to read the writing on the wall, but if he values his future as a leader he should come down on the side of moderation and co-operation and leave the militants to their lost cause.

In the newspaper OGGENDBLAD an article entitled "Big Gap" states:

There are surely not many whites who felt much sympathy for Chief Gatsha Buthelezi this weekend. He was threatened and driven away by his own people at the funeral of a recognised black nationalist leader.

But the incident cannot, however, merely be brushed aside with a little malicious joy.

The events indicate a wide gap between white and radical black views on the same matter.

For the whites, Mr. Buthelezi is someone who does still work within the established order, but only just. In fact, he is the black leader whose statements most easily annoy the whites.

Or course, it is partly because the black people who side militantly against the present order, are either abroad or not well-known personalities.

But Chief Buthelezi is regularly quoted whenever he thunders about something that he regards as unjust.

For the black radicals, however, he remains a man who works within the system and who can therefore not be identified with what they regard as their just struggle.

For this reason the white malicious joy and the radical stone-throwing.

It should be obvious, however, that if the politics of people like Chief Buthelezi attract such a varied reaction, then the gulf between the two points of view is big.

They also reproduced another cartoon from BEELD with the picture of me, Mrs. Suzman, and Mr. Leon with the banner carried by the Graaff Reinet thugs with the slogan: "Radical blacks only." Then the CURRENT AFFAIRS entitled "Graaff Reinet, New Brighton and Mongolia" also printed in full. I will not waste the time of the house by reading out the CURRENT AFFAIRS commentary to you. You know that sickening voice and the drivel it parrots. It is not my intention to make you nauseous.

I have in the past quoted instances in this house of the Department of Information's vilification campaign against me. I find it rather extraordinary that such people can then use my utterances out of context to prop up their apartheid policies. I do not support investment so that apartheid lasts long, as they do. My motives are just the opposite, as I stated the other day in this Assembly. My people have a long liberation struggle ahead of them and they must survive in order to triumph.

There was also an attack on me, during a BBC interview by Mr. Donald Woods, the former editor of the East London newspaper, THE DAILY DISPATCH, in which he stated in support of disinvestment that what I stated in favour of investment was not important as I am not representative of black people of South Africa. I defended myself from this attack, which had such a biting sting that he even claimed when I asked the audience at Jabulani Amphitheatre on the 29 January 1978 to stand, to honour the memory of Steve Biko, that I did so to exploit Biko's name. It is for this house to judge who exploits Biko's name, me or Donald Woods.

I just want members of this house to appreciate the number of storms that have broken over my head because of my support for investments. Also how the apartheid mass media have blunted the effect of my statements for investments by misusing them to support the status quo, which I reject.

Transkeian Claims on Zulu Territory

I was one of the leaders who were instrumental in the holding of the Umtata Conference in 1973. To me there have never been any doubts that the strength of blacks lies in their unity. This has been my gospel throughout my political career. Even at that time, there were rumours that the Transkei had decided to go for the Pretoria-type of independence. We all asked Paramount-Chief Matanzima, Chief Minister of the Transkei about those rumours, and he denied them outright. But in a couple of months time, we read of conferences the Transkei was already having with the Prime Minister the Hon. B.J. Vorster. There were joint communiques issued by the two parties concerned in the press, which left us in no doubt about the fact that the Chief Minister of the Transkei was not telling us the truth when he said that it was not true that he was already negotiating independence with Pretoria. We had a meeting of all the leaders at the Holiday Inn later and put the matter again to the Chief Minister of the Transkei. This time he told us that it was his people through their ruling party at their annual conference who wanted it. We were amazed, but could do no more at that point. We still continued to have meetings with the Chief Minister of the Transkei up to the 22nd of January 1975, and the Prime Minister, Mr. Vorster.

When we called another meeting in August 1976, the Transkei, then on the verge of independence, declined to be represented. We knew this. But we had called the meeting in order to discuss the violence which had erupted in South Africa from June 16, 1976. That was the last I ever saw, or had anything to do with, the Chief Minister of the Transkei.

I later received an invitation to attend the independence celebrations in October 1976. I declined not because I intended any slight on my brother, Paramount-Chief the Hon. K.D. Matanzima. Far from it, but I could not participate in an occasion which marked the first African connivance in an exercise which stripped them of their birthright as South Africans, by fellow countrymen who are descendants of foreign settlers to South Africa. I therefore declined to attend. To me it was a day for weeping and not for rejoicing, because it meant that millions of our people were going to be aliens in their own fatherland.

On the 7th of May 1976 the then Chief Minister of the Transkei had attacked me in the Assembly at Umtata. The Chief Minister described my joint statement with Dr. Beyers Naude as "verging on incitement to revolution and sedition". He described me and Dr. Naude as "a certain homeland leader and a politically active cleric". He stated that our statement constituted an attack on his policy and government. He called it "an immoderate left-wing manifesto ranging on incitement to revolution and sedition".

This was an unwarranted attack on me and on my integrity. The whole Nationalist Party establishment was tickled pink by these scurrilous attacks on me and Dr. Naude, which the Chief Minister of the Transkei levelled at us for the sole entertainment of his Nationalist Party friends, who also comprise the Pretoria regime. I had not attacked him, nor the Transkei government, nor his policy. I tried to keep a cool head even then. I did not want to descend to my black brother's level. I did not want like him to sling mud at an African brother for the sake of white entertainment. This unwarranted attack on me influenced me in making up my mind not to go to the Transkei for the independence celebrations. I felt that if I was that kind of seditions character and revolutionary, that I had no right to vitiate the celebrations with my presence. If I was seen as a revolutionary by him no one could know what my fate could be in the Transkei, particularly with Proclamation R400 still unrepealed.

All this has not changed the love and feelings of brotherhood I have for the Prime Minister of the Transkei. The Tembus originated here in Natal. He is also my Nguni brother and above all he is my black brother. Although he obviously despised me as a revolutionary, seditious character, I have never spoken about him in private or in public with the contempt with which he spoke about me. No black man is my enemy. We face one common enemy as blacks.

We have seen the drama that is unfolding before our eyes in which the Prime Minister of the Transkei, Paramount Chief K.D. Matanzima, and the Prime Minister of South Africa, Mr. B.J. Vorster, are the main actors. One can hardly believe what one reads in the newspapers. I have never called my brother Paramount-Chief Matanzima a liar, but this is what his benefactor and friend Mr. Vorster has now told the world and all of us that he is.

When the boundaries were drawn in Africa by imperial edict, no black man was consulted. That is why ethnic groups throughout Africa were cut into two by these arbitrary boundaries of the colonialists which run throughout the continent. We were even more surprised when Mr. Vorster determined boundaries between our territory in KwaZulu, and the Transkei and he never bothered even to consult us. It made us even more skeptical about his sincerity as far as ethnicity as the basis on which he determines his policies. We have a very serious problem at Umzimkhulu. The people of Umzimkulu are not Xhosas. The Chief of these people lives here in KwaZulu, and never was the subject of anyone in the Transkei. A lot of Umzimkulu people have KwaZulu citizenship certificates, and are members of Inkatha. I have had petitions and delegations from the Umzimkulu people who hate being forced to be Transkeians. It must be pointed out that there was no Transkei country before the whites conquered blacks. The Umzimkulu people owe allegiance to the King of the Zulus, and this has been the case for generations. I have attempted to play this whole thing low-key, for I know that nothing pleases whites in general more than black-on-black confrontations. I have referred this matter to the Commissioner-General more than once. Pretoria's response has been that this is Transkeian territory. No attempt has been made to investigate the representations of our people in Umzimkulu as this dispute can so easily result in unnecessary bloodshed between brothers, something that should be avoided at all costs. The Shakan territory extended right on to Umzimvubu River. We have not made a row about this since we know that if this dispute heats up between us and the Transkei, it would divert our attention from our liberation struggle to futile fratricidal self-destructive civil wars. This we will avoid at all costs. If any bloodshed ever results, it will be the responsibility of Pretoria, which has ignored the interests of our people in this matter.

Now, as if this were not bad enough, we have been told by Mr. Vorster that the Prime Minister of the Transkei is so fractious about East Griqualand because he believes that once this territory becomes part of Natal, it will be handed over to me. The Prime Minister of the Transkei knows more than anyone how hated I am in Nationalist circles, and how unlikely it is that Pretoria can ever hand over territory to me when right here in KwaZulu no part of Shaka's country now in white hands has ever been given back to us. There was a time when East Griqualand was Shaka's by conquest, as he cleared it of its population. That is a fact of history. We have, nevertheless, not used that to claim all the territory which belonged to King Shaka, some of which even now is given to the Transkei by Pretoria. We know that this policy is pursued by Pretoria to create enmity and internicine wars between blacks. Blacks must annihilate each other and prove that Africans cannot live in peace. We will not be baited into such a shameful orgy of internicine strife either by Pretoria or Umtata.

We will not deceive Pretoria, as others have done, that apartheid is good for us because through it Pretoria can cede us land that never belonged to us. We claim every part of South Africa as our joint possession with all other South Africans. We do desperately need land here in KwaZulu more than the Transkei, not just for the sake of establishing an empire but because our people are being expelled from white farms every day and they have nowhere to go. Our representations for our people fall on deaf ears because we fail to tell Pretoria the lie that we love apartheid. Pretoria seems to want to hear such lies from those who are capable of bluffing them. We do not believe in bluffs. They know that no self-respecting black man can really accept being made a foreigner in his fatherland. But those who have lied to Pretoria, and claimed that blacks love apartheid, have been Pretoria's curly-headed boys all the time. We prefer to be persona non grata than to tell lies and say our people love separate development. We do not gloat over the disillusionment Pretoria must have experienced in the past few days. We sympathize with them for their habit of liking only those who bluff them.

As if this is not enough, the Transkei's appetite for land that belongs to others has been whetted by some of our territory that Pretoria has dished out to them. The Prime Minister tells us now that the Prime Minister of the Transkei wants also some of our territory in Port Shepstone, Harding and Port Alfred. I just do not understand why our brother wants to use our land to extend his empire.

Why must he expect Pretoria to rob Peter to pay Paul? We will not allow one inch more of Zulu territory to be annexed to the Transkei as a price for restoring the cordial relations the Transkei has always had with Pretoria.

The letter I have recently received from the Transkeian Minister of Foreign Affairs speaks volumes for us. Here it is:

1978 POLICY SPEECH

MINISTRY OF FOREIGN AFFAIRS   FAM/A/1/1

Republic of Transkei
Umtata
Southern Africa

28 February 1978

The Hon. Dr. M.G. Buthelezi
Department of the Chief Minister and Finance
Private Bag X01
Ulundi
3838

Dear Sir:

At a recent Cabinet Meeting the appointment of Zulu Citizens to important posts in the Transkei Government Service was considered. During discussions, the remark was made that you do not ill-treat or in any way discriminate against Transkeians who live or work in your areas of jurisdiction. This remark was backed by a report which had emanated from our Consul in Durban.

Upon the motion of the Honourable the Prime Minister of Transkei, I was asked by the Cabinet to convey to you and your Cabinet the appreciation of the Transkei Cabinet for this brotherly attitude, which Transkei will always reciprocate.

Yours sincerely,

D.S. Koyana
Minister of Foreign Affairs & Information

We have never found it in our interest to make our people from the Transkei pay the price for the grandiose scheme of apartheid. This has been a political risk all the time but we believe in doing what is right in the eyes of God, and our consciences. So we have never insisted that Transkeians who are here should be discriminated against because of our belief in one South Africa. But I want my brothers and sisters from the Transkei to know today that although that is my attitude, we have constantly been under great pressure from some of our people here who want us to play Pretoria's divisive game. That was the object of apartheid in the first place and we have a duty not to fall for it.

We would like the international community to know that if there is any bloodshed as a result of this juggling around with land to placate the Transkei at the expense of their brothers in KwaZulu, the blood of such people will be upon the heads of the Pretoria regime. We are not armed for our people on the border of the Transkei who may be victims of the Transkeian megalomania. What has happened is our strongest indictment against Pretoria's balkanization of South Africa. We are in a difficult position because our people do not want to be part of the South African Defense Force and be seen to be prepared to die in defense of the apartheid society of South Africa.

Unless whites accept that the solution to South Africa's problems is through power-sharing in one legislative body, it is clear that we can expect the present policies to involve blacks in bitter self-lacerating civil wars. We in KwaZulu have indicated that we will not be satisfied with Pretoria's attempts to toss crumbs on to us. We want to share power with all other South Africans through the central parliamentary decision-making process. We would like to share the wealth of the country with all other South Africans.

Chapter 14

A BLACK HAND OF FRIENDSHIP

MESSAGE TO HONOURABLE C. MULDER

Ondini, 19 April 1978

Mr. Speaker Sir, Honourable Minister, in terms of the rules of this house it now falls on my shoulders to stand up before you to express the thanks of this Assembly to the Honourable Minister of Plural Relations and Development and of Information.

My first duty is to thank the Minister for coming here in spite of his heavy schedule to open this Assembly which to us is important, as it occurs after our first KwaZulu election. We appreciate that the demands of the Minister's office must make it very difficult to cope with the demands made on him.

This is not the first time that the Minister comes to KwaZulu to open our session. Our 1976 session was opened by the Minister, even before he held his present portfolio. We would like to flatter ourselves into believing that even then the Minister must have already had a special place for us in his heart.

The coming of a senior Minister to open our session is an event of great significance to us. When the Minister came to open our session last time I referred to him as the Crown Prince of South African white politics. We Zulus are a people who once wielded power in this part of the continent. It must be clear therefore that we appreciate the reality of political power and, however much as we may disagree with those who now wield political power in our country, we have to acknowledge the reality of that power.

Another significance is the stature the Minister has in the South African Parliament, and in the Nationalist Party hierarchy when coming here to open our Assembly. We realize that even when we talk within the limitations of a vote of thanks, whatever we state will go to circles that matter within the political power structure of those who govern all of us, both at government level and also at party level.

I am grateful that the Minister took the trouble to make it possible for us to meet privately and informally shortly after his assumption of the portfolio of Plural Relations and Development. I was favourably impressed with the

Minister's open approach. This open approach to our problems, which has come out in the Minister's speeches, has created an air of expectancy and new hopes. As I stated when I met the Minister on the 8th of February in Capetown, the humility with which the Minister approached issues I found to be most refreshing. The sound of the Minister's approach sounds good in our ears. I have, however, very grave concern, if these sounds do not measure up to what we see when it comes to performance. The Minister was this month quoted as saying:

> My main task is to get rid of my job and hand over to the people — not to build, but to break down an empire. As a white African, I demand my right to be accepted. I am not prepared to sacrifice my identity or right, just as you have the same claim to your identity.

This admission that your people the Afrikaners, as former victims of imperialism, have in turn colonized us blacks, is the kind of humility which I have referred to as a new feature in the new Ministerial utterances. Its frankness cannot be denied. We appreciate the fears the Minister's people have about losing their identity, although we have no such fears as far as our own identity is concerned.

I am, however, anxious that we should risk giving our people false hopes, because if it turns out that the Minister speaks of these changes within status quo politics, our people will turn against us. We will be accused of allowing ourselves through our plaudits for the Minister's words, to have allowed ourselves not only to be led down a primrose path, but also of having carried our people with us along that primrose path. When I last spoke to the Prime Minister in October 1976, I made it quite clear that:

> Let us now call a halt to such talk as there has been about the National Party's policy of self-determination within the framework laid down by the whites. Our people have not and never will desire self-determination within the framework laid down by whites, as the Afrikaners in particular never did during their own struggle.

We were just as heartened after the results of our elections were announced, to see the Minister quoted as saying that the Pretoria-type independence cannot be forced on us after our unequivocal rejection of it. The Minister was quoted saying that other alternatives will have to be looked at. This also pleased us. But in expressing my own pleasure to those who have jubilantly pointed to what appears to them to be a very healthy attitude of the Minister, I have been cautious. It has not been clear whether the Minister envisages such alternatives outside or within the framework of apartheid. If the changes we have heard so much about are envisaged within that framework, then I can only cry for this country and all our peoples. For that framework will never be acceptable to the majority of black people in South Africa. The Minister has said many hopeful things within the short time after his assumption of office. The Minister has been quoted saying that he believes in negotiation rather than in confrontation. We here in KwaZulu have bourne the brunt of all the denigration

160

that has emanated here and abroad from different quarters because of our policy of non-violence. We can only hope that the Minister envisages white South Africa turning a new leaf altogether when he talks of negotiation. Such meaningful political horse-trading can only take place between equals around a table at a national convention. Any other kind of negotiation outside those parameters would not be different from the negotiation that one would expect between a lion and a lamb. I remember as a child reading a story which illustrates this. The lion was drinking water at the river, and lower down the lamb was also having a drink. The lion, however, accused the lamb of dirtying the water although the lamb was down the river. I remember another story where the lion was resting in its den. The lion made professions of friendship to the lamb and asked the lamb to join him in his den. The lamb declined the invitation stating that he had observed that of all the animal footmarks on the ground none showed that animals that had gone into the den had returned. That is the kind of negotiation which I dread and which can get us nowhere.

There was a point I mentioned when I first met the Minister. This was the expression of the concern I have concerning his holding of the portfolio of Information. In a matter of weeks things have happened which have given validity to my concern. I refer here to the use of my photograph and an out-of-context part of my speech in Soweto on the 29th of January by the Department of Information. I do not want to bore the Minister and those present with the chequered relations I have had with that department throughout my political career.

This confirms just the kind of fears which prompted me to express that concern about this wearing by the Minister of the hat of the Department of Plural Relations and Development with the hat of the Department of Information. These things may be regarded by the Minister and the government as minor, but to me they are evidence of enmity, which makes it impossible for me to view with great belief whatever the Minister states he wants to introduce by way of change. The Department of Information's actions have the effect of undoing what the Minister seeks to achieve for South Africa through the Department of Plural Relations and Administration and Development.

It is true that this Assembly and the general conference of Inkatha have expressed themselves as all in favour of investments at the moment. It is also true that on the 29th of January, my audience of several thousands expressed themselves as in favour of investments at present. I discussed the pros and cons of disinvestment and the people expressed their point of view. To lift out some things I said then, and use that in the manner the Department of Information has used it, is grossly misleading. It is misleading because the support for investment expressed at the meeting, has nothing to do with the propping up of apartheid. It has nothing to do with the acceptance of the status quo. We believe that the Afrikaners are where they are today because they survived their own oppression. We believe that our people need to survive in their present struggle in order to carry on successfully their own struggle for self-fulfillment. I take strong exception that my photograph and part of my speech should have been used in the same context with one whose ideas and mine on apartheid and on the "homelands" so-called "independence", are as different as chalk and cheese. I viewed with disquiet the Minister's reply to Mr. Ray Swart's question in Parliament on whether my permission was obtained before this was done. According to a news item in the newspapers the Minister was reported to have said it was not customary to obtain a well-known personality's consent to quote from public speeches he had made.

How can this kind of handling of such sensitive issues create good relations between me and the Republican government? I feel insulted to be treated in this fashion, and in being used in such a way by the Department of Information, as if I support apartheid, which some of the people who appear in the advertisement support. I can only draw the conclusion that this was a deliberate and calculated attempt on the part of the Department of Information to damage my image as an opponent of apartheid in Canada, West Germany, the United Kingdom, the United States and France, where these advertisements appeared, by lending false authenticity to such expletives as "government stooge", which my opponents here and abroad have flung at me without any justification whatsoever. This amounts to undoing the work I have done for several years on the international plane. That to me, Mr. Minister, seems to be what the Department of Information wanted to accomplish with this fraudulant use of my photograph and utterance.

On the credit side, I want it to go on record that we are grateful for some of your senior officials, who have made it possible for our administration to function smoothly. I do not want to imply that there are no junior white officials who deserve as much credit as those officials in the higher echelons. They do exist. But I want it to go on record that a large number of the junior officials do not identify with us, and they have no empathy for us. I will quote a simple example, that some of these junior officials will not even exchange greetings with us when we meet. Today we have seen the financial problems we face. It is sometimes some of these junior officials at district level who contribute quite a lot to our financial woes because they do not care. There have been reports where, for example, building materials such as cement have been taken and used privately. I hope those officials who, as I say, do exist and do not do these things will forgive me. I do not imply that there are no similar wrong doers amongst blacks. There are scores of them as well. But the examples they get from their white seniors do compound our problems.

In January 1975, when we met the Honourable Prime Minister, he told us to work on our own people in the lower echelons of our society in order to build up good relations between the races. He, in turn, undertook that the government and himself would do the same within the white community. Do forgive me for going to such lengths, on what may be regarded by many as petty matters.

Again, Honourable Minister, our thanks for all the trouble you took to come to KwaZulu. We pray that the Almighty be with you as you return to Capetown. We realize that many people do not want to come to KwaZulu because we in KwaZulu believe that it is by speaking frankly to each other, as fellow countrymen and as fellow Christians, that this country may yet be saved from a conflagration. We do not want to see such a conflagration for if it ever occurs, its flames will consume all of us.

Jabulani Amphitheater, January 1978

164

Chapter 15

LIVING FROM CRISIS TO CRISIS

A MESSAGE OF BLACK SURVIVAL

Soweto, 29 January 1978

Hail to you, sons and daughters of Mother Africa! Greetings to you, rightful inheritors of this part of Mother Africa! I salute you, sons and daughters of Africa's warriors! I pay homage to you, descendents of Hintsa, Faku, Sekhukhuni, Moshoeshe the Great, Khama the Great, Soshangane the Warrior, Mzilikazi the Warrior, Somhlolo the Peace-Maker and of Shaka the great.

God in His wisdom placed us on this part of Africa and we owe it to the Creator Himself as well as to our great ascendants, some of whose names I have just mentioned, to struggle until this part of Africa is liberated.

We owe it to the founding fathers of the African National Congress, now banned, and their successors, some deceased, some exiled, and some incarcerated, to uphold the tradition of this titanic struggle for liberation.

I thank the Almighty for His mercy and the spirits of Africa's great sons and daughters, who have allowed me to be here amongst you today. Although the going is heavy and our losses heavy, I greet you in the name of freedom.

We last had this kind of get-together on the 14th of March 1976, when I issued a message to white South Africa from black South Africa, in what I then described as "this approaching hour of crisis," at this very Amphitheatre. I shudder now, as I shuddered then, and that warning was proved to have been very prophetic. On the 16th of June 1976, less than three months after my visit to Soweto, bullets and stones were exchanged in that first outbreak of violence which I had so desperately warned Mr. Vorster would occur unless blacks share power in South Africa. The hour of crisis came, and it came when we were all unprepared despite the fact that it was a logical sequence of events.

In true African tradition, my first duty today is to express my deepest sympathies to our black community in Soweto for so many human lives we lost in the crisis situation generated since that historic day of June 16, 1976. I have entitled my discourse with you today as "Living From Crisis to Crisis," and I have sub-titled it as "A Message of Black Survival throughout the Long Struggle for the Liberation of South Africa". We have lived from one crisis to another, ever since we came face-to-face with more than 152 years of white domination in South African and now 68 years of downright oppression by one white racist regime after another, up to the present apartheid regime. We have lost some of the very blossoming flowers of the black community in the current crisis, as well as adult sons and daughters of Africa, most of whom were victims of the riot squad police of the Minister of Police Prisons and Justice. We mourn their deaths. Their deaths are a challenge to each and every one of us, and none of us can sleep peacefully at night, for their sacrifice haunts all of us who have so far survived the current crisis. Their demise must nag at us every hour and at every moment of our lives, for we dare not rest until we can, through our own contributions, prove that their deaths were not in vain. I want to repeat whilst I am in the midst of our community in Soweto my deepest condolences to every family and to everyone who has had his next-of-kin pay this supreme sacrifice on behalf of all black people who are comitted to the liberation struggle which has been continally waged in various ways in South Africa in the past, and is being waged now and will be waged in the future, until we are all liberated.

As Lord Acton rightly said, power tends to corrupt, and absolute power corrupts absolutely. We have seen the callous manner in which blacks have been treated in the current crisis. Let us not lose heart as a result of the setbacks this entails for our struggle. Let us remember that this soil, recently drenched with the precious and innocent blood of the sons and daughters of Africa, has been drenched before during the 300 year white presence in our land. We live from crisis to crisis, and it should therefore be clear to all of us that more precious blood and more innocent blood will yet be shed in our efforts that will continue to be made to recover for us our rightful place, which the monster Oppression has consistently denied to us in the land of our forefathers.

There have been tough lessons we have learnt from all this. One thing that has come out very clearly is the determination of white South Africa not to get their jackboot off our necks. We have learned in the past two years the extremes to which the oppressors will go in order to entrench white domination. Let me remind you that the Prime Minister treated the Soweto tragedy like a non-event by maintaining a stony silence. At the end of his long and ominous silence he reacted to the whole tragedy by saying that: "law and order shall be maintained at all costs." This reminds me of what Herbert Marcuse, the political analyst, has to say in his essay on liberation, on this specific issue of "law and order." He states:

LIVING FROM CRISIS TO CRISIS

Law and Order: those words have always had an ominous sound; the entire necessity and the entire horror of legitimate force are condensed and sanctioned in this phrase. There can be no human association without law and order, enforceable law and order, but there are degrees of good and evil in human associations — measured in terms of the legitimate, organized violence required to protect the established society against the poor, the oppressed, the insane; the victims of its well-being.

Thus, in ordering of society in this land, no black has any voice. So that what is law and order is nothing more than a moat around besieged white self-interest. Stripped of its trappings this is nothing more nor less than a pretext by an oppressive regime to maintain the status quo. It means an excuse for unleashing violence against the powerless, ostensibly to maintain law and order. We, however, know that this is nothing more nor less than an excuse to open the doors of the arsenals at their command in order to perpetuate white privilege.

We had hard and callous demonstrations of what white power means in its naked ruthlessness. Although we have suffered these setbacks, we must remain undaunted in our determination to be free. We should not be foolhardy. But we should not allow ourselves, the majority of the population of South Africa, to be browbeaten by the ruthless minority just because they have arsenals.

When I last spoke from this podium, I warned those amongst us who thrive on thumbing the drums of division amongst us, against this habit. These people fall in various categories. Some do this on the basis of ideology, and some do this on the basis of ethnicity, and some of the basis of dividing us into rural or urban entities. The whole white establishment has their share as well in the thumping of these drums of division and tension amongst us. Both the white left wing and the white right wing have a stake in the fragmentation of black forces for liberation. This was well demonstrated during the current crisis. It was with a bleeding heart that I had to come up to Soweto in August 1976 as a result of a black-black confrontation at Mzimhlophe. There was a lot of drum-beating in an attempt to exacerbate the ugly situation that had arisen. There was a lot of negative, unconstructive talk and writings about contract workers from rural areas sabotaging the black resistance by urban blacks. This was done by people in the white establishment who normally want to be seen espousing our black cause. On the other hand, the white right-wing, led by certain members of the police force, bandied about ethnicity to justify the ugly situation that had then arisen here in Soweto. It had nothing to do with either of those two theories. The truth of the matter was that both the white left and the white right were quite wrong and each faction deliberately misassessed the position for their own ends. I am grateful to my black brothers and sisters who heeded my plea and laid down the lethal instruments that were used by those who participated in that tragic black vs.

black clash. In that instance our brothers became the unwitting tools of the oppressors. They enabled the powers-that-be to tell the world that the occupation of Soweto by the riot squad police, with all the countless things that were perpetuated against the black community in the name of law and order, was justified on the basis of what blacks were doing to other blacks.

This again can never be forgotten by any one of us. But we have lessons we can learn from it concerning the dangers entailed in beating the drums of division within our black community. We just cannot afford this. My brothers, my sisters, let us understand this very clearly. Without unity we can forget about ever being able to destroy the white oppression of blacks in South Africa. Without black solidarity we can forget any possibilities of enjoying freedom in our lifetime.

Let us understand one thing and that is that white oppression is operated on the basis of white intimidation of blacks. The worst thing we can do to retard the struggle is for us as blacks to indulge in acts of intimidation against other blacks. I do not for one moment deprecate debates about the methods which should be employed in order to liberate ourselves. One of the worst features of this phenomenon is our use of white mass media to denigrate each other. None of us here can deny that the majority of blacks in South Africa hate and reject the apartheid society which Mr. Vorster offers blacks on the basis of the balkanized, so-called independence. Most blacks are united in their rejection and opposition to apartheid and its consequences for ourselves and our future generations. Mr. Vorster seems to offer us nothing more than the very future which he himself described as "too ghastly to contemplate".

The big lesson we must learn here is that while we must avoid by all means falling into the trap of condemning all whites on the basis of a reversed racism, we must accept that our struggle for liberation is a black struggle, to be waged by the oppressed people themselves. Without developing political self-reliance we can abandon any hopes of this struggle's ever getting off the ground. As we move from one political crisis to another, let us remember that our only key to liberation is our black solidarity.

We can not refuse anyone who gives us a hand in this struggle provided we are certain of their sincerity. But let us understand this one thing. We must realize that we are capable of liberating ourselves. No one will do this for us. There tend to be too many expectations on the part of many of us that some one from somewhere will liberate us. In this connection I wish to quote to you the words of a well-known world statesman:

> The future of the Republic of South Africa will be decided by the social and political forces in that country. This can be influenced by outside pressure, but the main thing cannot be done from abroad.

LIVING FROM CRISIS TO CRISIS

These are the words of the Former German Chancellor and Nobel Peace Prize-winner Mr. Willy Brandt, which he uttered at a news conference at the end of his 10 day visit to Zambia on the 6th of January.

Last February, I was in Dar-Es-Salaam. I had a two-and-half hour discussion with His Excellency, the President of Tanzania, Dr. Julius Nyerere. An interview he gave just about that time sums up more or less what he said to me during the discussions we had on this very issue. Lee Griggs of TIME MAGAZINE posed the following question to President Nyerere:

> Do you see any possibility that you or the other frontline presidents might have to commit your own military forces to the armed struggle? And do you see a possibility that your own Tanzanian forces may be undertaking a combat role against security forces on the Rhodesian side — inside Rhodesia — do you see this? I mean as a possibility at some point if it is necessary if that is the only way to get rid of Smith?

President Nyerere responded:

> We have some experience of real fighting and we have some philosophy of the liberation. Both our experience and philosophy of liberation which we follow are against committing our troops in the liberation struggle. In the case of Mozambique, we gave them help but they did the fighting. We did not fight. We accepted certain risks. The Portugese used to cross the border. We had the camps here. We received the arms from the countries which were supplying us with arms and we passed these to the freedom fighters. This was done in the case of Mozambique and this is what was done in the case of Angola. That is our experience. But this experience is based on the philosophy that a people free themselves. You don't free them. They have to free themselves.
>
> It is no use our going into Rhodesia and fight. What happens at the end of that? Do we colonize that country or what? This is a war of liberation and the people have to liberate themselves. Nobody can liberate them. You see the philosophy? Those people have to liberate themselves and they do. This fighting is part of their liberation. It is no use the Tanzanians going in to fight for them. So both as a result of the philosophy and experience, we do not envisage the possibility of our going into Rhodesia to fight that war of liberation.

As far as black unity is concerned, you will recall that I said here in March 1976 that I intended initiating the holding of a few black national conventions. I proposed one on the so-called homeland independence issue, and another on economic matters. This was not to be as we were overtaken

With President Nyerere of Tanzania

by history when the unrest in the country erupted in June of 1976. In August, which is the month on which we were hoping to hold one of these, I came up here to defuse the black vs. black violent confrontation at Mzimhlophe. In spite of this situation I was involved with those of our brothers and sisters on the Reef, who founded the Black Unity Front. There was no progress in forging black solidarity links because of the crisis situation and action taken against various leaders and organizations. Just on the 11th of this month the Labour Party, the Indian Reform Party, and Inkatha have established an alliance of oppressed people. We set up a coordinating committee to identify areas in which we can adopt a common strategy and we intend having meetings regularly, not less than once every two months. The anger of the white right wing was clearly expressed by all the apartheid mass media. Some of you heard the bitter comments by

LIVING FROM CRISIS TO CRISIS

CURRENT AFFAIRS over the South African Broadcasting Corporation. Some of you may have seen the two-part scurrilous pieces in THE CITIZEN, the English Nationalist Party mouthpiece by the familiar megaphone, Aida Parker. There was also an editorial entitled "Dangerous" by the editor of the CITIZEN and another entitled "Dangerous" by BEELD. Attempts have been made by the white right wing to present our black unity moves as an exercise in ganging up against whites. The SABC. announcers, who now speak of the "Anglo-Afrikaner nation" and yet condemn our black unity moves, forget that what is good for the goose is good for the gander. To me these are all good signs. The anger of the mouthpieces of the racist regime shows that they are well aware that if we succeed in forging black solidarity, this will mark the end of our oppression, which has thrived for so long because of black disunity. We are not naive. We realize that anything can be done to frustrate us. But let us not be daunted.

My pretext for being with you here during this time when open-air meetings are banned is the KwaZulu elections. Because one has detractors who distort things and also because the African people have been betrayed so often on this issue of balkanized independence, I considered it a moral obligation to come here to explain to you that we in KwaZulu still stand with the majority of black people in rejecting this balkanized independence which Pretoria is trying to foist on the black majority of this land. KwaZulu is nothing more than local regional administration in which we are involved in order to do the best we can for the black people of KwaZulu. It is no different from what the Committee of Ten attempted to do for the people of Soweto. By proposing a plan for the administration of Soweto by the people of Soweto they were not thereby accepting apartheid. We in Inkatha stand four-squarely behind the Committee of Ten even at this hour. The question of whether the Community Councils are adopted or not in Soweto is an issue that should be decided by the people of Soweto. But I want to make it clear as President of Inkatha that no member of Inkatha should involve himself or herself in Community Councils whilst Dr. Nthato Motlana and his Committee are incarcerated. I would regard such involvement whilst members of the Committee of Ten are in jail as an indefensible act of treachery.

I have in the past tried to appeal to both the Minister of Justice and the Prime Minister to speak to the Committee of Ten. I was in each case not successful.

When I was last here I mentioned that the fundamental political issue in the country revolves around power-sharing and the destruction of apartheid. The incarceration and bannings of certain individual leaders and organizations and publications by the Minister of Justice on the 19th of October, represents the outright rejection of the concept of power-sharing by the Nationalist Party regime. Whilst the Nationalist Party continued to reject our black hand of friendship, one still hoped that whites as a whole might soon see the light. The result of white election last November has indicated to us that the majority of whites in South Africa approve the jackboot methods of the Pretoria regime, and the use of the draconian powers against the black people's leadership by the Minister of Justice. Not even the death of Mr. Steve Biko has touched white South Africa.

We have now reached the crossroads. The last election marked a watershed in South African black-white politics. White South Africans have responded to the sound of Mr. Vorster's bugle. The majority of the whites are prepared to defend white privilege to their last drop of blood. We must face up to this reality of South African politics. Whites in general are prepared to go into a shootout spree against the powerless rather than share power.

Some of you may have read in the newspapers that Mr. Kruger, the Minister of Justice, summoned me to the Union Buildings on the 19th of September 1977, exactly a month before he banned other black organizations. He invited me, as President of Inkatha, to inquire from me which way Inkatha was going. He threatened to take action against us if Inkatha takes on Africans as members who are not Zulus, as we have always done. The Minister was concerned about what he alleged was a possible infiltration of members of the African National Congress into the movement. I told the Minister that I believe in the ideals of the African National Congress as spelled out by its founding fathers. I told him that I made a clear distinction between those ideals and the present activities of the banned African National Congress. This was actually in response to General Gert Prinsloo, who was present during the interview, who tried to quiz me for what I stated in my aide-memoire to the Minister. I had stated:

> There are ideals that are dearer to me than life itself and most certainly are dearer to me than temporary political gains. I share these ideals with whomsoever holds them. Many of these ideals have been expressed by a long succession of those who have gone before me. I believe that these ideals have been embodied in the sentiments and activities of great South African organizations such as the ANC and the PAC. When I further these ideals, I do so not in order to further the aims of banned organizations, but to further the only common ground where all South Africans, black and white, can find each other.

That is the section of my memo which raised queries from General Prinsloo and to which I was responding. The Minister's view was that Inkatha should not take anyone other than Zulus. To do so, in the Minister's opinion, would amount to what he calls "polarizing against whites". He further stated that to talk about black people as an entity was racialistic. The Minister stated that Pan Africanism is a racialistic thing. He stated that it amounted to the black man polarizing against the white man. That the black man must take Africa and the white man must get into the sea or he must go over to Europe. He stated further that the African National Congress goes one better than that and that they want a communistic regime. He stated that he gets the impression that I want to broaden the base of Inkatha on to a black polarization and he told me bluntly that in that case there was going to be trouble. He said that he had no doubt about that because they have to react. He stated that they cannot sit quietly while the black man polarizes against the white man. He said that this will become a life-and-death struggle. I made it quite clear to the Minister that as black people we are one people as much as Afrikaners, the English-speaking South Africans, Greeks and Jews were one people. The whole conversation is most informative as far as the determination of the present regime to thwart black unity. In short, that is where we ended up in this argument with the Minister of Justice. I finally said that I was a black man of Zulu extraction inasmuch as the Minister of Justice is a white man of Afrikaner extraction. The whole transcript of the conversation has been printed by Inkatha and is on sale in the Office of Mr. Thula in Thembisa. I think there are probably copies on sale right here.

This is important in showing us the extent of white opposition to black unity and the struggle those of us who are committed to black unity will have to wage before we get our freedom as black people of South Africa. We have a long and tough struggle ahead of us. Whilst we appreciate the extent to which world bodies such as the United Nations, and individual countries in the East and West mouth diatribes daily against this racist regime, we must know that in the struggle itself, apart from their moral support, we stand alone. We must accept that the struggle will have to be resolved within South Africa by us, the oppressed people of this land.

In coming to Soweto today, I have brought to you the same message I have tried to convey to my brothers and sisters here through the past seven years. Our unity is an absolute prerequisite to our liberation. The privileged white minority power elite oppose it so much because they know that black unity is the key to our freedom. In emphasizing the urgency and necessity of black unity, I wish to reject outright the suggestion that in struggling to accomplish it we are doing so as an exercise in black polarization against the whites. Whites have guilty consciences because they know too well that they are the people who polarized along racial lines against the majority of the population of this country from 1910. In refuting all the white political propaganda, when we seek each other as black brothers and sisters, I want to repeat to you the Inkatha statement of belief which states, in concise terms, where we stand in our quest for a new and just society in South Africa. The following is our statement of belief:

—We believe that respect for individuals and the value placed on cultural and large groups is synonymous with progress towards a politically stable society.

—We believe that political rights of all national groups should be protected within a constitutional framework which outlaws discrimination based on colour, sex or creed.

—We believe in individual equality before the law, equality of opportunity and equality of benefits from the institutions of the state.

—We believe that the identity of an individual within a particular cultural military is essential to his identity as a South African, but we believe also that culture belongs to all men and that no social, economic or political impediments which hinder the free movements of individuals from one cultural milieu is essential to his identity as a South African, but we believe

—We recognize that there are privileged communities and under-privileged communities and we believe that it is the very special duty of the state to provide the opportunities and back those opportunities with resources to enable every individual who is underprivileged to develop the maximum of his ability.

—We believe that the resources of the country and the wealth which has already been created which is controlled by the state, belong to all the people of South Africa, and we believe that the resources and the wealth of the country should be utilized for the greatest good of the greatest number.

—We believe that we are facing a grave crisis in which the poor are threatened with greater poverty and we believe it essential that all men join hands and enter into a partnership with the state to effect the greatest possible redistribution of wealth commensurate with maximizing the productivity of commerce, trade, and industry whether state controlled or privately owned.

—We believe that fiscal control is essential to regulate the quantity and flow of money and near money, and we also believe that state control by equivalents of the Reserve Bank is essential for the utilization of land, water and power in the interests of the economy and in the interests of developing underdeveloped areas and populations.

—We believe in the elimination of secrecy in public administration and we believe an individual should have rights of appeals to the courts to protect his or her privacy in the pursuit of that which is lawful.

—We believe that practices acceptable in civilized nations should characterize the methods and the procedures used by the police in the enforcement of law.

—We believe that the enforcement of law is devoid of meaning outside of the rule of law, and we believe that there should be both a criminal code and a justice code in which rights to appeal to the highest courts of the land are the right of all persons, and we believe that upon pronouncement of an impartial law society, that the state should bear the costs of appeal where the appellant pursued a course of action to protect his individual rights.

—We believe that in living the good life in a just society an individual should be free to attend any educational institution in which he has entry qualifications, reside where he wishes, own ground where he wishes, become qualified in any trade or profession for which he has the required degree of competence.

—We believe that the development of trade unions, guilds and associations should be encouraged by the enactment of enabling legislation and courts of arbitration.

—We believe that the accumulated injustices of the past and the injustice now present in the institutions of our country have created a bitterness and anger among the underprivileged sections of our populations, and we believe that growing fears of this anger and bitterness make the privileged sections of our population intransigent in the face of the need for change.

—We believe, therefore, that the transition from an unjust society to a just society will be difficult.

—We believe that in this eleventh hour of South Africa, responsible leadership must publicly declare its commitment to bring about a just society within the foreseeable future, and we believe that leadership must meet the demands of responsibility by taking whatever steps remain from time to time to avoid a race war.

—We believe that the mobilization of constituency protest and a refusal to act within the restrictive confines of race exclusivity holds a promise we dare not abandon.

Whatever mischief the Nationalist Party wishes to brew against us, we would like the world to know that their scurrilous accusations and snide comments about me and Inkatha which they are constantly disseminating through all the apartheid mass media, are nothing more than raw and naked racist propaganda.

The Nationalist regime is full of this victory at the polls in November through Mr. Vorster's call to whites to get into his LAAGER. That demonstration of white solidarity is nothing other than a product of false propaganda. It is nothing more than the deliberate infusion of fear into the minds of most whites. We as blacks must appreciate the dangers of this situation. Political megalomaniacs are like cornered beasts, and a cornered animal is very dangerous. Let us not allow them to destroy our country. We must refuse to go into a suicide pact with the white minority power elite. To fall for the bait of fragmenting South Africa into independent mini-states, is the surest way to destroy the South African nation. Let us make it clear that we regard this development as an act of treachery. Let us make it clear that when it comes to the push that we will be forced to treat it as treachery and to regard those who are involved in it as traitors. That is why I find it impossible to come here to talk to you about any KwaZulu issues. There are no KwaZulu issues outside the parameters of one South Africa. The issues I have come here to talk to you about are South African issues as set out in our handout. This election can only deal with South African issues. I want to make the points in our handout clearer to you in more terse terms.

We in KwaZulu do not see ourselves as a separate entity from other black people of South Africa. We would like through this election to make clear to the world and to South Africa the black majority's rejection of apartheid.

As much as Government propaganda states that all the things I have espoused and have stood for all these years are not supported by the majority of black people, this election gives the people of KwaZulu a chance to make clear once and for all that I do not stand alone. They are called upon to demonstrate that what I stand for is the gut-feeling, not only of the people of KwaZulu, but of the majority of black people of South Africa.

We hope it will be clear through this election that when we demand development of reserves in KwaZulu which were deliberately bypassed, we demand the development of these areas not as countries, but just as one more region of South Africa.

Through our participation in this election we hope the people who will vote will, by supporting me and the candidates which Inkatha supports, be endorsing our rejection of the consolidation of these areas by the government under the 1936 Native Land and Trust Act.

Those who will vote for these candidates will in effect be saying that South Africa is one country, which should be shared by all the people of various racial backgrounds who have contributed towards her development.

Through this election we would like to reject the idea that there is any part of this land where blacks are foreigners. It must be made clear that blacks have a legitimate right to be in any part of South Africa.

Through this election we would like to emphasize the black rejection of pass laws and influx control relations, even under the new guise of "travel documents".

We want to make it clear that there can be no peace in South Africa unless blacks also have a free and compulsory education like other race groups.

We want to indicate through this election that the black people of South Africa reject job reservation and demand equal pay for the jobs they perform regardless of race, colour or creed.

We want the world to know that if trade unions are good enough for other race groups, then they are good enough for blacks.

Those who will support Inkatha in the forthcoming elections will be indicating that they endorse the call I have made over the years for a national convention, at which the future of all South Africans can be mapped out by delegates representative of all population groups and of all political persuasions.

If we get support for the candidates who stand for Inkatha policies, we will be endorsing a call I made to Mr. Vorster more than once that he should release all political prisoners and also allow our political exiles to return to their fatherland in order to determine the future jointly with all of us.

I thank you, my brothers and sisters, for your patience in listening to me. Let us not be intimidated by action taken against other political leaders and organizations. Let us make it clear through our black solidarity that there are things for which no price is too high for us to pay. Let us make it clear that we accept that in the history of any people there are things any people cannot flinch from, not even death. These are the things I have come to Soweto to explain, not just to the people who come from that part of South Africa called KwaZulu, but to all my brothers and sisters on the Reef who are gathered here today. Thanks for coming to hear me. Amandla! Ngawethu! Matla! Ke Arona! Ilizwe! Ngelethu! Lefatse! Laheso!

Chapter 16

AFTERWORD

TO MY AMERICAN FRIENDS
Los Angeles, 7 August 1978

I thank my dear friend Vernon Jordan, Jr. for inviting me on your behalf to participate with you at this international session of the National Urban League. I value the opportunity you have given me as your brother from that part of the continent whose history is similar to that of the United States, a part of Africa where slavery at one time was the norm, and where even today colour deprives one of opportunities readily available to others, merely because one is black. Your own struggles have been a great inspiration to us. You have overcome most barriers which to us are still very much a reality of our existence in that troubled land which is South Africa.

I regard this invitation and the financing of this trip by the National Urban League as a contribution towards the struggle of black people of South Africa for fulfillment. I bring with me the greetings of millions of your black brothers to this conference. I bring hopes of millions of your people in South Africa, who in their own struggles are inspired by what you black Americans have achieved in your own struggle against tremendous odds. I bring their thanks for this act of identification with their cause, which, as blacks, is also your own.

This is the eighth visit I have paid to the United States of America. After the last three or four times I have been here, I have returned home with deepening misgivings about the utility of these trips to the States, and were it not for the fact that on this trip I had been invited by black America, I would certainly not have found time in a crowded year to spend time away from home.

I would like to talk today about our blackness. The first thing I want to note in passing is that there are none as colour blind as those who recognize their blackness to be significant, and I share with you the underlying reasons for the apparent contradiction that it requires a blackness to be colour blind.

We have been minorities in those parts of the world where technological developments rapidly outgrew human wisdom and things of real value. It is this minority status which has given us a perspective which I sincerely believe will serve mankind in the broader sense. It is a significant fact that in a post Vietnam period, the United States of America has produced a President whose reliance on blackness is undisputed. I don't say that the black American GI differed from the white American GI in his commitment to his country, or that black and white American GI's were different people in Vietnam. The crass error of Vietnam, however, was more important to black American perception than it was to whites. The crass error of racialism was more important to the perception of black Americans throughout the history of your country than it was to the whites.

I want to talk about blackness within this context and I want to talk about it not only in a sense of sharing identities and perceptions of man, but I want to talk about it in a challenging and even more in a demanding sense. Black Americans have suffered because they are black and they have lost, or they are losing, a stigma attached to their blackness because they have valued being men amongst men and women amongst women more than being black.

I think it is important that we look at our future destinies each in our own way in the perspective of tracing the common cause we have, to its roots. Common to your experience as black Americans and our experience as black South Africans, is the fact that power and technology are not the repository of brotherly love and wisdom. The cotton grower in the South was not wiser or more humane than the slaves he imported. The American of today and tomorrow is striving, thank God, for the obliteration of the effects of a brutal and crass technology wielded by economic thugs seeking gain at the expense of their fellow humans. The slave traders who had the command of ships and guns were not wiser than the people they auctioned or bought and subsequently treated as things lesser than their dogs or cattle. Again, that which America is and will yet become is an apology to mankind for the brutality of those days.

If there is to be human progress, we will have of necessity to concede that observations such as this will stretch into the future. The stupidity of America's involvement in Vietnam has already been documented. The stupidity of Dr. Kissinger's shuttle diplomacy all around southern Africa is about to be documented, and the stupidity of America's involvement in southern Africa in a more general sphere will one day be documented. I believe that when that documentation is made, black Americans will have made their own peculiar contribution in South Africa. Unschooled Boers joined hands with the scum of Europe to behave with crass stupidity and as unpredictive of future mankind as did your frontiersmen who put themselves above God in the enslavement of their fellow men. Black South Africans have a particular perception of that which has a validity which future history will pronounce upon, and it is a validity which will one day be seen to be a particular kind of colour-blindness — an ability to see men as men and women as women.

It is tragic that when one looks into the past so many turning points away from human exploitation were missed. It is tragic that so many people have suffered and died before true perception shifted into focus. It is tragic that so many people have to suffer so very much before that which is wholesome and corrective can begin to work its slow changes in the conscience of man. Today when I look at man on the one hand as technological, and on the other as intrinsically different from machines and animals, I am appalled by the realization that we have not sufficiently learned the lessons of history, and we are now, as we were before, locked in a struggle between wisdom and technology.

In America's foreign policy and in its stance at international forums where its voice is so powerful and compulsive of events, it is the technocrats whose will is being done. It appears at times to me that American morality for Americans serves most usefully when it gives respectability to turning over the dollar. I am saying these things because I share with you a concern about men and the role of the powerful in determining the destiny of men. The powerful are meddling in the affairs of southern Africa and it is a meddling which is foreboding unless it is tempered with a greater degree of wisdom and understanding than has been the case up to now.

I would not like the tone of my opening remarks to colour the rest of what I have to say tonight. I did not come here to moralize and theorize about the good life or talk in terms lamenting the folly of the past and the folly yet to be committed in the future. My opening remarks should be heard as a preamble to urgent practical necessities. I hope that the relationship I have pointed to, between the suffering and despised and that which transpires in the evolution of man, is noted — noted not in a moralizing sense but in a pragmatic sense.

I am in a particularly disadvantageous position in which I have to correct false impressions before I can go on to talk constructively about what we ought to be doing. I am one of the people in South Africa who has gained particular insights into American misconceptions. There are not many journalists and commentators who come to South Africa who do not discuss matters with me. I am therefore frequently confronted with a rather tragic misunderstanding of South Africa and the nature of the struggle for liberation there. I was witness to the developing euphoria which was consequent upon June 16th, 1976. I was deeply aware at the time of the tragic losses being suffered and the futile heroism which so many of our young people were displaying in a false belief that victory over apartheid was within sight. I was painfully aware of the fact that American journalists and commentators, as well as prominent personages of your political system, were participants in a tragic folly.

I want to pause here and remind you that American commentators write for an audience and are not necessarily conveyors of truth. If you took the real American struggle to establish the dignity of man over the last 30 years, how much would have been achieved had you black Americans been at the mercy of newspaper and television commentators? Your own press, your own king-makers, your own little petty politicians without constituencies, misrepresented your suffering to the world and were incompetent in portraying the true nature of your struggle in American society. Why, in the name of God and all mankind, are you so persuaded about the facts of the matter in South Africa by this same mass media? I have suffered at the hands of Americans, and the liberation of South Africa has suffered at the hands of Americans, and you and I have a common cause in reducing that suffering and maximizing the forces of justice which are struggling to emerge in a morass of conflicting vested interests.

I did not ask that South Africa be internationalized, but it has been internationalized. I think it is very important to note that it has been internationalized by the West, not by the Communist blocs or the socialist blocs of the world. It is the Western powers who rig scenes in southern Africa. It is the Western powers who are busily engaged with the frontline presidents of central and southern Africa in secret wheeling and dealing. It is the Western powers who are redoubling their efforts to lock South Africa into a north/south economic and political axis. It is the Western powers who are turning South African into frontier territory of their capitalist interests.

You black Americans have not completed your own liberation. You black Americans will only complete your own liberation by bringing to bear on the Western powers the shame of their vested interests and a deepening awareness of responsibility to man beyond the interests of Western technocrats and Western investors. You as black Americans have common cause with us black South Africans to establish justice. Your liberation and our liberation are coterminous. While we suffer, you will have failed. On the other hand, our partnership in success with you is equally dependent upon the opportunities we afford you and the doors we open for you. I therefore do not come with a cringing, whining, you-owe-me-something attitude. But a political spade is a political spade, and I am not convinced that black America has taken its responsibility in southern Africa as seriously as it might have done.

Let us go back to June 16, 1976. At the time I was very aware and you were very aware that in all the annals of man's history, we find no example of an 18 to 25 year-old group successfully transforming a society on their own. Nowhere in the history of man were the American expectations of our youth justified. I can understand an empathy with militancy displayed at great personal cost in a country as hideous as South Africa. I can understand applause for death and suffering. I can understand many things but I cannot understand the tragic lack of realism which swept the world after June 16, 1976. Nor can I understand a sense of responsibility which passed the buck to kids.

Your mass media must learn to put the South African struggle for liberation in its true perspective. Singularly the most important perspective of the South African situation is that the struggle for liberation is the responsibility of those who suffer under apartheid. In this perspective, those who suffer will come forward in wave after wave of endeavors. There will be no final force of liberation in South Africa that has not its roots in generations of liberation. The suffering and endeavors of the black people of South Africa since 1910 when, through the Act of Union, blacks were excluded from any meaningful participation in the affairs of the country, is like a vine with deep roots. It will bear fruit and it is one thing. We need, more desperately than ever before, the coalescence of these forces. You Americans have fragmented these forces. There is one tradition in the struggle for liberation. At different times that same tradition has expressed itself in different forms but there is an accumulation of resistance and an accumulation of wisdom.

The struggle itself will display offshoots and upstarts by the bitterness of failure. We had our Sharpeville; there will be more Sharpevilles. We had our June 16th; there will be more June 16ths. We had our 19th October; there will be more 19th Octobers. Unfortunately, each such event has produced a kind of transient arrogance which has been subsequently tortured by humility arising out of a recognition of failure. As President of Inkatha, I regard myself as the custodian presently charged with the responsibility of preserving that which went before and sharpening it for that which is yet to come. In this position, I urge you to recognize the fact that it was your permissiveness, it was your failure, it was your lack of specific involvement which made it possible for the South African government to drive the African National Congress and the Pan-Africanist Congress underground and into exile. There is your failure to provide hospitality to the oppressed from these organizations which prescribed the bitterness and the long years in exile. What has the United States of America done that is noteworthy in reinforcing the central tradition of resistance to apartheid? Where have you put your hand of brotherhood? Where do you now put your hand of brotherhood? Inkatha is a grass-roots organization building on the traditions of the past, embodying the suffering of today and the aspirations of tomorrow. Where is your hand of friendship?

Inkatha has a paid-up membership unparalleled in the history of South Africa among blacks. The same Inkatha was in its infancy in June 16th 1976. It was then only one year old. The prophets of doom abounded, telling me that I had better hastily resign from my position as elected leader of the KwaZulu Legislative Assembly and as President of Inkatha. I was assured that the end was nigh and that I had no political future on the platform of my choice. You Americans connived with these prophets of doom. You amplified their voice. You printed their accusations. You poured thousands upon thousands of dollars into their coffers. You excluded me and Inkatha from participating in forums you have organized. You poured thousands of dollars into scholarships, the terms of which excluded Inkatha.

When our Inkatha bulletin was banned, by the Publications Board, our black brothers in one of your influential bodies would not assist us to finance a court case in which we tried to challenge the banning of this bulletin. Because they had chosen to be selective in giving assistance and were carried away by the euphoria of political king-making, they would not help us. This is the handiwork of you black Americans. I hold you responsible and I challenge you to look again at South Africa to seek again a wisdom which will make your contribution relevant to the future.

I have a deep and abiding belief that right, and that which is good, will yet emerge to temper both black and white insanity with wisdom and understanding. So I return again to the United States of America and I appeal again for us to sit down and talk about South Africa. I appeal again for us to join hands and defeat inequity in that form which apartheid has presented it. I make an appeal to morality, but I do so as a hardbitten politician. Any politician who effectively represents a real constituency is aware of the fact that in one sense politics is not only the art of the possible, but also the management of vested interests. I am not so naive as to appeal to black Americans and America at large to fly against their deep and widely accepted vested interests. If I did not think the vested interests of my people have overlapped with the vested interests of you here in the States, I would not have come here at all. Political husbandry means pruning superfluous vested interests in favour of those which deserve to survive. In saying that there are overlapping areas of interest between your people and my people, I am not denying that they should be condoned in your society.

I believe that the vested interests of the United States of America would be served better and more effectively in the future if there is a real and meaningful participation by yourselves in the struggle for liberation in South Africa.

We are faced lately in our country with a chorus of voices from the United States on the question of human rights, and demands for rapid movement towards majority rule. But we have yet to witness any kind of effectiveness in partnership between America and those who struggle among us to liberate our country from oppression. I said earlier that we black South Africans have a responsibility to you as black Americans, and that you have a reciprocal responsibility to us. Both on our side and on your side, we have an obligation to be creative in that which faces us as a joint responsibility. Black Americans have made commendable efforts. In Congressional committees and associations throughout the United States the voice of conscience has been kept alive, but I am moved to say that much of this initiative is a black American endeavor to beat white America with a stick of apartheid. The focus of the endeavors has for the most part been more intimately related to politicking amongst yourselves for your own purposes, than it has been related to the liberation of South Africa.

Every sense of realism I possess says to me that it is highly unlikely that the United States will abandon its commitment to bring about change in South Africa through peaceful means. It is unlikely in the extreme that in a post Vietnam America, we will see a direct American participation in an armed struggle in our part of the world. Your corporations will continue to export to South Africa the nuts and bolts of Mr. Vorster's war machinery. Your corporations will continue dealing with the oppressive powers in such

184

a way that they gain added strength. Your corporations will do these things in the name of free enterprise, and they will do so upholding the right of big business to be free of political manipulation. Your diplomats in our country will continue to proclaim the illegality of direct American participation in political systems other than your own. Your diplomats will continue to invite black South Africans to their cocktail parties, before which, and after which, the real business of their presence in our country is concluded with big business behind closed doors. But you will not get involved in a South African Vietnam, and you will not be seen to be participants in an armed struggle in our part of the world. This is why we black South Africans find the voice of Ambassador Andrew Young so refreshing. He has done more for President Carter's credibility in our part of the world than all his predecessors have done for their Presidents. He has done more diplomatic work for the United States amongst us blacks than all your diplomats put together.

Current America's concern with human rights and a hardening of heart towards Mr. Vorster, the public stance of the United States on majority rule in our country are all promises of things to come. Unless black Americans become far more creative and effective in their creativeness than they have done in the past, your promises to us of today will become your lies of tomorrow. In this matter, you have a responsibility which you cannot pass on to us. We in turn have a responsibility which we cannot pass on to you. I have re-made this point about our separate responsibilities because I want to talk about that which we share as a responsibility in the right context.

You Americans cannot have it both ways. You cannot on the one hand confine your support to non-violent means; you cannot go on refusing to give material and diplomatic aid to our great banned organizations and on the other hand feed the machinery of Mr. Vorster's power over us. You cannot claim to be willing participants in a non-violent struggle to justify your non-participation in the violent struggle if you do not add the deed to the word.

The crucial question I have to ask today is what you are doing for us in our situation, not what you are doing for us in your situation. Definitions of problems are spurious when they do not isolate factors relevant to remedial action. I will go further to say that definitions of problems which do not spell out the answers to those problems amount to a deliberate negation of responsibility. Furthermore, and worse still, the definition of real and pressing human problems which denies the only possibilities which do exist for remedial action is mischievous and worse. One could define the South African problem in such a way as to excuse the Americans for not participating in the armed struggle. This would incur a responsibility to go on to indicate what steps should be taken to eliminate the need for violence. If the armed struggle in South Africa is so hideous that Americans cannot become involved in it, then Americans must be obligated to remove the need for armed opposition to apartheid.

You all know that apartheid is enforced by draconian laws and the inhuman application of power by ministers unfettered by democratic constraints. You know the detentions without trial; you know of police harrassment; you know of many of the political prisoners. One is justified in looking at pass offenders in jail as being prisoners of the system. They are also political prisoners. You know that apartheid is so ugly that it can only survive if it is enforced with the barrel of a gun. This degree of ugliness you are aware of, and you are indignant about it. You must therefore understand the growing feeling amongst black South Africans that oppression by force can only be removed by force. You must respect those who have opted for an armed solution to South Africa's problems. If you are unwilling to participate in that which is for you too ghastly to be involved in, then you must necessarily feel a deep commitment to help others to stay out of it as well. In my travels around the world when I meet many people who advocate violence in South Africa, I cannot help feeling that they have an interest in such violence taking place, which can be compared to that of spectators in a bull fight, who neither care for what happens to the poor bull nor to the matador, but who love to watch the spectacle for their own entertainment.

The definition of the South African problem now perforce must be in terms of avoiding the escalation of force. An analysis of the South African situation leads me to believe that it is still possible to avoid the uncontrolled escalation of violence in our country, and also leads me to believe month by month and year by year that there are fewer options open to us in the alternatives to violence. I see no reason to believe that the natural course of events in South Africa will bypass uncontrolled violence. In violent situations, there are always two sides: violence and counter-violence. The forces of violence as they increase precipitate an ever greater tendency towards counter-violence. Counter-violence is always limited in its beginning and therefore ineffective. Defeated counter-violence does not eradicate the need for violence. The defeat of counter-violence is the cultivation of it. Counter-violence, on the other hand, breeds the need for a greater degree of the violence which produced it.

South Africa is locked in this vicious circle of violence and counter-violence ever spiralling upwards. Neither you nor I dare hope that the forces of violence will peter out. South Africa is rushing headlong into the final violence of a race war, and I repeat that if we do not participate in violence, we are obliged to defuse it. There is no morality and no justification in an attitude so widely displayed by the West that they cannot enter into violent solutions in South Africa but continue an engagement and a stance which they wrongly maintain is working for evolutionary change. The status quo in South Africa has given rise to, and will continue to give rise to, violence and counter-violence. The status quo is nothing other than the balance of violence and counter-violence.

The threat of violence against those who oppose apartheid and the threat of violence against those who employ apartheid are very real factors in our political setup. I perceive quite clearly the real dangers of playing brinkmanship with disaster which is so implicit in a violence posturing. No matter how grave this danger is, the kind of brinkmanship which is taking place is not a parlour game played out between isolated political leaders. The white popluation is playing brinkmanship with the black population. Mr. Vorster's constituency has an underlying willingness to fight to maintain its racial supremacy. My constituency has got an underlying willingness to fight to defend itself against rabid racialism. The current heightening of brinkmanship and the consequent possible folly of misjudgment which will take somebody beyond the point of no return is inherent in our society, and has been produced by many decades of specific actions and counter-actions.

If there is one lesson we in South Africa have to learn it is to be learnt in Mr. Smith's failure. There was a time when he and his white Rhodesian compatriots sincerely believed their control of institutionalized violence ensured the survival of an indefensible socio-economic system, and a political structure which housed it. Logistically, it is dangerous to draw comparisons between the Zimbabwen and the South African situations. It is also just as dangerous to make the assumption that the only form of violence is to be found in the strategy adopted by Zimbabwe. Violence is possible in South Africa — violence on an ugly and destructive scale yet unseen in any part of Africa.

I am dedicated to non-violent change in the country. I am still dedicated even now in this eleventh hour, because the twelfth hour has not yet struck. Neither you nor I nor anybody else willingly espouses violence. Violence is that which people turn to when there is nothing else to hand. I want therefore to look briefly at nonviolent options open to us, and to appeal directly to you for a partnership in whatever non-violent strategies yet remain open to us. A last word on the question of violence is that the whites in South Africa cannot implement their apartheid policy to its logical conclusion by any other means. If they persist in pursing the ends of apartheid, they are already committed to a violent solution. Administratively, it is not a system which can be implemented. Its implementation requires guns and barbed wire and jackboots. With those they will fail. Guns and barbed wire have not been the nursery of democratic societies. Those who live by the sword will die by the sword! Those who live by the gun will die by the gun!

I want to make now a simple statement. Apartheid cannot be brought to its logical conclusion unless the South African government brings all the so-called black homelands to the point where they voluntarily opt for Pretoria-style independence. If every homeland other than KwaZulu opted for independence, the blacks who remained in a common South Africa, i.e., the Zulus alone, will still outnumber the whites. KwaZulu will not become independent Pretoria-style. Inkatha nominated candidates for the Legislative Assembly in an election earlier this year who all adopted anti-independence platforms. Every Inkatha candidate was returned. The people have expressed their opinion and the point has been made to Mr. Vorster. Not only politically is it impossible to implement apartheid; it is impossible to do so socially and economically. Integration is taking place in the social and economic spheres. That integration is fundamental to white standards of living being maintained. The basis of the nationalist government a decade ago that the number of blacks in so-called white areas will be reduced to leave a white majority there has proved an empty base. It is no longer seriously talked about. Black cities are rapidly expanding. White dependence on black workers has passed a threshhold. Black/white worker substitution is a necessary condition of economic growth, or even the maintenance of existing levels of economic activity. Commerce will be crippled if there is not a continued expansion of black consumer spending.

Whether it be in the sphere of politics, the social sphere or the economic sphere, there is already a white dependence on blacks. This dependency on blacks is white society's Achilles heel.

Inkatha is a well-organized, disciplined organization with a paid-up membership of over 150,000. For every one paid-up member, there are thirty, fifty sympathizers of Inkatha and its strategy. It is a grass-root movement; it has by far the best organized and largest constituency South Africa has ever seen and it continues to grow. It pushes beyond so-called homeland boundaries, beyond professional boundaries, beyond tribal boundaries and beyond racial boundaries. The South African government is also perturbed about this and Mr. Kruger, the Minister of Justice, Police and Prisons, had this to say when we met in September last year:

> But we must get our basic things right. If Inkatha wants to become a nationalist organization like my people have had nationalist organizations, then I am not going to do anything against Inkatha. I believe that nationalism is correct. I am nationalist and I believe that the Zulu people must have a nationalist organization but if he (Chief Buthelezi) wants to broaden his base, like I get the impression I think, I don't put it higher than that, but I get the impression that Chief Gatsha Buthelezi wants to broaden the base on to a black polarization, then of course it's going to, there's going to be trouble. No doubt about it. Because you can understand, we've got to react. We cannot sit quiet while the black man polarizes against the white man. It will become a life and death struggle then. This is our difficulty.

The South African Black Alliance which sprung from this viability is going to be an increasingly important development. The mobilization of consumer spending and the organization of worker attitudes is now a real possibility for the first time in the history of the country. It is in that direction in which Inkatha is making its way. Those who have seen the vulnerability of South Africa to mass action at an economic level have hitherto been subject to the limitation of not having well-organized constituencies as a power base. They have called for strikes which they could not sustain. In the history of the Western industrial society, it has been amply shown that strike action is unviable where there are inadequate strike funds. The call for boycott action to which people have responded came only in flash endeavors. This inability to mobilize people, to organize them, and to sustain their action has led to resorting to outside aid. Appeals have been made to international trade union movements; appeals have been made to foreign governments to apply economic pressure on Pretoria which the people themselves have failed hitherto to do.

I empathize with those who have sought to bring about change through economic pressure but I am adamant about one thing, and that is that the people themselves who are carrying the yoke of apartheid ultimately must be the people who exert the economic pressure, and they must do so in their own strength, following their own strategies. We in Inkatha are determined not to run before we can walk. We are determined not to hold out to the black people of South Africa promises of easy victories which will not be had. Step by step we will consolidate the strength we have and that strength is considerable. The struggle for liberation in our country will still be a long and hard struggle, and it will be our struggle.

Any pressure group in your country working to bring about economic pressure on Pretoria is deeply aware of the fact that they cannot obtain the necessary information to be effective in their campaigns. Inkatha is the information they seek. Inkatha's membership are the migrants of South Africa; they are the urban dwellers of South Africa; they are found on the factory floor, in commerce, in the utilities and the civil service. We do not gather information. We do not have to seek the cooperation of bosses. We bear the heavy hand of their treatment, and we can tell the story as it is. For the first time, therefore, the consumers and the workers in South Africa have amongst them an organization and leadership which is not dependent on foreign aid. This will be our contribution. Our contribution is aimed at assuming a rightful place in the economic affairs of the country and the acquisition of decision-making powers about the wealth of South Africa.

Because foreign investment is so important an element in South Africa's economic viability, there exists the possibility of a fruitful partnership between ourselves and people like yourselves. The owners of capital in South Africa are to be found scattered through the whole of the western world. These people know that the present situation offers no security for their enterprises. What they have so far located is a belief in alternatives to running the country by guns and barbed wire. Strikes in South Africa are notoriously unexpected. When they do take place, they take place to surprise management. If the South African situation is allowed to develop along its course of spiralling violence, many enterprises will be destroyed and the owners of capital will have proved that South Africa is a risk area. The owners of capital in South Africa, I am persuaded, are now ready to talk before the shooting and destruction starts.

Before the shooting and destruction escalates beyond control, a national convention is something everybody wants but is also something which they lack the necessary hope and determination to make work. South Africa will produce a national convention of all parties, both those inside the country and outside the country. It will have to do so if it is to avoid violence. I am not so naive as to believe that we can sit around conference tables today and hold a national convention which will produce a blueprint for the future. I do, however, believe that such a national convention is going to take place, and the hard work we do now in preparation for it will be the determinant of its success. The more possible we make it, the greater likelihood it will occur, and the more we prepare for it, the greater the likelihood will be that it will succeed. It is in the preparation of this national convention, in collaboration with growing consumer and worker resistance to apartheid, that I see the partnership between blacks in South Africa and blacks in America.

When I speak to your industrialists and your investors they talk about the possibility of scholarships, goodwill and so on, and they seek my blessing of their investments. I have not yet had a meaningful response from them to my utterances on the extent to which they are jeopardizing their own enterprises by non-participation in the struggle for liberation. I expect from them a kind of creativeness which they have employed in exploring their avenues of investment. The free enterprise system must not be free only to one enterprise at the expense of others. A free enterprise system must necessarily mean a distribution of wealth and opportunity. A free enterprise system in the United States of America is conscious of this responsibility and endeavors to meet the demands of labour and the interests of the average citizen. It is true that the demands have to to be made, but once made and made insistently, there is a creative response to them. Somehow you must find a way of persuading the industrialists and financiers in your midst to take the need for a national convention very seriously and prepare for it determinedly and expeditiously.

Our starting point is going to be the monitoring of employer codes of conduct. We have started here because these codes of conduct are the products of employer thinking. We are persuaded that they contain more than an element of hypocrisy, but we are also persuaded that if this hypocrisy is moved there could be a first step in the right direction. There is an urgent need for Inkatha to meet employers in serious dialogue about the improvement to these codes of conduct. You must remember that apartheid is breaking up; that on the factory floor it is no longer possible to implement apartheid as the Department of Labour has formulated it. South Africa's industry runs on exemptions more than rules. We know what is being done and your employers cannot tell us what is legal and what is not legal. We will tell them what we are doing and what we are prepared to do, and we in Inkatha will carry the brunt of Mr. Vorster's objections should he have any. Until such time as you have persuaded your investors to take us seriously, I do not believe that they will be moved to have discussions with us. I am quite prepared in the first instance to meet them privately and set the scene for the dialogue I am suggesting. That dialogue I know is something we cannot enter into lightly and must not enter into at all unless we are prepared for it and are serious about it. This preparation and the imbuing among investors of the degree of seriousness that is required is something which is your responsibility. They are your investors; they represent your society. If you cannot do this much for us, labour unrest will move through various phases to the point where organized labour becomes party political and ideological. If that is to come it will come, but I do not believe that the interests of South Africa and its workers will best be served by labour movements having political bosses. Inkatha offers affiliate membership to black trade union movements. Your employers must see the advantage of (a) establishing black trade unions and (b) having them affiliate to Inkatha. Inkatha is not a takeover bid in the field of labour. Inkatha's responsibility will be discharged when we have shown what can be done.

I said earlier and I repeat here again that it is Inkatha's intention to organize and mobilize worker and consumer resistance to apartheid, and it is Inkatha's intention to do this within the limitations of its own strength and within the timetable of its own determination. This move is a grass-roots move and does not emanate from foreign sources, nor will it be subjected to foreign control. If the workers see such initiatives as failing, foreign influences will play an ever greater part among us.

South Africa has already been internationalized by the West as I pointed out. I appeal once again to you Americans to heed what I say about a kind of ill-conceived Western liberalism which connives with the forces of oppression behind our backs for our own good. There can be no achievement in the direction of non-violent opposition to apartheid without involving us. We remain suspicious of secret CIA studies of the South African situation. We remain suspicious of the shuttle diplomacy between apartheid bosses and the frontline presidents without consulting us.

Things I have talked about are matters of grave concern and should exercise our minds. The victory which I know can be ours, I repeat, is not easily obtained, nor will it be obtained with no price being paid. We will pay a price. The investors will pay a price. I want to end on the note that beyond any particular organization or beyond any particular leader in black South Africa, there is a tradition of liberation of which we are the custodians. There is a growing and accumulated wisdom which will serve us. The authentic voice of that tradition is not to be found in minority protest groups, no matter how articulate they are. It is not to be found amongst the youth. The youth cannot be the custodians of the intricacies of involvement in bringing about the necessary conditions for a national convention. They are but one symptom of the disintegration of apartheid. They are not the answer to apartheid. They are important beyond refutation, but their importance lies within a wider context. It is that context we search for and will achieve.

Church groups have not been able to subsume in them the wisdom of a suffering people over generations, and the churches cannot mobilize people. That is not their job. It never has been their job. The churches will not lead South Africa into a new future. The churchs will not organize people into coherent constituencies with defined leadership and political roles. They lack the perspective and they lack the know-how. The United States of America cannot be guided by the clerics and the youth in the grave responsibility of creating a better society. I hasten to add that both the clerics and the youth are essential ingredients in any formula themselves. Speaking as a churchman, I have frequently had occasion to call the church to order in its non-participation in the struggle for liberation. I would, however, be extremely foolish to abdicate my leadership role in favour of a cleric, no matter how renowned he might be. I say this very much mindful of the fact that your country has witnessed the emergence of a number of outstanding clerics, whose common touch rallied men not only in church, but in the streets and ghettoes where you struggled for freedom. One remembers Dr. Martin Luther King, Jr. who abandoned the comfort of the pulpit for the harshness of the pavements and the jails. I am also mindful of that unique contribution men like the Rev. Ambassador Andrew Young, and the Rev. Leon Sullivan, are making, and the contribution now being made by such clerics as the Rev. Jesse Jackson.

When Martin Luther King, Jr. stood with his people in the face of a firehouse onslaught and baton charges when he faced prosecution, he did so in the service of a cause which was the cause of his people. He died at the hand of assassins, still serving that cause. He did not do so as a stepping-stone to political power. He did not prostitute the suffering of his people.

There are clerics of this stature; we have them in South Africa. We have got men like Beyers, Naude, David Russell, and Archbishop Denis Hurley. But none of these people of stature has sought to use the suffering people as stepping-stones to secular power for its own sake. To be a political force is the role of every true Christian, but to aspire to be a political boss is quite another thing.

If America, and in particular you black Americans, continue to look at South Africa only through the eyes of impotent youth and the eyes of impotent clerics, you will not discern the true South Africa. You will only see a kind of Alice-in-Wonderland scene. There is a power to be derived from the youth, but the employment of that power does not lie within the wisdom of the youth and the clerics, and both the youth and the clerics at all costs must avoid the further lopsided internationalization of the South African scene. There is a misguided belief among many of these children and gentlemen that international acclaim is more than hypocritical lip service to our struggle. The time has arrived in South Africa where acclaim should be afforded to the fruits of political action, and not the promise of ideological statements.

The revolution is an earthly thing and the revolutionary politician is a pragmatist who starts with hard work which achieves that which cannot be destroyed. It is a false claim to fame when one seeks acclaim for the kind of martrydom which results from being squashed and destroyed in strategies which have no chance of success. These people and their failure may feed the conscience of the West when the West acclaims them and their failures, but those failures are not protective of Western interests. To state these home truths is not to deny that amongst them we now have a string of martyrs whose names will remain an inspiration in the struggle, despite their faulty strategies and despite the fact that their strategies did not achieve anything concrete in our liberation struggle. I am deeply moved as I say these things because I am aware of the tragic situation which necessitates their telling. It is tragic that Mr. Vorster and his predecessors have abused Christianity to bring about a *broederbond*-inspired apartheid system. It is tragic that the mechanisms of a democratic parliamentary system have been used to usurp the rule of law. It is tragic that the deeply valued cultural characteristics of people have been abused in bringing about divisions of people along ethnic lines. Because Mr. Vorster has abused the Church, I will not abandon it. Because Mr. Vorster has abused democracy, I will not abandon it, and because Mr. Vorster has abused rich cultural diversity in South Africa, I will not abandon that either. These things must be used as positive elements. We must reduce our shame in being democrats, and we must reduce our shame in having a culture, just because South African racists try to prostitute our culture to create divisions amongst us.

In talking to you, I have noted that human wisdom was outstripped by technological developments and that those with power did not represent the pinnacle of man's achievement over animals. I pointed out that our liberation is intimately related to your final liberation as American citizens. I pointed out that the crass stupidity of gun-wielding thugs, whether they be your frontiersmen or our frontiersmen, or the Vorster regime, or other agents of oppression, is doomed to failure. I pointed out that their failure can be demonstrated by another gun. I also, however, pointed out that we have common cause, you and I, in bringing about change by nonviolent means and that we have an obligation to do so in opposition to violence. I have indicated the areas in which your creativeness and our creativeness can lead to a partnership protective of everything you value and we value and finally I appealed for a perspective that broadens that of just youth and cleric. There is a road ahead which bypasses the minefields of today. Let us take that road together.

IDEA INDEX

Struggle in Southern Africa

"Above all this, I want to emphasize that I love my people and share their suffering. So that when there is nothing left but to fight a just war, people all over the world, right down through the centuries of history have done just that, not least amongst these the founding fathers of the United States. We black South Africans are people among the rest of humanity. My people's options are my own options." p. 135
also. pp. 79, 80, 89, 90, 114, 118

Soweto riots, pp. 20, 84, 114, 129, 165

Stability, pp. 30 , 64

Turning the tables, pp. 27

Detente in Africa, pp. 24, 39

Apartheid Laws and Problems

"No black has any other purpose in South Africa. We exist only to struggle for the total overthrow of apartheid and all the injustices it means in the daily lives of the black people of South Africa." p. 15

"Political treachery stalks the land. Treachery by the government, secret police, bribery, manipulation and detention without trial. The banning of people, the banning of organizations are political treachery as far as the majority of South Africans are concerned." p. 27
also pp. 3, 6, 26, 30, 32, 113, 117, 134, 136, 176

Detention without trial, pp. 27, 147, 176-7

Economic Aspects

"I would argue that some form of a free enterprise system in which the private sector is permitted to play a creative role would be the best option for South Africa. I would, on the other hand, argue against unrestrained capitalism in which the dependency of the South African economy would be perpetuated." p. 9

"If my people have to remain in South Africa, they must eat; they must buy clothes; they must educate their children. They need work. I am not speaking for white South Africa. But I do speak for black South Africa. Any drying up of the stream of foreign investments in a country still so dependent on them would impede economic growth of the country generally, injure those economic activities which have been the largest absorbers of foreign capital, such as the mines and secondary industries, and so cause a decline in the volume of employment. Black people, and Africans in particular, who are the only race group subject to the pass laws and influx control regulations, would suffer more than whites or other racial groups. White employment is protected by the government, whereas the Africans are the first to be fired and always the last to be hired." p. 80

"Frequently those who are most ardent in their defense of the capitalist free enterprise system are the greatest enemies of that system. If ever there is any demise of capitalism here, white capitalists will fully share in the blame. It must be a matter of common sense that if, as in the case at present, the majority of the people who are black are not participants in the capitalist free enterprise system, it cannot survive in the southern Africa that is now unfolding. The South Africa we have known is bound to crumble in the face of the new southern Africa that is coming into being. It is, however, not too late to do something to ensure a continuing democracy within which a responsible free enterprise system can evolve. It is, however, important to emphasize that it is now too late to perpetuate the status quo." p. 139
also pp. 5, 7, 8, 10, 11, 15, 17, 75, 76, 79, 100, 153

Foreign investors role, pp. 75, 79, 80, 140, 150

Free enterprise, pages: pp. 9

Foreign Big Power Pressure

"Whilst we appreciate the extent to which world bodies such as the United Nations, and individual countries in the East and West, mouth diatribes daily against this racist regime, we must know that in the struggle itself, apart from their moral support, we stand alone. We must accept that the struggle will have to be resolved within South Africa by us, the oppressed people of this land."
p. 173

"Some seek ideological cleanliness at the expense of black people, the very people they claim they want to assist. When, for instance, people overseas say that they cannot help blacks in education because the South African government can do it, I am often in a great dilemma as to their sincerity. The South African government should do it, yes and a big yes, at that. But the South African government is not doing it. Must we the victims of apartheid suffer because the racist regime does not do it for us? Must we be deprived of whatever valuable assistance is available in order that people may aim for ideological puritanism?" p. 114-15   also pp. 97, 99, 135, 142,

Black African Pressure, pp. 79, 80, 145

Well intentioned help, pp. 6, 15, 118, 134-40, 142

War and Armies

"We blacks do not believe that the social and moral elitism produced out of the fabric of our society can be defended militarily in a situation of real conflict. The majority of blacks will not find it in their hearts to die on the country's borders to defend a system which is to them morally repugnant, a system which dehumanizes them and which mocks God Almighty for creating us blacks also in his image." p. 27

also p. 4, 15, 24, 26, 76, 89, 135, 137, 172-3

Formulas for Peaceful Liberation

"I have, for moral and Christian reasons as well as pragmatic reasons, chosen the path of peaceful change. I must confess, however, that after a meeting I had with the Prime Minister on the 8th of this month (Oct. '76), I am now even more skeptical that those of us who believe in a peaceful change can ever succeed in the face of such white greed, and white intransigence as came through so distinctly in the attitude of the Prime Minister to all our suggestions about a peaceful change." p. 4

"Those who have ears to hear what I say will understand that I am offering a black hand of friendship to the whites of South Africa. Yes, it is a black hand, but it is still a hand of friendship." p. 25 also pp. 26, 42, 64, 70, 75, 87, 92, 100, 135, 173

Non-violence/violence, pp. 4, 74, 78, 119, 127, 148

Co-operation still possible?, pp. 25, 142, 171

The Advancement of a People

"It is high time the privileged in this country heard the voice of the underprivileged. They have failed to do this so far. Theirs is, I am afraid, a willful failure. It is this willful persistence in social and political stupidity which is productive of despair and anger, which in turn create racial tension." p. 15

"Before we can begin doing everything we need to organize ourselves into a disciplined body. We need to come together to support each other, plan with each other and act with each other." p. 32

"We need a workable plan—a strategy which will win—we do not need to be told we suffer. This we know. We also know that the time is ripening for effective political action. We also know that the hard work of organizing the people has arrived. The discipline of being organized is something we lack. We are attending to that lack because we have seen that mass disorganization cannot be thrown against the organized forces at the command of the state." p. 1

also pp. 26, 30, 74, 80, 110, 115, 116, 143

Inkatha, pp. 32, 33, 108, 109, 119, 145-6, 149, 171

Homelands System

"That is why at the outset, I want to make it very clear that blacks in this country have one homeland which they all share together — South Africa. The myth that we blacks have no rights in so-called white areas can no longer be sustained. South Africa will never be divided into a number of black mini-states dominated by a sprawling white monster state. This is a figment of the white man's mind, which is more a sympton of his political megalomania than of political reality." also pp. 2, 6, 22, 35, 36, 51, 76, 89, 99, 118, 119, 133-4, 138, 146

Western Democracy and Christian Civilization

"Let the Church in South Africa support the majority in their movement towards constructive unity. The Church has in the past only paid lip service to this ideal. Some churches have not even done that much. It is perhaps necessary for black Christians to recognize that they have to take the lead at a national level. There may be protests from some white churchmen when they hear what I have said today about the Church. My answer to these protests is that the Church is rapidly losing credibility among blacks in South Africa. If churches are convinced that they have acted properly, then they have only convinced themselves. The Church has not been effective in their support for the black liberation struggle." p. 31
also pp. 24, 71

Role of the Church, pp. 65, 66, 68

Zulu and Other Nationalities

"I have no hatred in my heart for any section of our population. I accept that we are all South Africans before we are Zulus, Jews, Afrikaners, Sothos, Indians, Coloureds, etc." p. 93

"Whites from various parts of the world settled in South Africa and seized land by imperial edict, supported by military superiority. In their present intransigence they are again relying entirely on their military strength. Whites, as you know, did not fight only with blacks, but they also squabbled among themselves for a whole century before coming together in the Act of Union in 1910. This was mainly done in order to consolidate their white interests. While they themselves are heterogeneous, coming as they do from different cultural backgrounds, it suited their scheme of white domination to declare themselves to be one white nation, while blacks are conveniently being divided into a mini-nations on the basis that they have different cultural backgrounds." p. 133
also pp. 33, 34, 55, 89, 91, 105, 120, 148-9, 155, 156, 157, 167, 174

The Afrikaners, pp. 38, 39, 86, 93, 94, 132

British Land grabbing, pp. 134

ENERGY
THE CREATED CRISIS

Antony C. Sutton

YOUR TAXES ARE GOING UP; YOUR ELECTRIC AND GAS BILLS ARE COSTING MORE; AND THE GOVERNMENT IS TELLING YOU TO USE YOUR AIR CONDITIONER LESS IN THE SUMMER—WHY?

FOR AN ENERGY CRISIS THAT DOESN'T EXIST

In ENERGY: THE CREATED CRISIS, Antony C. Sutton confirms the suspicion long held by many Americans that the energy "crisis" is a hoax perpetrated on the American people by big government aided and abetted by big business.

Inside are the details on:

- *America's present energy reserves— enough for the next 2000 years*
- *How and why the U.S. government works to obstruct energy development*
- *Which huge multi-national oil companies are most politically active in supporting the government's efforts to encourage the energy "crisis"—and why*
- *Nuclear energy—far cheaper and safer than oil, coal and gas*
- *The Carter energy plan—a taxation plan in disguise*
- *The ruling elite—who they are and how they're working against you*

To order, send $10.95 (plus 80¢ p. & h.) to: BOOKS IN FOCUS. 30 day return privilege.

∙∙∙

POWER IS OURS

Buthelezi Speaks on the Crisis in South Africa

"The speeches of *BUTHELEZI* provide a tremendous source of material . . . on the South African Problem . . . The reader will gain new insight as he is led by this gifted mind and articulate person . . . It's extremely important that (he) is heard and understood . . . he has earned the right to be heard."

    Rev. Leon H. Sullivan
    Director, General Motors Corporation
    Minister, Zion Baptist Church
    Author of the Sullivan Code of Ethics for American Companies operating in South Africa

An epic struggle is unfolding in South Africa—a struggle destined to affect the entire world. At the forefront of this movement a leader has arisen.

A *MAN* whose existence cannot be ignored by the South African or world media;

A *MAN* too powerful to be dealt with in typical Apartheid fashion;

A *MAN* who combines rare qualities of leadership, intellect, organization, and courage;

A *MAN* whose hour has come.

This man is Gatsha Buthelezi. He is the leader of 5,000,000 Zulu people in South Africa; he is the Chairman of INKATHA and of the South African Black Alliance.

This book contains some of his most powerful speeches, covering every topic of importance in the South African dilemma. As you read through its pages you will be drawn into Gatsha's struggle and life, and will share his moment in history.

Topics are indexed by a unique "Idea Index."

To order send $12.95 (plus 80¢ p.&h.) to Books In Focus. 30 day return privilege.

HONEST MONEY NOW!

DONT TREAD ON ME

**SELECTED ESSAYS By
HOWARD S. KATZ**

*Arise then ye freemen, use liberty's hand
And drive this vile paper from liberty's land,
And let the gold dollar be coin for the poor
And circulate freely to every man's door,
Awake up to freedom and not be controlled,
Submit not to bankers to pocket your gold.*

100 years ago it was common knowledge that gold money was in the interest of the average citizen and that paper money served the interests of bankers and charlatans. History shows that the struggle between paper money and hard money had been the dominant political issue in the United States until World War I.

Today, the fight between hard money and paper money is again becoming the primary political issue of our time.

Honest Money Now! is the first shot fired in the action-phase of this struggle. In **The Paper Aristocracy**, Howard Katz explained why the gold standard was essential to our nation. In **The Warmongers**, he showed how the paper money interests were moving our nation toward war. In **Honest Money Now!**, he explains how the Gold standard can be acheived now, and what you ought to be doing about it!

To order send $3.95(plus 80ᶜ p.&h.) to Books In Focus. 30 day return privilege.

· ·

RUDEBARBS

By
RANDY HYLKEMA

RUDEBARBS are cartoons with a message! Some of the funniest economic, political, and social lampoons ever created; thanks to the genius of Randy Hylkema. Guaranteed to have you in stitches or your money refunded.

To order, Send **$5.95** (+80ᶜ P. & H.) to: BOOKS IN FOCUS. 30 Day Return Priveleges.

The elite that controls America's money system.

THE PAPER ARISTOCRACY
by Howard S. Katz

A simple explanation of what is happening to your money.

Katz has written a new classic as important to the development of economic thought as Adam Smith's *Wealth of Nations*, or Marx's *Das Kapital*. For in this book Katz carefully documents the development of a powerful elite, which through the mechanism of paper money, has come to control the economies of Nations. This group, which Katz calls the paper aristocracy, reaps unearned benefits from this control at the expense of the people. For the first time ever, economics is not viewed as a cold science, but is evaluated within a moral framework. What's more, Katz does it in clear language easily understood by the layman or student.

The Paper Aristocracy represents a major revolution in economic thinking. Howard Katz deserves the praise and thanks of all honest men. Order his book now.

"Your presentation is about the most penetrating and stimulating of any I have read in years. You are absolutely right—paper money inflation makes the poor poorer and the rich richer."
—ELGIN GROSECLOSE, PH.D., Institute for Monetary Research, Inc., Washington, D.C.

To order, send $7.95 (plus 80¢ p. & h.) to: BOOKS IN FOCUS. 30 day return privilege.

Another classic by Howard S. Katz.

THE WARMONGERS

They started World War I.
They engineered World War II.
They are moving the world toward war now!

<u>Who</u> they are, <u>how</u> they have operated, and above all <u>why</u> they are warmongers, is carefully documented in this brilliant analysis.

THE WARMONGERS re-examines <u>history</u> and discovers a distressing link between the creation of paper money and major wars. Detailed facts expose a fascinating and frightening intrigue in which bankers, big business and government create wars to increase their power and wealth.

THE WARMONGERS analyzes the <u>present</u> and uncovers a consistent trail of actions on the highest level, designed to lead the U.S. into major war.

THE WARMONGERS projects the <u>future</u>, convincingly predicting that America and China will be fighting Russia and Japan; tells what major policy shifts must occur; and explains why 1981 and 1985 are the most likely years for the U.S. to be brought into the war.

THE WARMONGERS is a non-fiction book.

To order, send $11.95 (plus 80¢ p. & h.) to: BOOKS IN FOCUS. 30 day return privilege.

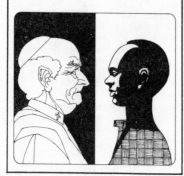

Conflict of Minds
Changing Power Dispositions in South Africa

by Jordan K. Ngubane

Conflict of Minds is a brilliant redefinition of the South African Crisis in terms of two conflicting philosophies of life, rather than a racial struggle.

Ngubane shows how the Sudic philosophy of Africa, and attitude toward the person evolved from ancient Egyptian theology, being passed on from generation to generation through the oral tradition; and he traces it to present day Zulu philosophy.

Conflict of Minds is the first written presentation of this philosophy ever, and therefore represents a major cultural achievement. It is a clear demonstration that there is a unifying world view throughout Africa, and that contrary to popular belief this view is in respects actually in advance of the Judeo-Christian structure. This has implications for that structure which cannot be ignored.

ABOUT THE AUTHOR:

Conflict of Minds represents a labor of 10 years for Mr. Jordan K. Ngubane. During this period he has been in exile from his home and people in the Zulu areas of South Africa. Living in Washington, D.C. and lecturing at Howard University, Jordan has maintained an objective attitude and has remained very much in touch with Black leadership within South Africa.

This is Jordan Ngubane's fifth book. He was the editor of a South African Black newspaper for eight years and was the correspondent for Mahatma Ghandi's newspaper. He has written 10 articles for the McGraw-Hill New Encyclopedia of World Biographies.

To order send $10.95 (plus 80¢ p.&h.) to Books In Focus. 30 day return privilege.

"It is by far the best and most comprehensive statement for liberty I have come across."

Leon Louw
Founder and Executive Director
Free Market Foundation

In Search of Liberty

FRED MACASKILL

IN SEARCH OF LIBERTY advances the concept that the more liberty a society enjoys, the stronger it will be, with greater material and moral benefits available to its individual members.

THE PRINCIPLES AND CONCLUSIONS of *In Search of Liberty* are based on the solid bedrock of individual rights. Taking nothing for granted, the author proceeds from the most basic right - the right to live. Then, considering more complex derivative rights, *In Search of Liberty* examines the most pressing issue of our time - the proper role of government in the life of man. Statism is shown to be destructive to individual rights; the free market is demonstrated to be an approach consistent with man's nature. These free market conclusions are underscored by the fact that author Macaskill lives in the highly authoritarian South African society. The concluding chapter appropriately shows how the individual rights approach (without regard to color or nationality) is the best and possibly the only hope in the South African situation.

"It's no exaggeration to say that the future of Western Civilization depends on ideas set forth in this book."

James U. Blanchard
Chairman, National Committee
for Monetary Reform

To order, Send $8.95 (+80¢ P. & H.) to: BOOKS IN FOCUS   30 Day Return Privelege

Immortal Light of Genius

Flight

In this volume
you will find the immortal light
of genius at its moments of greatest
inspiration discovering truth, creating
beauty, moving Humanity to fulfill its
dream of Glory... freedom, achievement
and joy.

Touch this blue fire of genius, this
immortal light, this glory, with your
mind and with your heart and it will
set fire to your spirit.

The immortal light of genius
is the energy for life.

To order send $5.95 (plus 80ᶜ p.&h.) to Books In Focus. 30 day return privilege.

BARNARD
SOUTH AFRICA: SHARP DISSECTION

Christiaan Barnard, the world renowned
South African heart surgeon speaks his mind
on the dilemma in his country, and other
trouble spots in Africa.

"In an unquestionably heartfelt expression of
his views as a white Afrikaner proud of his
heritage and land, he asserts his reasoned
opinion that apartheid should be ended
immediately — for practical as well as moral
reasons."—PUBLISHERS WEEKLY (review)

Here is a view of South Africa for the reader
who wants to form his own judgment, a view
based on practical knowledge of the situation
as analyzed by an intelligent mind. As the
situation there threatens to explode and in-
trude more and more into our lives, concerned
persons will want to understand this viewpoint.

To order, send $8.80, hardback (includes
postage) to Books In Focus. 30 day return
privilege.

AMERICAN JUSTICE IS IN TROUBLE

THOUSANDS OF NEW LAWS ARE BEING ENACTED EACH YEAR, YET JUSTICE IS DISAPPEARING FROM THE AMERICAN SCENE. WHY?

JUSTICE OR REVOLUTION examines justice in America—not in terms of legalistic structure—but from the viewpoint of our inalienable individual rights, and comes to some surprising conclusions:

- That the greater part of the American system of justice as achieved by the American Revolution, has been obstructed.

- That complex laws are MORE OFTEN THAN NOT, enacted to serve one special interest group or another, and are actually one of the greatest barriers to justice in our society.

- That a revolt is building, because Americans are fed up and are taking matters into their own hands, as with California's Proposition 13.

- That unless this action is based on the sound principles of individual rights, it will lead to an even greater loss of justice, to a condition of dictatorship.

JUSTICE OR REVOLUTION traces the concept of justice as understood by the great minds of the past, particularly those thinkers who developed the philosophy of rights on which America was based. JUSTICE OR REVOLUTION points out the injustices of the present system, and presents the way to re-establish political and economic rights, in a principled and peaceful way. *The alternative is revolution!*

To order send $9.95 (plus 80ᶜ p.&h.) to Books In Focus. 30 day return privilege.

• •

Adventures with Liqueurs

Lucienne M.L. De Wulf
and
Marie-Françoise Fourestier

For centuries liqueurs have provided a special flavor to sophisticated living and have been valued as elixirs, potions, curatives, digestifs, and even as aphrodisiacs.

ADVENTURES WITH LIQUEURS introduces you to the world of liqueurs. It gives their fascinating history, telling the story of how they were discovered and are made, and best of all **ADVENTURES WITH LIQUEURS** describes in detail how you can use liqueurs to add to your enjoyment of food and beverages, and enhance your lifestyle. Hundreds of elegant food and beverage recipes using liqueurs are presented, from simple mixtures to gourmet productions!

ADVENTURES WITH LIQUEURS has been written by two French Ladies to help you bring the sensuous intriguing and sophisticated tastes and experiences afforded by fine liqueurs into your life. Join Francoise and Lucienne in this adventure with liqueurs, as they share their knowledge and experience on this exquisite topic.

To order send $11.95 (plus 80ᶜ p.&h.) to Books In Focus. 30 day return privilege.

SPECIAL DISCOUNTS TO READERS

The following quantity discounts are available to readers who want to help spread the message of this book. (The same discount applies to all books available through Books In Focus).

10 copies	20%
25 copies	30%
50 copies	40%
100 or more	45%

Add 25¢ per book for postage and handling. New York residents add sales tax also. Mail your order and check to: BOOKS IN FOCUS, P.O. Box 3481, Grand Central Station, New York, N.Y. 10017.

- -

To Order Books

Send The Following Information:
(You can send this sheet or photocopy it)

Book Title(s)	Quantity	Cost

Total quantity: _____

Name: _____

Address: _____

City: _____ State: _____

ZIP: _____

Total Cost: _____

Minus % Discount: _____

Plus Postage: _____

Total Due: _____
(check included)

Send your personal check or money order payable to:

Books In Focus, Inc.
P.O. BOX 3481
GRAND CENTRAL STATION, New York 10017

If you have a question, phone (212) 490-0334

THE LIBRARY
ST. MARY'S COLLEGE OF MARYLAND
ST. MARY'S CITY, MARYLAND 20686